BLACK ENTERPRISE
GUIDE TO
TECHNOLOGY FOR
ENTREPRENEURS

Black Enterprise books provide useful information on a broad spectrum of business and general-interest topics, including entrepreneurship, personal and business finance, and career development. They are designed to meet the needs of the vital and growing African-American business market and to provide the information and resources that will help African-Americans achieve their goals. The books are written by and about African-American professionals and entrepreneurs, and they have been developed with the assistance of the staff of *Black Enterprise*, the premier African-American business magazine.

The series currently includes the following books:

Lessons from the Top: Success Strategies from America's Leading Black CEOs
by Derek T. Dingle

Black Enterprise Guide to Starting Your Own Business
by Wendy Beech

The Millionaires' Club: How to Start and Run Your Own Investment Club—and Make Your Money Grow!
by Caroline M. Brown

The Black Enterprise Guide to Investing
by James A. Anderson

Against All Odds: Ten Inspiring Stories of Successful African-American Entrepreneurs
by Wendy Harris

Take a Lesson: Contemporary Achievers on How They Made It and What They Learned Along the Way
by Caroline Clarke

Black Enterprise Guide to Building Your Career
by Cassandra Hayes

Wealth Building Journal: A Day-by-Day Journey to a Brighter Future, a Better You
by the Editors of *Black Enterprise* Magazine

BLACK ENTERPRISE GUIDE TO TECHNOLOGY FOR ENTREPRENEURS

Bernadette Williams

John Wiley & Sons, Inc.

ISBN: 0-471-44358-1

Printed in the United States of America.

10 9 8 7 6 5 4 3 2 1

To my "wonder twin" and brother,
Marzette Williams,
for your love, support, and laughter.

ACKNOWLEDGMENTS

I started writing this book over 5 years ago, not thinking that I would be blessed enough to capture the attention of Black Enterprise or John Wiley & Sons, Inc.

This work was inspired by what has become my personal and entrepreneurial mission: to educate business owners about new technology and its benefits. As an author, speaker, and president/CEO of my own company, I fully understand what it means to wear many different hats over the course of a day. While many technology-related subjects are exciting to me, I am certainly sensitive to other entrepreneurs who have been overwhelmed and confused by it. Hopefully, my passion for the subject comes through in this effort and my readers will share in this passion and allow technology to make a difference in the development of their businesses.

Many thanks to my literary agent, Malaga Baldi. You're the best!

I am grateful to the managers at Black Enterprise, who continue to serve African American entrepreneurs by providing inspirational and educational information. Your vision and partnership with John Wiley & Sons made this possible.

Thank you to the editors at John Wiley & Sons for being so patient as I worked to complete the manuscript while running my business and traversing the globe.

Thank you to all of the entrepreneurs who took time out of their busy schedules to be interviewed, and to the experts who contributed their knowledge and opinions. Continued success to each of you.

Thank you to my mentors and cheerleaders for keeping me inspired and on track. My best-selling buddy, Mimi Donaldson (author of "Negotiating for Dummies"), Rene Amoore, Loesha Bromley Ringoir, Dr. Sharon Badenhop, and Julie Williams—your guidance and support have been and continue to be invaluable.

To my grandmother, Sallie Mae Kimbrough, thank you for your wit and wisdom.

To my mother and father, Louise and Arthur C. Williams, Sr., thank you for everything.

BERNADETTE WILLIAMS

CONTENTS

INTRODUCTION:
HELPING OURSELVES

It has been interesting to watch the initial hiccups and the subsequent snowballing efforts to bridge the chasm between technology's developers and the overwhelmed and somewhat disconnected masses. I am pleased that the Digital Divide issue has gained such widespread significance and support. Technology is absolutely vital to the development of African American business.

My purpose for writing this book is twofold: (1) to educate African American business owners and managers about technology's potential impact on African American economic development, and (2) to provide African American entrepreneurs with a methodology to effectively and productively integrate new technology into their businesses. African American entrepreneurs need to know that technology programs and resources are available to assist them, and that technology can be used to create an extremely meaningful impact on our businesses, communities, and culture. We cannot afford to dive into every new technology product and service the way mainstream America does. We must be more strategic in our technology integration efforts lest we stand to further contribute to the Digital Divide. We also cannot stand aside while government and Corporate America determine what we need and how we should have it. The task of minimizing the effects of the Divide trickles down to the individual—in business, at work, at home, and within the community.

Just as it is important for African Americans to know the value of what it means to be "connected," it is equally important to be aware of how we are viewed as a market for technology products and Web content. While unfortunate, it should come as no surprise that the initial reaction to my book proposal four years ago was: "Black people aren't into technology" and "African Americans don't invest in computers." Time and again, my proposal fell on deaf ears. Certainly, things have changed in the past few years. The question is: "How much?"

African American spending on computer-related products has definitely surged in the past six years. With this news, plus all of the

1

worldwide efforts in place to bridge the Divide, one could easily consider this issue closed and assume that all will quickly return to status quo. That is a problem in and of itself. Status quo for African Americans typically means (99.99 percent of the time!) being labeled "disadvantaged." It is possible that the Digital Divide may have narrowed over the past few years, but many issues remain. Access to hardware, software, and the Internet is important, but what we do with technology access matters most. Odds are pretty high that, as access continues to increase, government and corporate representatives will feel that their efforts are successful when, in actuality, all they have done is provide high-tech paperweights to communities in need of education.

REVIEWING THE DIGITAL DIVIDE ISSUE AND ITS IMPACT

Let's take a look at the origins of the issue. The Digital Divide is a clear case of the Haves versus the Have-nots—technologically speaking, that is.[1] Numerous studies have shown a very clear disparity between those who are technologically connected versus those who are not. And, according to these studies, the African American community tends to fall on the disconnected end of the spectrum.

The exponential growth of the Internet has forced the disparity of access to computers and to the Internet into the limelight. It is no secret that the Internet's initial targeted audience was 30-something, educated white males with $60,000 in annual income. It's also no secret that women quickly became a primary Internet target market and even surpassed their male counterparts in accessing the virtual environment. Subsequently, seniors, Generations X and Y, and the affluent joined the targeted ranks as technology businesses developed new products and Web content.

Not until NetNoir, BET.com (formerly MSBET.com), Afronet, BlackVoices.com, and BlackPlanet.com were declared widespread successes did major corporations—technology or otherwise—begin to focus on communities of color. (At best, we might have seen a person of color in a technology product advertisement, but rarely did we see aggressive efforts to market to African American consumers and entrepreneurs.) The simple truth is: Despite skyrocketing sales of cellular telephones and pagers in minority communities, and computer vendors' promises to put a personal computer (PC) in every home, the technology industry's marketing efforts most often targeted folks who looked like the companies' founders.

EXPECTATIONS

But what could we really expect? Despite the amount of money that we spend as a group, it took decades for major corporations to recognize African Americans as a viable target market. Should we have expected anything different in the virtual realm, from newer technology companies? As pessimistic as it seems: Of course not! New technology companies are more concerned about remaining solvent than they are about social responsibility.

There have been so many other viable niche markets for these firms, there was little reason to aggressively market to communities of color. As a group, African Americans have been notorious for investing in clothing, shoes, and cars—not computers. So, it makes sense that we were not initially viewed as a prime target for technology products and services.

THE DIGITAL DIVIDE: STUDIES AND OPINIONS

Prior to 1995, there were few reports on computer usage among African Americans and other ethnic groups. Obscure reports of telephone penetration in rural and urban areas took place as far back as 1980. In the mid-1990s, when the term "Digital Divide" was first bandied about, several technology and telecommunications usage reports detailed access challenges and issues in homes, libraries, and schools. The most popular of these reports, the "Falling Through the Net"[2] series, was compiled and presented by the U.S. Commerce Department's National Telecommunications and Information Administration (NTIA).[3] Heavy emphasis was placed on Internet access at home and at work, but these reports also included information on telephone access and computer ownership and usage.

Since the first NTIA report was introduced in 1995, several other relatively high-profile reports have been released, including the Benton Foundation's "Losing Ground Bit by Bit: Low-Income Communities in the Information Age" (1998) and Vanderbilt University's "Bridging the Digital Divide: The Impact of Race on Computer Access and Internet Use" (1998). Joining the bandwagon in the new millennium were CyberDialogue, Pew Internet, Forrester Research, International Data Corporation (IDC), and eMarketer, all seeking to note how communities of color were (or were not) getting connected.

As NTIA and other groups reported their findings, ethnic groups were conclusively lumped into the "have-not" category. According to these reports, more often than not, African Americans and Hispanics, whether they lived in rural or urban areas, were "disconnected" and lacked the disposable income to purchase big-ticket items like computer products.

Initially, the debate over numbers seemed to take on a greater momentum than efforts to create solutions. The only consensus was that, as a group, we were definitely "disconnected." Since the late 1990s, conflicting Digital Divide data have been all too prevalent. No one seemed to know exactly how many African Americans had computer and Internet access, or whether the situation was as dire as the reports and hype proclaimed. (The ballpark number of African Americans accessing the Net in late 2000 was around 5 million.[4] The number is projected to reach 8.5 million by late 2001.[5])

GLOBAL IMPLICATIONS

Regular reports of the ever-increasing hundreds of millions of North American Internet users cast a foreboding shadow on the remaining disconnected billions on the planet. While many Americans complain of high-speed access issues, Internet access is a luxury that few outside of the United States have been able to afford (Table I.1).

As an example, look at any country on the African continent (Table I.2), where the Digital Divide's effects are most extensive. South Africa tends to be among the more progressive of Africa's countries, but access issues in all African countries can be attributed to the lack of appropriate equipment and infrastructure, a lack of security regulations, and a low level of awareness of the benefits of the Internet.

Nearly every country in the world has been experiencing some sort of technology infrastructure challenge. The so-called digital changeover has been an especially daunting task in Third World countries, where the prevailing issues are poverty and illiteracy. Now, in addition to meeting basic health and education needs, Third World

Table I.1   Internet Access Worldwide

World total	513.1 million
Africa	4.15 million
Asia/Pacific	143.99 million
Europe	154.63 million
Middle East	4.65 million
Canada & USA	180.58 million
Latin America	25.33 million

Source: NUA Internet Surveys, as of August 2001. www.nua.com.

Table I.2   African Internet Access

Country	Connected Population
Algeria	180,000
Angola	30,000
Benin	10,000
Botswana	12,000
Burkina Faso	10,000
Burundi	2,000
Cameroon	20,000
Cape Verde	8,000
Central African Republic	1,500
Chad	1,000
Comoros	1,500
Congo-Brazzaville	500
Djibouti	1,000
Egypt	560,000
Equatorial Guinea	600
Eritrea	5,000
Ethiopia	10,000
Gabon	15,000
Gambia	4,000
Ghana	30,000
Guinea	8,000
Guinea Bissau	1,500
Ivory Coast	20,000
Kenya	200,000
Lesotho	1,000
Liberia	300
Libya	20,000
Madagascar	30,000
Malawi	10,000
Mali	10,000
Mauritania	2,000
Mauritius	87,000
Morocco	220,000
Mozambique	15,000
Namibia	30,000
Niger	3,000
Nigeria	100,000
Reunion	10,000
Rwanda	5,000
S. Tome & Principe	6,500
Senegal	40,000
Seychelles	6,000

(continued)

Table I.2   (Continued)

Country	Connected Population
Sierra Leone	20,000
Somalia	200
South Africa	2,400,000
Sudan	28,000
Swaziland	3,000
Tanzania	115,000
Togo	20,000
Tunisia	280,000
Uganda	25,000
Zambia	15,000
Zimbabwe	30,000

Source: As compiled by NUA Internet Surveys, as of March 2001. www.nua.com.

governments are faced with the tasks of wiring their countries, gaining access to equipment, and finding qualified IT trainers to bring the country's educators and entrepreneurs up to speed.

The focus on North American Internet access statistics tends to underscore the Divide's primary elements, namely telephone and computer access. Needless to say, one must have the appropriate wiring and equipment to access the Internet. A quick assumption is that "everyone has a phone" but that's definitely not the case (see Figure I.1). In America, images of teens, seniors, and businesspeople walking around with cell phones, pagers, and handheld devices are commonplace, so we tend to forget that there are people in the world who don't have homes, let alone telephone access. There are, in fact, 7 to 15 percent of American households without telephones (depending on race, income, and geographic location).[6] In many other countries, the number of families without telephones is much higher.

One proposed solution is wireless access, but disposable income to purchase the appropriate equipment, an awareness of access benefits, and a desire to learn are still needed before the Divide can be bridged.

Slowly but surely, efforts toward change are leading to increased telephone penetration and Internet access throughout the African continent. The number of Internet users in all of Africa has increased from 2.5 million in 2000 to nearly 5 million in 2001. All African countries are now online, up from only 11 countries in 1996.

Numerous articles and reports maintain that the Digital Divide is more about income, education, and geography than race. The truth is that wherever an uneven distribution of resources can be found, the Divide surely exists. The Digital Divide's effects extend well beyond

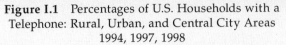

Figure I.1 Percentages of U.S. Households with a
Telephone: Rural, Urban, and Central City Areas
1994, 1997, 1998

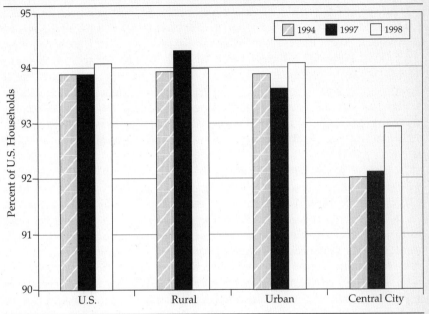

Source: U.S. Department of Commerce, NTIA.
Note: This study did not track ownership of cellular telephones or other wireless
devices.

America's borders and affect people by geography, income, race, education, gender,[7] and disability. Bridging this Divide is not as much about gaining access to hardware, software, and the Internet as it is about providing access to information and opportunity to individuals and countries around the world.

WHOSE ISSUE IS IT, REALLY?

The damaging effects of the Divide can be seen in nearly every facet of our lives—employment, business development, education, communication, and so on. The chasms between those who have high-speed access to the Internet, better job opportunities, greater access to valuable information, and enhanced experience of new technologies will continue to widen as the tech elite distance themselves from those who were late to the game. It is critical that African American business owners learn to successfully integrate technology in order to survive in the quickly changing landscape of the new economy.

Some entrepreneurs and community leaders argue that it is the U.S. Government's and Corporate America's job to create programs and workshops to bring African American business owners up to speed technologically. Others, like Michael Batie (Successnet, Los Angeles, CA), Floyd Webb (e22 Digital, Inc., Oak Park, IL), and Marlon K. Brownlee (JMMS Enterprises, Inc., Maplewood, NJ), are not convinced that it is Corporate America's job to help the African American community bridge the Divide. To these entrepreneurs, handouts only serve to create more codependence for African American businesses. Ultimately, they feel that the responsibility falls on the shoulders of the community itself.

Hence the need for a solutions-oriented guidebook to help African American entrepreneurs to help themselves. This book is less about the Digital Divide than it is about what each of us can do to work toward digital inclusion. It is my intention to provide a variety of bootstrapping techniques to help business owners become more productive and efficient. Here is a chapter-by-chapter synopsis of what you can expect:

In Chapter 1, we will review some of the specific technology obstacles facing African American entrepreneurs. Some reports claim that African American entrepreneurs still lag behind in the adoption of new technologies, thereby negatively affecting the economic future of the community. Others claim that we are right on par with mainstream (white-owned) businesses. We will also look at the changing landscape of the new economy and review some key points for business owners to keep in mind as they adopt new technologies.

Chapter 2 provides a strategic methodology for assessing your company's current technology resources and for integrating new hardware and software into your company, for growth. We review the process for creating computer equipment profiles, evaluating IT human resources, and budgeting for upgrades. We will also review methods for keeping up with the constant influx of technology information.

Numerous options are available to mobile professionals. Chapter 3 sheds light on some of these options and provides a means for selecting from among the wide variety of devices that provide access on the go. We also review the services of community technology centers, Internet kiosks, and cybercafés as access alternatives; and learn more about the growing interest in m-Commerce and its possible business benefits.

In Chapter 4, we get to the nitty-gritty of hiring, retaining, and promoting technology talent. We take a close look at the so-called IT (information technology) workforce shortage in the United States. Readers will find out where to locate IT employees and vendors, as well as how to assess IT skill levels. Learn about the accomplishments of some amazing African American "technopreneurs": Donna Auguste of FreshWater Software and the Leave A Little Room nonprofit organization; Ken Granderson of Innercity Software; Angela Walton of Melador Technologies, Inc.; and Vercell Vance of Alpha Data Corporation.

Chapters 5 and 6 focus on the promotion of business products and services on the Internet. Learn how to create the right Internet presence for your company, and how to develop a successful integrated marketing strategy. Learn how to properly target markets and effectively project the right corporate image online. (Find out whether "passing" is the way to go for your business.) Also, discover when it's time to upgrade your company's Internet strategy and presence. We'll take a closer look at Internet business models and virtual branding using Internet advertising and online public relations.

Business is about vision, long-term planning, and thinking outside of the box. It is not enough to provide solutions to current problems without preparing for the future. Chapter 7 provides a framework for effectively managing an e-business. We'll take a look at where things are headed, now that the "dot-com" community has taken a nose dive. Find out how to position your business for success, no matter where technology developments and IT companies are heading.

The Networking Directory provides a categorized list of several hundred Web sites with content and resources for business owners and managers. Many of these sites are tailored specifically to African American entrepreneurs; others are general business sites that provide useful information in the areas of technology, finance, public policy, marketing, human resources, and business management.

The Appendices include a number of useful tools and tips for searching online, validating information, avoiding scams, and successfully communicating in virtual space.

The Glossary presents a laundry list of definitions for commonly used technology terms. For all acronyms and interspersed technology terms, check the Notes and Glossary for clarification.

Unless a specific technology is referenced, the terms *IT* (information technology), *technology,* and *new technology* are used synonymously, throughout the book, to describe all aspects of managing and processing information using telephones, computer hardware, software, the Internet, wireless devices, and handheld devices. *Technology industry (-ies)* refers to the collective of telecommunications and new media companies responsible for the development and sale of technology devices.

I was inspired to write this book because, as an entrepreneur, I understand that business owners and managers are already overwhelmed with day-to-day business operations, let alone having to understand the jargon, constant developments, and goings-on within the

---

WEBSEARCH

As you read, watch for the WEBSEARCH sections, which will provide you with Web sites, keywords, and other resources to further explain some concepts and to help you find additional information about previously discussed issues.

---

technology sector. Whether we like it or not, technology literacy has become tantamount to business management skills. It is important for entrepreneurs to be computer-literate no matter what industry they're in—be it law, construction, dentistry, or hair care. But, it is not your job to become a network engineer, a Webmaster, and/or a data security expert. I wrote this book with the mind-set that entrepreneurs are not "dummies" or "idiots"; we simply need to have consolidated information and a basic strategy for technology integration so that each new development doesn't become a setback.

Once they get past the hurdles of awareness and access, African American entrepreneurs who implement strategic technology integration are able to utilize the technology in creative ways that can strengthen their businesses and their overall community. The greatest potential of new technology is its ability to close the gap between the more advantaged segments of society and those that have traditionally been left behind. At this point in time, basic computer equipment, Internet access, and creativity far outweigh the need for excessive amounts of cash to start and develop new businesses. Now, more than ever, opportunities are available for us to do business without boundaries.

Technology can be fun; it will be as profitable and beneficial to us as we make it. Let's tap into this medium, stay informed, make our voices heard, and, last but certainly not least, get paid.

Part I

DIVISION IN THE MARKETPLACE

1

DEFINING THE TECHNOLOGY CHALLENGES FOR AFRICAN AMERICAN ENTREPRENEURS

No matter what industry you are in or what you do, your life is being touched at this very moment by new technology developments. Cars now have navigation systems that can prevent us from getting lost; appliances warn us of needed repairs; handheld devices sound an alarm to prepare us for an upcoming meeting; and cell phones serve double duty as contact managers. We can "beam" messages across the room to PDA[1]-wielding colleagues, and, at any time of day or night, we can send e-mail messages and documents to people on the other side of the world, in places to which we've never dreamt of traveling. We now have the ability to expand our global networks with ease and do business anywhere we wish. It is no wonder that our world has become fascinated with all things technological.

Nearly 30 years ago, computer systems were large enough to fill rooms; now they are small enough to fit into our hands, and they are a million times more powerful. Everywhere we turn, there is news of the current ups and downs of the technology industry, from initial public offerings (IPOs) to impending dot-com layoffs; from voice recognition developments to viruses that could potentially cripple computer systems worldwide. We have become a society that is obsessed with transforming our world into a futuristic, automated, Jetsons-style reality as quickly as possible. There's no end to where we can go. Did the notion of moving into a new millennium spark the breakneck speeds of technology developments? Or was it the numerous news reports of 20-year-olds who achieved the American dream and acquired billion-dollar portfolios? Whatever the reason, technology has become a focal point in our business and our personal lives.

Young people nowadays cannot imagine life before the PC. What was once considered a luxury found only at the offices of major corporations and government agencies is now a fixture in the lives of most individuals in the modern world. Or is it? Contradicting stories of computer access and Internet usage by minorities make you wonder whether the situation is still as dire as was originally reported. Does the African American community still lag behind in computer access and Internet usage, as Digital Divide experts would have us believe? Or, are we finally keeping pace with our mainstream counterparts?

One thing is certain. We have become bonafide consumers of computers and electronic equipment. According to Target Market News' *Buying Power of Black America*, African Americans' expenditures on computers have increased exponentially over the past five years. African Americans spent $1.3 billion in 1999 on computer-related products— a 143 percent increase over computer-related expenditures in 1998. Jupiter Communications, in *Assessing the Digital Divide* (September 2000), predicted that the gap between African American and white households with Internet access will be reduced within the next five years when only 18 percent more white households will be online. The study showed a continuing double-digit growth rate for African Americans' Internet access through 2005. It is fairly reasonable to accept the results of these studies. These are exciting times, and it makes perfect sense that we would jump on the bandwagon. Besides, African Americans are quite resourceful and wield an incredible amount of buying power.

My concern for the community is not about the Digital Divide's access issues as much as it is about what I call the Knowledge Divide. The vast majority of Digital Divide issues and efforts have focused on providing access to computer equipment and the Internet for schools and under-served communities. Although it has taken a few years for these access efforts to gain momentum, it is much easier to solve computer and Internet access problems than it is to provide people, especially busy entrepreneurs, with the skills needed to make the best use of technological advances. Our biggest dilemma is how to close the gaps between the informed and the uninformed, between those who produce and those who consume, while still increasing the computer literacy levels of technology's latecomers. I am quite happy that African Americans have become digital consumers, but I have to question where we stand as technology producers, and to what extent we are integrating these developments into our lives and businesses in ways that encourage productivity and economic development.

News media and technology industry pundits have been preaching about the opportunity for a level playing field for minority and women business owners since the advent and incredible growth of the Internet. And while it's true that being connected opens up global possibilities to business owners, we have yet to see a truly level playing field. If that's not enough, as barriers to entry continue to decrease, competition will increase. Surely, opportunities exist as never before, but if we are not able to fully capitalize on technology developments, it will make an extraordinarily negative difference, not a positive one.

DOES THE DIGITAL DIVIDE AFFECT AFRICAN AMERICAN BUSINESS DEVELOPMENT?

In my opinion, the answer goes without saying.

Effective technology integration is one of the foremost challenges facing business owners in the new millennium. Technology is not only driving the new economy; it is fostering social transformations. Even small business owners are addressing globalization issues and increased workplace and organizational structural changes. Gaining technology access is only the tip of the iceberg. It's what we *do* with the

Table 1.1 Comparison of Business Ownership by Minority Group: 1997

Minority Group	All Firms Firms	All Firms Sales and Receipts ($ millions)	Minority-Owned Firms Firms (%)	Minority-Owned Firms Sales and Receipts (%)
All minority firms	3,039,033	591,259	X	X
Black	823,499	71,215	27.1	12.0
Hispanic	1,199,896	186,275	39.5	31.5
American Indian and Alaska Native	197,300	34,344	6.5	5.8
Asian and Pacific Islander	912,960	306,933	30.0	51.9

Source: U.S. Census Bureau, 1997 Economic Census. Released July 2001. (NOTE: All firms' data include both firms with paid employees and firms with no paid employees.)

technology that can truly move us toward digital inclusion as well as bridge several other gaps that have contributed to our disadvantaged status.

The numbers that will tell the real story of the Digital Divide's closure, and technology's positive impact on the African American community, are based on business and economic development. The U.S. Census Bureau's 1997 Economic Census clearly showed that, in comparison to other minority groups, African Americans have had the smallest percentage in new business development and the smallest growth in annual receipts (Tables 1.1, 1.2, & 1.3). In my humble opinion, we need

Table 1.2   Comparison of Minority-Owned Firms to all U.S. Firms: 1997 and 1992 (Excluding C Corporations)

	All Firms	
	Number of Firms	Sales and Receipts (millions of dollars)
All U.S. firms		
1997	18,431,456	4,661,018
1992	17,253,143	3,324,200
Percent change	6.8	40.2
All minority-owned firms		
1997	2,786,098	335,316
1992	2,149,184	209,740
Percent change	29.6	60.0
Black-owned firms		
1997	780,770	42,671
1992	620,912	32,197
Percent change	25.7	32.5
Hispanic-owned firms		
1997	1,121,433	114,431
1992	862,605	76,842
Percent change	30.0	48.9
American Indian- and Alaska Native-owned firms		
1997	187,921	22,441
1992	102,271	8,057
Percent change	83.7	178.5
Asian- and Pacific Islanders-owned firms		
1997	785,480	161,142
1992	603,426	95,714
Percent change	30.2	68.4

Source: U.S. Census Bureau, 1997 Economic Census. Released July 2001. (NOTE: All firms' data include both firms with paid employees and firms with no paid employees.)

Table 1.3   Average Receipts per Firm, by Race, Hispanic
Origin, and Gender of Owner: 1997

	Male	Female	Equally Owned
	Thousands		
Black	115.1	43.3	98.5
Hispanic	199.8	80.9	131.8
American Indian and Alaska Native	193.1	126.0	188.8
Asian and Pacific Islander	437.0	153.7	307.2

Source: U.S. Census Bureau, 1997 Economic Census. Released July 2001.

to see a greater increase in successful national and international African American-owned business efforts before we feel that the digital transformation has truly succeeded. We need to see increased and better utilization of technology for saving, surviving, and thriving in the African American business community.

Can technology solve all the issues that impede African American business development? Certainly not. Nor does it create a completely leveled playing field. Technology can, however, play an integral role in the number of new companies started by African Americans, as well as the number of African American businesses that grow beyond the million-dollar revenue mark. It also levels the playing field more than ever before by lessening businesses' start-up, marketing, and growth costs. With access to the right technology and proper integration along the way, more and more of our businesses stand a chance to succeed.

ACCESS CHALLENGES AND ISSUES

So, what are some of the obstacles that prevent African American entrepreneurs from obtaining or using computer equipment and Internet access? Overall, the challenges are awareness, infrastructure, money, and attitude. A closer look reveals the following specific obstacles:

- Lack of disposable income, and greater concern about basic survival (e.g., basic operating expenses, making payroll, business development). As is the case for most business owners, access to capital is the primary deterrent to start-up and growth for African Americans. If an entrepreneur has to choose between buying a new printer or paying an employee, the odds are pretty high that the printer will wait. A possible remedy to this dilemma: Utilize one of the many access alternatives that we'll review in Chapter 3 (e.g., borrowing, bartering, repairing old equipment, using equipment at a local tech center or a copy center). In addition, a much-needed shift in priorities has to take place before African American businesses become truly competitive. It is vital for entrepreneurs to revise their company budgets to account for miscellaneous equipment expenses throughout the year.

Despite the fact that the African American community generates billions of dollars in income each year, we are still less likely, overall, to invest our money in stocks, real estate, and computer equipment than in anything else. Heaven knows that we've had plenty of obstacles standing in our way—for starters, access to capital—but prioritizing is a key factor. Prior to all of the hype inspired by the Internet, it was easier for entrepreneurs to dismiss the adoption of technological advances. This is no longer possible. It is not only counterproductive for business owners to put technology on the back burner; it can be detrimental to the viability of one's business.

- Concerns about security and privacy, including fear that "Big Brother" is watching (government interference in personal activities) and that credit card and identity theft are rampant. Security and privacy are the leading areas of concern for computer and Internet users worldwide. While e-commerce is growing by leaps and bounds, millions of consumers still refuse to shop on the Web because of what may happen to their financial information. Also, Web surfers are concerned about how their contact information is being used or sold for marketing purposes. This is an important issue for entrepreneurs because it is our job to assuage any consumer fears about security and privacy. Ways to protect your information, as well as that of your potential customers, are given in Chapter 5 and in Appendix A.
- Fear that computer and Internet access will lead to antisocial behavior. Extended computer usage still frightens many people into thinking that they'll become the digital equivalent of the couch potato. Geeks may be "en vogue" financially, but no one wants to become a full-fledged member of this much-maligned group that spends countless hours staring into a computer screen with minimal, if any, human contact. Computer and Internet addiction are real byproducts of technology developments and have inspired the creation of countless studies and therapy groups. In Chapter 5, we'll look at ways to create

balance in our digitally influenced lives and to alleviate user apprehension and addiction.

- Entrepreneurs with home offices fear kids' access to pornographic or adult-oriented Web sites. A number of software packages monitor and filter inappropriate material and Web sites for PC and Macintosh operating systems. Some are even available free, via download. Others are available at neighborhood computer software stores. Software titles include: CyberSitter, Net-Nanny, SurfWatch, The Internet Filter, CyberPatrol, and Cyber Sentinel. Naturally, few things are foolproof, but this software is worth a try.

- Intimidation based on the assumed learning curve. What with the speed of technological changes, many people believe that they don't have the skills needed to operate computer equipment and to effectively use the Internet.

QUALITY TIME By Gail Machlis

www.uexpress.com   ©1998 Gail Machlis Inc. by Universal Press Syndicate

Whatever you do, you can't let the computer sense your fear

"Many African American entrepreneurs have a fear of technology and this new way of thinking and doing business," says Bridget L. Wall, Assistant to the Secretary for HUB Outreach, State of North Carolina/Office for Historically Underutilized Businesses. "With proper exposure, knowledge, and education, we can help our business owners make a smooth and gradual transition to becoming technology-based businesses."

Ms. Wall goes on to say, "Technology can have a positive effect on African American businesses whose owners and managers know how to use it to their advantage. African American firms with limited sales and marketing forces, limited office and warehouse facilities, and limited capital resources can use technology to market their businesses, services, and products to markets in which they would not otherwise have access. Technology can allow a small, local, one-man operation to have the presence of a national, multistaffed, multifaceted business.

"On the other hand, technology may have an adverse affect on African American business owners who do not realize that in order to grow a viable business entity, they have to integrate technology into their business processes and operations. Through e-procurement and e-commerce, technology allows many government agencies and corporations to electronically advertise bids and purchase orders, select vendors, make awards, issue purchase orders, verify shipment of orders and deposit checks via transfer of funds to a company's financial institution. If African American businesses do not incorporate some aspects of technology into their businesses, they may continue to exist, but by no means will be viable."

One of the biggest challenges for North Carolina's HUB program has been informing small and minority business firms about how to access bid and contract information via the State's Internet site. Ms. Wall partly attributes this to the fact that because there are so many MBE/WBE/DBE programs throughout North Carolina, it is difficult to coordinate outreach among the programs and deliver timely information to minority suppliers, especially to businesses that are without Internet access.

She also points to a lack of awareness and follow-through on the part of some African American entrepreneurs. Many times, when she shows the HUB program's Web site to minority entrepreneurs, they are amazed at the number and variety of bids posted. A lot of the entrepreneurs are unaware of all of the goods and services that the state purchases or of the bid result information, which could be helpful for future bidding. "Many of the businesses don't have marketing, business development, or sales departments. Therefore, it is incumbent upon the owner, or one or two salespersons, to identify leads, follow up on them, and put the bids together."

Ms. Wall adds: "If your business has inadequate technology—a slow computer, an Internet Service Provider that kicks you out of the system or locks up on you—a business owner can become frustrated with trying to access information. Some businesses have actually missed out on bid opportunities because bid files were too large for them to access or the bid files were condensed[2] and they didn't know how to "unzip" them to access the information needed to review the bids.

- Entrepreneurs are overwhelmed with decisions about what type of equipment and software to buy; how often to upgrade, and so on. According to Alma Lorraine Bone Constable, owner and President of First Friday of Seattle (www.firstfridayofseattle.com), the prevailing technology challenge for First Friday of Seattle

---

WEBSEARCH

HISTORICALLY UNDERUTILIZED BUSINESS PROGRAMS

Epylon (San Francisco, CA)
www.epylon.com/corporate/partners/partners_hub.shtml

North Carolina HUB Program
www.doa.state.nc.us/hub/

Ohio Department of Administrative Services HUB Program
www.state.oh.us/das/eod/hubcert.htm

Tacoma, Washington HUB Program
www.cityoftacoma.org (Click on "Business," then on "Business Opportunities")

Texas Water Development Board HUB Program
www.twdb.state.tx.us/about/HUB/HUB.htm

Texas Department of Health HUB Program
www.tdh.state.tx.us/hub/default.htm

U.S. Small Business Administration HUB Zone Home Page
www.sba.gov/hubzone

To locate other HUB Programs, search the Web using the keywords "historically underutilized business," **"HUB program"** or **"HUB zone."**

---

members is a lack of knowledge about what to buy. "I haven't found fear as much as a lack of information in a form they can relate to themselves, like what type of computer should they buy? How do they learn to use the software applications? Do they really need a class, or can they teach themselves?"

On a daily basis, we are bombarded with countless product advertisements and reviews, so it would make sense that already overwhelmed business owners would feel incapable of selecting from among the myriad equipment and application options available. This book has been designed to facilitate product selection for African American entrepreneurs. (See Chapter 2 for a strategic method to assess future hardware and software purchases.)

- Greater faith in "traditional" media for information and marketing. For many business owners, print media, radio, and television are tried and true. Whether or not they've been privy to the countless reports of the billions of dollars generated in e-commerce and Internet advertising, some folks just haven't bought into the promises of virtual space yet. What needs to happen is a realization that no form of communication is without fault or flaws. We must learn to validate information without resisting change (to our detriment). I'll discuss validating online information in Appendix C, and, in Chapter 6, I'll look at ways to strategically brand a company in virtual space without breaking the bank.

- Lack of exposure to the latest technological developments. Sometimes you just don't know what you don't know. It is my guess that many African American business owners realize the importance of technology but simply don't know where to begin to collect information and to properly integrate developments into their businesses. One could just as easily blame the system or the consumer. As pointed out earlier, until a few years ago Corporate America made no great effort to market technology products and services to African Americans. Nor did we aggressively seek out technology information. Now that we have begun to spend more on computer products, we are on the marketing radar screens of technology companies. However, this doesn't entirely solve the problem.

Some entrepreneurs fault African American professional organizations with shoddy attempts at providing technology information. Brian Stevens, Executive Director of The Telecom Opportunity Institute (www.ttoi.org), in Houston, Texas, feels that many African American professional organizations "are more challenged by technology than many businesses." President/CEO Nathan Burrell, of VirtuPass in Fort Lauderdale, Florida, agrees: "Many of these organizations have not effectively utilized new technology themselves. Futhermore, they lack the technology alliances in the industry to assist and create solutions for technology challenges. There needs to be a dedicated division for technology incorporated within the business organizations or alliances made with technology organizations like The Minority E-Commerce Association to provide information and solutions at Internet speed." In Chapter 7, we'll take a closer look at the role of Corporate America, professional organizations, and entrepreneurs in creating more technologically proficient minority businesses.

- Business owners fear employee "time theft." Rather than enhancing productivity, some entrepreneurs see many technological advances as big time wasters. Studies show that corporations lose millions of dollars each year because employees waste time surfing the Web, reading personal e-mail, and handling personal problems on the job. Employee time theft is actually one of the most common yet often unreported labor costs. To tackle this issue, entrepreneurs can use a variety of techniques, without keeping their firm in the technological dark ages. We'll look at some options to minimize employee time theft in Chapter 2.

- Some entrepreneurs don't see the value in many IT products and services. At the root of such problems is the continuing "access to capital" issue. But the real question is whether, in a perfect world where access to capital wasn't as big an issue, African American business owners would make the necessary IT investments to strengthen their businesses for mainstream competition. I personally feel that this issue can be attributed to lack of appropriate technology education and prioritizing. Once African American business owners have a full understanding of the benefits and features of specific technological advances, they may be more likely to prioritize for the integration of these advances into their businesses.

There are, no doubt, hundreds of reasons why people find themselves disconnected from, or out of, the technology loop. At this point, African Americans might be latecomers but we're not out of the game. Awareness is just the beginning.

So What; Now What?!

As a very dear friend of mine says, "So what; now what?!" We know that these challenges exist, but what should we do about them? The Internet and telecommunications industries are revolutionizing communication as we know it; they are fundamentally changing the way that we learn, interact, do business, and spend our leisure time. For the African American business community to play a more integral role in this emerging revolution, four things have to happen:

1. We have to know about the technology.
2. We have to see the specific value in it for our community.
3. We have to have access to it.

4. We need to know how to effectively integrate it into our businesses.

KNOWLEDGE AND EXPOSURE

The Internet and other new technologies have steamrolled into the headlines and don't appear to be going away any time soon. One would think that it is next to impossible for anyone to be unaware of the power and importance of today's technology, specifically that of personal computers and the Internet. However small in number, this group of people does exist. Many people just don't know where to look for relevant and comprehensible technology information; others are resistant because they feel overwhelmed. Oftentimes, for a variety of reasons, information takes a bit longer to filter into communities of color.

As for the African American community, it is my belief that the greater issues are more about awareness and value than access.

Luckily, within the past few years, efforts to provide access in traditionally underserved communities have picked up steam. Churches, community centers, government agencies, professional organizations, and technology companies have developed programs and continue to distribute integral information to increase awareness of technology developments in the African American community.

As I write this, many organizations are actually reporting that the Digital Divide is closed or is no longer a big enough issue to receive support from the government, technology and telecommunications companies, and nonprofit foundations. As always, studies and reports can be slanted to say whatever people want or need to believe.

Apparently, major technology and telecommunications companies think otherwise. In 2000, Microsoft launched its "Big Day Tour," which targets African American and U.S.-based Hispanic entrepreneurs and showcases Microsoft's bCentral and business desktop products. According to Mitchell R. Duncan, Group Program Manager at Microsoft, "This national event generates awareness and excitement about Microsoft's commitment and leadership in bringing technology to African American and U.S.-based Hispanic small business owners."

Other corporations have stepped up their efforts to bring technology to community businesses through sponsorship support of African American professional events; collaborative efforts to offer discounted products and services; and free seminars, workshops, and product demonstrations.

Corporate, government, and personal efforts to educate minority entrepreneurs must continue. Those of us with access need to pass

EFFORTS TO BRING TECHNOLOGY
TO AFRICAN AMERICAN BUSINESSES

Microsoft Big Day
Phone: (877) 435-7638
E-mail: bigday@microsoft.com
www.msbigday.com
www.msbigday.com/africanamerican.htm
FREE day-long seminar for small business owners and managers based in the United States and Canada. Seminar demonstrations show how Microsoft's products and technology solutions can help improve small business efficiency.

Places of Color
Phone: (877) 426-4762
www.placesofcolor.com
Places of Color is a hardware distributor and Internet Service Provider (ISP) focused on offering affordable computer equipment, customized Internet services, and bundled PC/ISP packages starting as low as $249.00 for individuals, households, and small businesses. Places of Color is the brainchild of DME Interactive Holdings CEO Darien Dash; it is part of DME's ongoing effort to provide technology access to those affected by the Digital Divide.

National Rainbow/PUSH Coalition Silicon Valley Project
Phone: (510) 486-1095
E-mail: info@rainbowpush.org
www.rainbowpush.org
Launched in 1999, Rainbow/PUSH launched the Silicon Valley Project to focus on the technology industry and to ensure that all people and communities participate in the 21st century's Digital Revolution. The primary goals of the Silicon Valley Project are to transform the Digital Divide into digital opportunities and to build digital connections between minority-owned businesses and the high-tech industry that will open up access to capital for minority businesses, venture funds, and technology entrepreneurs.

along new technology information and resources through churches, professional organizations, community and recreation centers, work sites, schools, e-mail messages, and however else we can get the word out. We must also refer to the "global drum" to pass information to our disconnected friends, relatives, and colleagues.

THE VALUE OF BEING CONNECTED: WHAT'S IN IT FOR US?

The benefits of constant multitasking and continuous access to seemingly limitless amounts of information mean nothing to some people. If anything, these efforts might seem more overwhelming than beneficial. Being the information junkie that I am, having the convenience of a global resource at my fingertips is absolutely invaluable. For others, value needs to be more clearly defined and must target immediate and specific personal and professional needs. In my opinion, the major selling points of having Internet access were not initially well translated to many African Americans.

In all of the hype about the Internet, major technology vendors failed to realize that African Americans might seek access for different reasons or that they might have trouble getting access. Let's look at our expectations again. Despite Corporate America's finally figuring out that we like to see people who look like us in advertising and that we like to see value in products and services advertised specifically for our community, new technology providers initially forgot or completely ignored this.

There is an incredible desire to see technology as the great equalizer. While it makes sense that business owners would typically use printers, scanners, and PDAs in similar ways, in virtual space this assumption was quite wrong. In the beginning, the Internet community was seen as one homogeneous group of people, all seeking access for the same reasons. Obviously, this was a big mistake on the part of traditional corporations and Internet companies. African Americans *are* different and our needs are different, as are those of other communities of color. People should be given reasons to purchase technology products and to access the Internet based on these differences.

Here's a short list of personal and professional reasons for African Americans to stay informed about emerging technologies:

- Reduce business start-up costs. Access to computer hardware, software, and the Internet allows entrepreneurs to develop a big image with a small budget.

- Find information on specific health problems and medical disorders (e.g., diabetes, cancer, high blood pressure, AIDS), including herbal and nontraditional treatments.
- Join African American investment clubs and get help with money and credit management. Also, find information about African American-owned banks.
- Compare vendor prices. Get information on office products, automobiles, appliances, electronic equipment, and real estate.
- Recycle black dollars. Surf Afrocentric Web sites to buy products from African American vendors.
- Find books on specific topics, as well as reports and articles featuring a potential client, industry, or issue.
- Enhance communication for business owners and managers on the go. Laptops, wireless applications, and handheld devices provide a means to stay in touch with clients, employees, and corporate managers.
- Get your degree online. Take technical, language, or other continuing education courses online. Increase your computer literacy for employment and productivity. Take a "virtual tour" of universities and colleges online, and find helpful financial aid information.
- Receive "filtered" news in your e-mail box, or, at your leisure, seek out additional info on local, national, and international issues.
- Network. Develop professional relationships and friendships with people all over the world via e-mail, chat, instant messaging, and newsgroups.
- Get background information on business or vacation destinations before you go.
- Put your tax dollars to work by surfing government agencies' Web sites for programs and resources that can help your family and business. The United States Government is slowly but surely transferring its programs and resources to Web-based systems. Individuals and businesses will need Internet access to receive the benefits of available programs and to do business with the government.
- Create your own collateral pieces, including business cards, letterhead, postcards, and a regularly distributed newsletter.
- Seek out and get involved in social and professional organizations.
- Market your company's services, and find government and corporate bid opportunities.

- Perform research for your new or developing business. Get competitor information, find business resources, and network with your peers.
- Trace your family history with online genealogy resources.
- Let your voice be heard about corporate and organization discriminatory policies. Also, e-mail your political leaders and let them know what's on your mind.
- Tired of hearing HIStory? Within a few seconds, a quick search on the Internet will turn up valuable information on Kwanzaa, Juneteenth, African American patriots, the Negro Leagues, and millions of other African and African American historical topics.

Needless to say, I could go on. Access to new technology gives us an opportunity to bootstrap like never before. No longer do we have to pull up the rear, spending generations trying to catch up with mainstream America. We can play an active role in shaping the virtual and economic landscapes, inject some much-needed information into our community, and focus on becoming more self-reliant.

BACK TO REALITY

Conflicting reports aside, the reality is that millions of African American consumers and entrepreneurs *are* "connected." They use computers, handheld devices, and wireless applications on a daily basis. They have Internet access and surf the Web for information. They hold degrees in the sciences, manage IT departments, and run their own businesses, often employing African American technology professionals.

A July 2001 report[3] from the Tomas Rivera Policy Institute showed that minority businesses are, in fact, embracing the Internet. According to the study, minority-owned businesses are aware of the Internet's benefits and have computers, Internet access, and Web sites at rates similar to those of majority-owned businesses. More than 60 percent of the African American, Asian American, Latino, and Native American entrepreneurs interviewed recognized and understood the benefits of e-commerce, and up to 91 percent of the businesses were connected to the Internet.

The report also showed, however, that barriers block the complete integration of minority businesses into the digital economy. Only 10 to 13 percent of the entrepreneurs interviewed were engaging in e-commerce. This is reportedly due to the fact that many of these businesses target minority consumers who may not be "connected," and thus limit their online sales opportunities. Some interviewees claimed that their products do not lend themselves to e-commerce. Others pointed to their limited capital and lack of Internet-skilled employees, or questioned the viability of e-commerce.

THE CHANGING LANDSCAPE OF THE NEW ECONOMY

Considering the rather volatile state of the technology industry, it is no wonder that many African American entrepreneurs are treading lightly before doing business with dot-coms or integrating the latest technologies into their businesses. How do you know whether the vendor will be around in six months? What about all the mergers and acquisitions? Will product and service pricing structures change? Will you be able to get customer service from a business after you've purchased its product? These are all valid questions in light of the fact that technology businesses are going down in flames 10 times faster than new ones are popping up.

In their desire to shrink the get-rich-quick cycle, technology and new media industry movers and shakers have also shrunk the failure cycle. Traditionally, small businesses that survive beyond five years are deemed, at the very least, moderately successful, and are potentially in it for the long haul. Nowadays, a technology or new media business that survives beyond a few months and claims even the slightest profit is a rare animal.

Initially, it seemed that any 20-year-old with a dot-com dream and a business plan sketched out on a cocktail napkin could get millions of investment dollars. The once high-flying dot-commers have since fallen out of grace and are now expected to prove themselves, in the name of customers and profits, before getting any accolades from the media or money from investors. The media focus has turned somewhat from high-tech initial public offerings (IPOs) to widespread layoffs and company closures. Web sites have been created for the sole purpose of tracking industry rumors and company failures. As these companies began to crash and burn, old economy businesses—law firms, event planners, property management companies, advertisers, and so on—began to feel the fallout as well. Many of their technology customers cut back on spending or disappeared entirely.

So, how does this affect the African American business community?

In a sense, because we are typically deemed disconnected, this whole crash-and-burn process may affect us a lot less than other entrepreneurial communities, especially that of mainstream America. The African American community has always expected success to come at a higher cost, so the fact that our technology businesses will have to "prove" themselves before securing funds is no major issue.

What *is* of utmost importance to African American entrepreneurs is the variety of reasons that so many of these companies have gone bust—mismanagement, poor business plans, and easy access to capital, to name a few. While it's true that no entrepreneur would turn down expansion or operating capital for his or her business, the dot-com fallout proves that creativity and good management can go a lot farther than all the cash in the world.

If anything, the stock market "correction" of April 2000 restored some common sense to the entrepreneurial and venture capital communities. It is important for African Americans to pay close attention to the goings-on in the technology industry because, despite this backlash, technology continues to fuel the economy, create jobs, and influence all modes of global communication.

Remember these key points when you are selecting technology products, vendors, and investments:

1. The rules haven't changed for us. Technology levels the playing field somewhat, but we must continue to be strategic and proactive in our business development.

2. Despite simplified global communications and constant technological changes, this new economy requires a shift in mindset and practice on the part of the customer. We cannot push our customers to unfamiliar territory when they have so many familiar options. (Take the technology pulse of your primary target markets before you establish your Internet strategy.)

3. Your Internet strategy should be a *part* of your overall business strategy. Many businesses set themselves up to fail because their Internet strategy and business strategy are one and the same. Regard the Internet as an extension of your business. A Web site needs to be marketed, but it is itself a marketing tool. To succeed, you must integrate your marketing plan to include traditional and online marketing methods. (See more about marketing in Chapters 5 and 6.) Companies that rely solely on the Internet to drive sales are more likely to find themselves in trouble.

4. Most content-based Web sites are labors of love trying to disguise themselves as ad-generating portals. The days of the free Web-based services are numbered, so a business model based

solely on advertising may *not* be the way to go. Be wary of virtual companies that put all their eggs in the ad revenue basket.

5. Investment money isn't there for the taking anymore. This means that future technology and Web-based businesses should be better managed and built on more solid ground. To survive, companies will be more customer-oriented and financially responsible.

6. There's always going to be something new. By the time your staff has managed to get beyond the learning curve of the most recent technologies integrated into your business, the new "big thing" will have already hit the marketplace. The key is to make sure that your company has a specific technology integration plan that is focused on savings and productivity, and not on "keeping up with the Joneses." Gadget mentality can take your business off course and put you in the poorhouse.

Access to technology and utilization of it are two entirely different things. As the African American business community continues to gain access to the Internet and other new technologies, we cannot breathe a sigh of relief. We must use the technology to our advantage so that the success of efforts to provide access do not overshadow the growth of a "Knowledge Divide."

RESOURCES

Benton Foundation—www.benton.org

Closing the Digital Divide—www.digitaldivide.gov

Community Technology Center Network (CTCNet)—www.ctcnet.org

Digital Divide Network—www.digitaldividenetwork.org

NUA Internet Surveys—www.nua.ie/surveys

Pew Internet and American Life Project: "African Americans and the Internet" (2000)—www.pewinternet.org

U. S. Department of Commerce: National Telecommunication and Information Administration *"Falling Through the Net"* reports—www.ntia.doc.gov/ntiahome/digitaldivide

Part II

INFORMATION TECHNOLOGY (IT) STRATEGIES TO GROW YOUR BUSINESS

2

EFFECTIVELY INTEGRATING INFORMATION TECHNOLOGY INTO YOUR BUSINESS

People have always seemed to have extraordinary expectations for technological advances. No matter where we are in time, we can easily envision where technology should go next. Looking back 20, 30, or even 40 years ago, it is very easy to see that society has been on a quest to automate nearly every function and process of our daily lives. There is an intense desire to simplify and expedite everything. We are fascinated with the idea that we may actually be able to "beam" ourselves to distant places in the near future, à la *Star Trek*.

In their amazement at what we humans have been able to create, developers and consumers of technology products seem to underestimate the need for humans to prepare themselves to handle constant interaction with computerized equipment. Computers and other technological developments are nothing without human direction (with the exception of "Hal" in *2001: A Space Odyssey*). Our attraction to personal computers and their capabilities seems to overshadow the need for a paradigmatic shift in human beings. We are not always so charmed with the idea of changing to accommodate technological developments, despite our fascination with them. With each new generation, more and more education is required for communication, employment, and entertainment. (Think of the numerous VCRs and DVD players that keep blinking "12:00am" because consumers don't know how to program their equipment.) Most of us love the idea of moving into a futuristic world, but we hesitate to learn all that is needed to function in such a world.

Our situation is somewhat of a Catch-22. Life-changing technological innovations are created almost daily, and we are excited by the possibilities these innovations offer. Yet, we are hesitant to change. We are moving as fast as the speed of light in our personal and professional lives. We like the idea that new technologies create more time and streamline our day-to-day processes, yet we use more and more time, and we work at faster and faster paces. Personal computers and other new technologies have contributed richly to our lives, but they also seem to encourage immediate gratification. We want all of the benefits of these innovations right now—the savings, the information, the entertainment, the return on our financial investment. The challenge is that, in order to reap the benefits, we have to adapt by educating ourselves.

Entrepreneurs and corporate managers seem to have the greatest technological expectations because there is a need to be productive and profitable, as quickly and as much as possible. Given the well-hyped fortunes and savings created by technological developments, business owners and managers want returns on their investment immediately. Millions of entrepreneurs around the world have found out the hard way that a much greater investment is needed beyond the development or purchase of equipment or software. There is a much-needed investment of time and education, for and by the end user. These expectations and oversights exacerbate a number of the technology challenges facing entrepreneurs, especially in small businesses with limited capital.

There are plenty of reasons for integrating technology into our businesses; the principal benefits are savings of time and money. Here are a few examples of business owners and managers who have incorporated technology to enhance productivity, increase sales, and save themselves time and money. As can be expected, there is a flip side to integrating technology into a business. Some of these examples will show the advantages as well as the counterproductive effects of computer and Internet usage:

- Antonio Cox has been able to increase productivity in a variety of ways for his New York-based graphics company, Kinetic Media, Inc. (www.kineticm.com). The company's production cycle has improved because clients receive project information much faster. With high-speed Internet DSL service, his staff now sends and receives client information via e-mail. In the past, information was copied onto Zip disks, which cost around $16.00 each, and the disks were shipped via first-class mail or messenger.

- While Bridget Sullivan credits technology integration with saving her business money on postage and gasoline, she also credits her increasing time spent on the computer with keeping her out of the sales field. Using e-mail and the Web has greatly minimized her phone calls and face-to-face meetings, saved wear and tear on her car, and substantially reduced her dry cleaning bill. But, Ms. Sullivan feels that some of the time that she spends answering e-mail is time that she could spend making presentations and marketing her business in traditional space. Ms. Sullivan is President of Possibilities, an Austell, Georgia-based event management and public relations firm (www.possibilitiesbbs.com).

- Justice & Sustainability Associates, LLC (www.justicesustainability.com), a Washington, DC-based strategic planning and organizational development firm, uses videoconferencing technology to be more competitive. Don Edwards, the firm's founder and managing partner, feels that this keeps clients coming back. The firm also uses the Internet to save money on postage, communications, and messaging. "As a company advising clients on how to be greener, sustainable, and just, using and promoting information and Internet technologies is a part of our mission," says Edwards. "We spend much less time wandering around by communicating through the computer."

- Floyd Webb of e22 Digital in Oak Park, Illinois (itutu.com), feels that early adoption of new technology may have inherent incompatibilities not yet recorded, so he and his staff are slow to upgrade during the first quarter of any new technology product's release.

- Perry LeBlanc's strategic consulting business, i4 Consulting (www.i4cg.com), uses a Lotus Notes collaborative solution that allows his employees to work from home as efficiently as if they were in the office. Travel time and communications expenses have been reduced substantially. The company also uses Lotus Notes to streamline research and work product development processes. Palm Pilots and laptop computers, in conjunction with Lotus Notes, have allowed staff members to improve account management and effectively integrate schedules.

- Kamyra Harding, an organizational development consultant in New York, uses listservs (aka "electronic mailing lists") to market her company's services online and reduce promotional expenses. However, she laments that product crashes cost her time and money.

- False advertising is a negative effect that has caused serious problems for Paul Williams' Dayton, Ohio-based JNAD Web Design (www.jnad.net). "When a technology product fails to operate as advertised, it definitely has a counterproductive effect on a business," says Williams. "For example, when host servers go down, our clients' Web sites are not available for viewing. Luckily, this doesn't last for a long time but it is definitely inconvenient."

- Linda Cousin's Brooklyn-based Cultural Travel Publications & Promotions business was negatively affected when downloaded software crashed her computer system. Luckily, she didn't lose any data but she did have to send the computer out for repairs.

- Using the Internet to locate free and state-of-the-art resources is a great way to save money and enhance presentations. Just ask Iya-Sokoya Karade, owner of Splendid Rain Enterprises and Karade Village for Children in East Orange, New Jersey (www.splendidrainenterprise.com). Karade has also used technology to lower her company's phone bill, streamline the bill payment process, market a retreat via e-mail, and improve recordkeeping.

- Lisa Shepard, owner of CulturedExpressions.com (www.culturedexpressions.com), an Afrocentric decorating business in Union, New Jersey, feels that technology allows her to do "too much." As a result, she often develops more ideas and contacts than she has time for.

- Gordon Lewis, freelance writer and photographer, notes that he lost four months of productivity due to a defective film scanner. The necessary replacement part was on backorder. Although the scanner was under warranty and was eventually repaired by the manufacturer, the downtime was both inconvenient and costly. He now uses a digital camera to take care of most of his digital photo needs.

- Printing costs have been greatly reduced at Brian Joseph's Austin, Texas-based Bydee Art Gallery (www.bydee.com). Rather than print new brochures annually, Brian simply updates the Web site with new artwork and information. He is also able to send samples of commissioned work via e-mail so he can get an immediate response and increase sales.

No method of technology integration can eliminate all of the things that can and do go wrong. But a little strategy can go a long way to minimize the technology challenges that arise.

A NOVEL CONCEPT

Strategy seems to have been the last driving influence in technology development and integration in the late 1990s. My suspicions were confirmed when panelists at technology conferences started to use the word "strategy" as though it had been discovered by a linguist only a few weeks prior. *Hmmm. Let's see here. You mean technology developers and business owners should apply strategy to their product development, purchases, and Web sites? What a novel idea!!* All sarcasm aside, strategy and a healthy dose of common sense are absolute necessities if you don't want to be overwhelmed (and bankrupt) by technology. Thus far, industry growth, hype, and peer pressure have made billionaires out of a few business owners and confused paupers out of many others. Believe it or not, there is a happy medium between having age-old, inefficient equipment and going broke by upgrading every four or five weeks.

TO UPGRADE OR NOT TO UPGRADE?

Confusion leads many consumers to stick their heads in the sand and simply not deal with technology upgrades. Hype and peer pressure lead others to upgrade, purchase, and download everything they can get their hands on, whether they plan to use it or not. Computer and high-tech salespeople are now akin to used-car salesmen. "Of course, you'll use this machine/software," they say. "I'm sure that everyone else in your industry has had it for a few months now." Yeah, right.

How are you, a hard-working professional, to know when you should upgrade, and exactly which piece of your computer equipment needs the upgrade? If you're like most business owners, upgrades take place on an as-needed basis. If you run a larger firm and can afford an IT Director or Management Information Systems (MIS) Director, this decision might be a lot easier. (Delegating is wonderful work, isn't it?) Whoever is handling your technology integration, the trick is not to let technology manufacturers, media hype, and computer salespeople answer these questions for you. Computer hardware upgrades and new purchases should be application- and productivity-driven.

ASSESSING YOUR CURRENT SITUATION

Before deciding to integrate any new technology product into your business, you need to completely assess your current situation.

Look around your office; take stock of your equipment and the software currently residing in your company's computers. The odds are pretty high that you'll find many things that you don't use and/or don't need. Most people can't give a technical support person a basic profile of their computer equipment, yet they are certain that they need that new device or software package. This certainty is usually the result of media hype and technology industry pressure.

Here's a five-step technology integration strategy:

1. Establish your immediate application needs.
2. Evaluate your computer equipment, software, and mobile devices.
3. Assess your human resources.
4. Look at your budget.
5. Consider all available options.

NOTE: After you've created your initial equipment profile and reviewed your available resources, the process becomes a lot easier.

Let's take a closer look at each step in the strategy.

Step 1

First things first: clearly define your goals. What are you trying to do? This step may depend on recent technology challenges and/or long-term goals included in your company's business plan. Are you trying to streamline internal processes to save money or time? Are you expanding your staff? Are you trying to correct recurring technical problems?

Whatever you're trying to do, it is likely to fall into one of the following categories:

- Add or upgrade a software product.
- Add a peripheral device.
- Optimize your system for speed, storage, or efficiency.
- Connect your machines via a network (for file sharing).

- Add one or more new stations to the company's network.
- Add Internet access to one or more computers (via dial-up, ISDN, DSL, wireless, or a tiered network).
- Protect company files from hacking, viruses, or disasters.
- Recover from a hack attack, virus, or disaster (e.g., fire, flood, theft, earthquake).
- Create better staff and client communication (via e-mail, Intranet, Extranet, PDAs, wireless communication).
- Design or renovate a company Web site.

An important question to ask is: "Why are you doing this?" Naturally, if you've hired several new people, you may need to buy new equipment or add a few nodes to your network. But, if the answer to the above question does not immediately contribute to your company's bottom line through savings, increased productivity, or increased revenue, consider alternatives. (We'll address alternatives in a later section of this chapter.)

Also, when I say, "immediately contribute to your company's bottom line," I mean within the next three to six months. Typically, integrating technology involves a learning curve, so you must account for some lag time between the actual integration and any return on your investment. The point of the exercise is to get you to be realistic and specific about your needs.

Step 2

Create a hardware and software profile. It's time to take inventory. What types of computer hardware and software do you have? When were they purchased? How long ago were they upgraded, and which parts and programs were upgraded? How does your equipment perform? Are there any recurring problems? What versions of your primary software packages are you using?

Your computer profile should consist of the following information:

- *Operating system (OS).* Some of the more widely known operating systems are: DOS, OS/2, Microsoft Windows (3.1, 95, 98, 2000, ME, XP), Macintosh OS, and Linux. (Mac operating systems are numbered. The most current at the time of publication is OS 10.1.)

  Some of the more popular network operating systems are: Novell Netware, Microsoft LAN Manager, LANtastic, Macintosh OS, Unix, and Microsoft Windows NT.

- *Microprocessor (CPU).* The microprocessor is sometimes synonymous with (and often referred to as) the central processing unit (CPU). There are quite a few microprocessor brands including AMD and Cyrix, but Intel's Pentium (II, III, 4, Pro) and the PowerPC[1] (G3, G4) are the most popular. (Prior to the release of the Pentium, Intel's microprocessor models included the 8086, 286, 386, and 486.)

  In addition to their brand name, microprocessors are often differentiated by bandwidth (16-bit, 32-bit) and clock speed. The microprocessor's clock speed, given in megahertz (MHz), refers to the number of instructions the processor can complete per second. Examples of clock speeds are 33, 66, 133, 166, 200, 333, 450, 750, 900 MHz, or 1 GHz.

- *Random access memory (RAM).* Refers to the computer memory that is available for application use. RAM is measured in megabytes, gigabytes, and terabytes.

- *Available disk drives.* Most personal computers have an internal hard drive and a floppy drive (3½"). An inventory list should also note whether your hard drive is partitioned. CD-ROM and DVD (digital video disk) drives, technically speaking, are optical disk drives and are noted by speed (e.g., 10x, 24x). There are also external or detachable floppy drives (e.g., Zip and Jaz, among others).

- *Peripheral devices.* These pieces of equipment are attachments to a computer—for example, monitors, keyboards, mice, and printers. This category also includes extras such as scanners, speakers, CD burners, digital cameras, and other multimedia devices.

- *Internet access.* Note whether your company accesses the Internet through a dial-up network, ISDN, cable, DSL, wireless, or a leased line (T-1). For dial-up connections, be sure to include the modem type and speed.

- *Software.* Because most computers have dozens (if not hundreds) of software programs, focus on the primary applications used. When preparing this list, be sure to include the software brand and version number. Software programs may include: office suite (e.g., Microsoft Office, Lotus SmartSuite, Corel WordPerfect Suite), anti-virus, e-mail reader, Web browser, utilities, Web publisher, file transfer, photo editor, financial manager, fax, graphics, Internet connection, file compression, media player, scheduling, project management, and firewall.

Computer profiles can be as simple or as complex as users prefer (Figure 2.1). Hardware and software are upgraded often, so it's best to

WEBSEARCH

For more information about computer hardware and software, go to these sites:

CNet
www.cnet.com
CNet's vision is to educate and empower people and businesses by unlocking the potential of the technology world to make things easier and faster, and by helping them to make smarter buying decisions.

MacWorld
www.macworld.com
The only Macintosh-oriented Web site providing in-depth, lab-tested product reviews and how-to advice, including original, on-line-only content.

TechTV
www.techtv.com
A Web site for the only cable television channel covering technology information, news, and entertainment from consumer, industry, and market perspectives, 24 hours a day, 7 days a week.

Webopedia
www.webopedia.com
Online Computer Dictionary for Internet Terms and Technical Support.

WhatIs
www.whatis.com
Definitions for thousands of the most current IT words.

ZDNet
www.zdnet.com
Full-service destination for people looking to buy, use, and learn more about technology.

Linux Central
linuxcentral.com
The /root for Linux resources.

Figure 2.1   XYZ Corporation Computer Profile (Sample)

Station: <u>Mary Smith, Administrative Assistant</u>

<u>X</u> Desktop   ____ Laptop

<u>HARDWARE</u>

Manufacturer, model: Gateway v1000se
Microprocessor: Intel Pentium III, 1000MHz
RAM: 64MB SDRAM
Disk drives: Hard drive (10GB)
                                       3½" floppy drive
                                       48x CD-ROM
Peripheral devices: 15" Monitor
                                       Millennium 104+ Keyboard
                                       PS/2 Mouse
                                       Hewlett Packard OfficeJet 600 Printer
                                       Boston Acoustic 735 Speakers
Internet access: WireSpeed DSL modem (external)

<u>SOFTWARE</u>

Network: N/A
Operating system: Windows 98
Office suite: Microsoft Office 97
Anti-virus: McAfee VirusScan (version 5.12)
E-mail reader: Microsoft Outlook Express (version 5.0)
Web browser: Microsoft Internet Explorer (version 4.0)
Utilities: Norton Utilities (version 3.0)
Web publisher: Microsoft FrontPage Express (version 2.02)
Financial manager: Quicken 99 (Release 8.0)
Fax: Symantec WinFax (Basic Edition)
Internet connection: Earthlink DSL 5.0
File compression: Aladdin Systems (StuffIt/Expander—version 5.1)
Other: HP OfficeJet Manager
                                    Adobe Acrobat Reader 2.1
                                    Microsoft Windows Media Player 6.1

<u>MAINTENANCE</u>

1. December 4, 2000: Added new printer (Brother HL-630)
2. January 10, 2001: Computer crash due to software upgrade,
   repaired by CompUSA
3. January 26, 2001: Upgrade browser to version 5.0
   _____
   _____
   _____
   _____

(As of: <u>March 12, 2001</u>)

Computer Profile

Station: _____

_____ Desktop   _____ Laptop

HARDWARE
   Manufacturer, model: _____
   Microprocessor: _____
   RAM: _____
   Disk drives: _____
   Peripheral devices: _____
   Internet access: _____

SOFTWARE
   Operating system: _____
   Network: _____
   Office suite: _____
   Anti-virus: _____
   E-mail reader: _____
   Web browser: _____
   Utilities: _____
   Web publisher: _____
   Financial manager: _____
   Fax: _____
   Internet connection: _____
   File compression: _____
   Other: _____

MAINTENANCE
_____
_____
_____
_____

(As of: _____)

make them as simple as possible. The whole point of the exercise is to establish better familiarity with your equipment, which will lead to better decision making. Profiles may also prove useful during emergencies such as theft, fires, widespread viruses, and natural disasters such as floods, earthquakes, and so on.

Most often, all the details that you will need for your computer profile are listed on purchase and maintenance receipts. Another quick way to compile computer profile data is to review the "System Information" file on your computer's hard drive.

A blank copy of a computer profile, for you to photocopy and use for your company's equipment, is on page 45.

A copy of this profile should be kept near the equipment for easy reference should a computer emergency arise. Naturally, it's a good idea to keep a backup electronic copy. You should also maintain equipment and software warranty information, as well as technical support information for your computer consultant, ISP, Webmaster, Web hosting service, and local computer stores. Remember to update the computer profile whenever any equipment (hardware, software, and peripherals) is upgraded or replaced. Note the date and new version number of the upgrade, as well as the name and contact information of the person who installs the equipment or software.

For larger businesses that use LANs or WANs, a profile should be kept for the servers and for each workstation. If your company has an in-house MIS Director, make sure that part of his or her job is to maintain these equipment profiles. IT employees come and go, and equipment profiles might facilitate a smoother transition from one computer person to the next.

Reassess your equipment and productivity every 9 to 12 months. If your equipment has become problematic or if you become aware of upgrades that may contribute to your bottom line, ask your IS manager or computer consultant for a recommendation. Your computer's operating system or software may require regular optimization [2] to maintain efficiency.

Step 3

It's time to take stock of your employees' skills. How familiar with the company's hardware and software are you and your employees? Are there areas where you could be more efficient? When was the last time that you or your employees had computer training classes?

The odds are pretty high that most employees learn new technology skills and repair computer problems on-the-fly. With dozens of things to do, who has time to wait (or money to spend!) for the computer consultant to come out again? It is all too familiar, in the course of a business day, to implement a quick fix to computer software and hardware that we learned from a friend or from someone in an electronic discussion list. A band-aid approach to developing tech skills may work in the short term, but some time should be invested in developing employees' technology skills for the long term.

More often than not, computer users are not making good use of their available equipment simply because they're not fully aware of all of the features of their software applications. What's more, assigning duties to employees who are only moderately familiar with software or hardware can cost more money, in the long run, than outsourcing the task or sending the employees to a training workshop. If you factor in the amount of time it takes an employee to learn a new application (just well enough to perform the task at hand), plus the amount of time it could take to fix anything that goes wrong, you could have invested that amount in the services of an IT professional.

How should an entrepreneur or manager deal with this?

1. Consider implementing a policy where at least once every three to six months, your employees must attend a one-day intermediate or advanced computer software course. A variety of courses are available through computer training schools, community colleges, community technology centers, and via the Internet. (If you have a larger staff, your best bet may be to have someone come into your company to present a workshop.)

2. Set a time limit for employees to troubleshoot tech problems that arise. If the problem cannot be solved within this specified time frame, contact the appropriate IT professional (e.g., computer consultant, network engineer, ISP).

3. Make a note of regularly occurring problems. Also, record how the problem was finally solved and ask how the problem can be avoided in the future.

4. Keep computer hardware and software manuals handy. Rather than guessing, it makes more sense (and it might save some money!) to go straight to the source. Along these lines, it also helps to stay abreast of manufacturers' warranties. If your equipment or software is still covered, you may be able to contact technical support without incurring fees.

5. Maintain bookmarks for manufacturers' Web sites. These can prove to be quite useful and can save the money that you'd spend on the phone with technical support if your equipment or software is no longer covered by a warranty.

There are, indeed, learning curves associated with most technology equipment and software applications, but computer training should be considered a regular business expense. The important factor to keep in mind is that enhanced productivity, combined with properly optimized applications, saves your business more money in the long run. Alta J. Cannaday, CEO and Principal of eFundsAssist.com (Bowie, MD), notes: "Initially, integrating technology products into your business may seem to be counterproductive because of the down time as staff trains. This, however, later improves productivity and affects the business' profit margin positively."

WEBSEARCH

COMPUTER TRAINING COURSES

Computer Training Schools
www.computertrainingschools.com

Community Technology Centers Network (CTCNet)
www.ctcnet.org

New Horizons Computer Learning Centers
www.newhorizons.com

Online Learning:

CyberLearning Universe	www.cyberlearning.org
CyberU	www.cyberu.com
FreeSkills	www.freeskills.com
Learn 2 University	www.learninguniversity.com
OnlineLearning.net	www.onlinelearning.net
TutorialFind	www.tutorialfind.com
Virtual University	www.vu.org
Virtual University for Small and Medium-Size Enterprises	www.vusme.org
ZD University	www.learnitonline.com
Software Advisors	www.softwareadvisors.com

In addition to these online sources, look for manufacturer-sponsored or local computer stores' seminars and workshops.

Step 4

Take a look at your budget and ask yourself: How much money has your company spent on hardware, software, upgrades, and training this year? How much did you spend last year? Will this upgrade affect your bottom line positively? When can you expect a return on your investment?

When asked about their upgrades, entrepreneurs typically fall into two categories:

1. They only upgrade when their equipment or software becomes completely inoperable.
2. They upgrade their equipment and software as often as possible.

As we all know, cash flow is the primary challenge for most businesses. This is usually the area that keeps companies from integrating technology into their businesses. When you're worried about day-to-day survival—making payroll, financing projects, and paying office rent—the idea of having your computers networked, or paying for computer training, takes a back seat. The problem is that antiquated equipment and computer illiteracy can cost your business a fortune. On the other hand, overspending on technology can lead to frustration, lengthy learning curves, and diminished productivity.

Most technology expenses are sudden rather than planned, and sudden expenses can really add up. It's best to be aware of technology expenses so that you can plan how much your company will spend each year. This will also help your decision making in emergency situations. The key is to be proactive, not reactive.

Daryl Tarik Wiley, President of Pittsburgh-based My Man Printing, LLC (www.mymanwear.com), is lucky to have friends and colleagues who advise him when technology emergencies arise. He realizes the major dependence that most businesses have on technology. In an effort to minimize service interruptions and other technology problems that can arise, he budgets for ongoing consulting and equipment maintenance. "If you do not have proper consultation prior to buying and setting up your technology, you may not know what measures to take to cover yourself in the case of a malfunction," says Wiley. "Also, if you are not prepared for the financial burden of correcting problems and/or training employees so they do not harm your system or equipment, it will cost financially."

Your company's annual projections should account for technology expenses, such as:

- Computer equipment purchases or lease payments (including peripheral devices).

- Software programs (including upgrades and phone support).
- Employee training.
- IT vendors' fees (computer consultant/network engineer for scheduled and emergency maintenance and support).
- Salaries (for dedicated IT departments).
- Internet access.
- Mobile devices: PDAs, pagers, phones, wireless access.
- Domain name registration.
- Web site/Intranet/Extranet development and maintenance.
- Web site hosting.
- Merchant fees (online transactions).
- Web-based tools (e.g., fax, voice mail, unified messaging).
- Equipment insurance.

Intangible technology expenses include loss of time, based on learning curves (which can be minimized by providing computer training; see STEP 3), and time theft by employees who spend company time surfing the Web aimlessly and answering personal e-mail. To minimize time theft through Internet usage, consider using an Internet monitoring and blocking tool, like WebBlocker (WatchGuard Technologies, www.watchguard.com) or Disk Tracy (WatchSoft Incorporated, www.watchsoft.com), to restrict access.

Your company can also implement an Employee Acceptable Computer and Internet Use Policy. Such a policy clearly outlines the permissible parameters of employee computer and Internet use, prohibited uses, rules of online behavior, and penalties for violations of the policy, including security violations and vandalism of the company's computer equipment. Since this is a legally binding document, your business attorney should be responsible for drafting it, and a copy of the policy should be signed by each employee and kept on file.

Now, let's get back to your budget. If equipment is stolen, destroyed, or inoperable, the best that you can do is to find an inexpensive solution. If there isn't a lot of money in the budget, consider alternatives, which we'll discuss shortly. If you are merely considering an upgrade to gain enhanced product features or a current deal at a local computer store, your budget should play a significant role. Consider the following questions:

- Is the money available in the budget (after you have accounted for all other expected technology expenses)?
- Will the upgrade solve an immediate problem? In other words, are you getting the most out of what you've already got?

- How long is the expected learning curve, if any?
- What are the memory and equipment requirements?
- Are there any known problems with this particular upgrade?
- Will the upgrade provide a return on investment before the next fiscal year?

The answer to whether you should upgrade or integrate a new technology into your business will be very clear after you answer these questions.

Step 5

Before finalizing the decision to integrate a new technology product or service, consider all of your available options. First and foremost, consult with the company MIS Director or technology consultant. And, ask colleagues what solutions they've used under similar circumstances.

Find out what you can get for free or on the cheap. An easy way to cut software costs is to use one of the thousands of freeware and shareware software programs available. It might be possible to rent the necessary equipment for a few hours or days. A local community technology center, cybercafé, or Kinko's might provide the needed access or service. Also, see whether a colleague would be willing to loan you some equipment or barter a few technology services.[3]

A Web-based option might be available. A wide variety of Web sites offer free or low-cost services to businesses, including Intranets, fax, voice messaging, e-mail, accounting, employee benefits solutions, press release distribution, broadcast fax distribution, graphic design, and Web site development.

Rather than invest in custom-developed software, check for the availability of an application service provider (ASP) solution. Application service providers are companies that develop, manage, and distribute software services over the Internet or a private network. ASP solutions range from payroll processing to operating systems, from enterprise resource planning (ERP) packages to vertical or horizontal industry management software.

If you're in a high-growth business that requires frequent upgrades, consider leasing hardware instead of purchasing it. Contact the Equipment Leasing Association for a list of equipment leasing companies in your area. The Association can be reached at (703) 527-8655, or view its Web site at elaonline.com.

If your company needs one or more computers, check out Places of Color (www.placesofcolor.com) or the Used Computer Mall (www.usedcomputer.com) for low-cost options. Also, many equipment

DON'T FORGET TO RECYCLE!

If you buy new computer equipment, don't just set that old equipment out for the next garbage pickup. Consider donating it to a relative, student, employee, local school, community technology center, shelter, or library.

A number of nonprofit agencies are eager to collect old computers and peripheral devices, which they then refurbish and give to schools, libraries, or technology access centers. Here are a few:

Another Byte, Inc.
Directory of Non-Profit Computer Recyclers
www.recycles.org/byte/others/index.htm

CompuMentor
San Francisco, CA
(800) 659-3579
www.compumentor.org

Computer Bank Charity
Seattle, WA
(206) 365-4657

The Computer Recycling Center
Locations throughout northern and central California
www.crc.org

The Detwiler Foundation
Computers For Schools Program
Locations throughout the United States
(800) 939-6000
www.detwiler.org

Gifts In Kind America
Alexandria, VA
(703) 836-2121
www.giftsinkind.org

The National Cristina Foundation
Stamford, CT
(203) 863-9100
www.cristina.org

PEP National Directory of Computer Recycling Programs
(415) 382-1818
www.microweb.com/pepsite/Recycle/recycle_index.html

Share the Technology Computer Recycling Project
Rancocas, NJ
(856) 234-6156
sharetechnology.org

manufacturers have programs that allow purchases to be paid over an extended period of time (24 to 36 months).

When you are comparing product and service offerings, review prices with at least three to five vendors. It's best to limit the number of vendors because it's easy to spend an exorbitant amount of time trying to find the best deal. For future reference, maintain a list of the vendors that offered the best products and services at the best prices.

Take into account computer product reviews in your industry publications. There may be specific pieces of hardware or software that are better suited to the needs of your industry. It goes without saying that you should choose the product or service that is the most cost-effective and best suited for your company's needs over the long term.

If these steps seem like a healthy dose of common sense, it is because that is exactly what technology integration is all about. An occasional review of these steps might prove helpful because, as all entrepreneurs know, it is very easy to become overwhelmed by day-to-day activities. Besides, common sense and common practice are entirely different things. Collectively, they can go a long way to save your company money and increase its productivity.

SAFEGUARDING YOUR INVESTMENT

Any new technology that is integrated into your business should be an investment toward your company's success. That said, I'd be remiss if I discussed computer hardware and software without touching on some of the most basic ways to safeguard your investment.

Performing regular software backups and using current virus protection software are the easiest ways to protect your hardware and software. Despite this fact, these are two of the most overlooked tasks in computer ownership. When was the last time you backed up your files? How current is your virus protection software? If you have to think for more than one second, you should back up your files and update your virus protection software *immediately.*

Remember the "Melissa" virus, in 1999? People were running scared; meanwhile, the virus made its way around the world and back in a very short period of time, and paralyzed computer systems in its wake. Virus creators are becoming more and more ruthless, developing programs that wreak havoc—and sometimes permanent damage—on computer software systems. Other examples of these nasty little critters include: "Happy99," "Anna Kournikova," "Naked Wife," "Bubble Boy," "I Love You," "Love Letter," and "Hare Krishna."

Not all virus warnings are what they're purported to be. I'm sure that many of you remember the "Good Times" virus scare that began in 1994 and has circled the Internet more than a few times. The "Good Times" virus is, in fact, a hoax. That verdict has been confirmed by a variety of reputable sources, including several government agencies, America Online (AOL), and a number of anti-virus software manufacturers. Incidentally, no copy of the virus has ever been found.

How can you know whether a virus is real, and what can you do about it? A computer virus is a program designed to spread itself by first infecting executable files or the system areas of hard and floppy disks, and then making copies of itself. Most often, the damage is done without the immediate knowledge of the computer user. Viruses spread when files are shared via floppy disks, CD-ROMs, e-mail, or computer networks. For the virus to cause damage, the infected executable file must be opened (run). The virus is then triggered to execute (since it is a program) and infect other programs on the computer. As each newly infected file is opened, other files are subsequently infected, and so on.

In addition to replicating itself, a virus can be programmed to damage files and interrupt a computer's operations. There are different types of viruses. For example, macro viruses infect word processing and spreadsheet documents that use macros. Anita Paul, Principal of San Diego-based The Write Image, had a close call. Her computer contracted a virus that put her out of commission for a few days. She also lost a few files. Luckily, the situation was easily remedied with updated virus protection software.

A lot of people don't know that, in addition to viruses, a few other programs can cause problems—namely, trojan horses (aka "trojans") and worms. And if that's not enough, many viruses, worms, and trojans have variants. Variants are basically mutated versions of viruses, worms, and trojans that may travel in slightly different file formats, and they may have more destructive effects than their predecessors.

A trojan horse is a program that pretends to be something else and causes damage when the infected file is executed. For example, a trojan horse might be programmed to look like a screensaver file, but when you open it, it formats your hard drive, exposes hidden files, or sends out a mass e-mail exposing normally encoded information. Trojans are commonly confused with viruses, but they are not the same.

Worms, like viruses, are programs designed to replicate themselves. The primary difference between worms and viruses is that worms are independent. They do not have to attach themselves to another file to execute or spread through computer networks. The notorious Sircam and Code Red worms threatened computer systems around the world during the summer of 2001. The Sircam worm traveled the Internet via e-mail with a random subject line and an attachment by the same name. Sircam infected systems by sending copies of itself to all addresses listed in an infected user's address book and in temporarily cached Internet files. The Code Red worm posed little risk to personal computers but caused a flurry of panic. Threats and predictions failed to materialize, but computer users were reminded of the vulnerability of networks and Web sites. Code Red compromised network security in Internet Information Service Web servers. Its effects were triggered by a network system's date; depending on that date, Code Red either executed a distributed denial of service attack (DDoS) on a government Web site or sent copies of itself through insecure network ports. Microsoft responded by creating patches for users to protect their networked systems and Web sites.

The differences between viruses, trojan horses, and worms seem quite clear, but the terms are typically used interchangeably. Truth be told, I have seen each of the above-referenced "viruses" (e.g., "Happy99") referred to as trojans and worms.

You can protect your company's computer equipment from viruses, trojan horses, worms, and their variants by inoculating it with anti-virus software. And keep it current! New viruses are created each and every day, so age-old virus protection software is not going to help you. Also, run a virus check on **every** file that you download as well as every disk and CD-ROM that comes into your office, no matter who or where it comes from. Most virus protection software can be updated by going to the corporate site, downloading the most recent release, and installing it on your computer. (Yes, I realize the oddity of this—downloading a virus protection software update—but what else can you do?) You can also request to have update disks or CD-ROMs mailed to your office (usually, for an additional fee).

Please note that downloading files does not cause damage to your computer. The damage begins when you open (execute) an infected file. This is why you must check **every** e-mail attachment (and files distributed in chat rooms) before you open it, even if the file comes from a major corporation, a trusted relative, a colleague, or a client.

Some additional notes:

- If your e-mail reader (e.g., Netscape Messenger, Eudora, Microsoft Outlook) is configured to automatically open (execute) attached files (especially JavaScript, Word macros, or other executable code contained in attached messages), you should disable this feature to avoid contaminating your computer system.
- Configure your anti-virus software so that it scans all files when your computer boots up.
- If your computer is infected by a virus, trojan horse, or worm, an updated version of your anti-virus software should be able to inoculate your system. If you need additional assistance, check

---

WEBSEARCH

VIRUS PROTECTION SOFTWARE

Central Command
www.centralcommand.com

Computer Associates' EZ Anti-Virus
www.etrust.com

McAfee VirusScan
www.mcafee.com

Proland Software's Protector Plus
www.pspl.com

Symantec's Norton Anti-Virus
www.symantec.com

Trend Micro
www.antivirus.com

If you receive a virus warning message, go to one of the following sites for more information:

HoaxBusters
HoaxBusters.ciac.org
A public service of the U.S. Department of Energy's Computer Incident Advisory Capability (CIAC)

HoaxKill
www.hoaxkill.com

Virus List
www.viruslist.com

Vmyths
www.vmyths.com

---

the Web site of your anti-virus software manufacturer for more information about the specific virus, trojan horse, or worm.

If you think viruses are bad, consider what would happen to your business if an employee decided to have his or her way with your equipment. I've had to deal with a disgruntled employee who left a going-away "present" in the form of a stolen database and malicious letters sent to clients and colleagues on company letterhead. Unfortunately, there is little that you can do to prevent this type of thing. Recall the Employee Computer and Internet Usage Policy previously discussed. At the very least, if your company maintains signed copies of such a policy, you can file charges. The point is that no matter what you do, the deed has been done. Aside from reactive spin control, the best that you can do is to make sure that your company's hiring and data storage practices are top-notch. Believe me, far more things can go wrong than one immediately imagines.

Speaking of data storage, what would you do if there was a fire and everything in your office was destroyed? What if one of your employees accidentally formats your computer hard drives or maliciously unleashes a worm that deletes or damages important project information? What would become of your company's hardware, software, and client files. It's one thing to lose equipment; losing client data is a whole other ball of wax. Think about the amount of sensitive and proprietary data that resides on your company's hard drives. A colleague lost tens of thousands of dollars in accounts receivable because her house burned down and all of her home-office equipment and files went up in smoke. Needless to say, she hadn't backed up her files in months.

When you add it all up, software can cost you thousands of dollars. To protect your investment, you **must** back up your operating system and client files on a regular basis. Consider keeping software disks, CD-ROMs, and backup disks in a fireproof safe. Also, it might be useful to keep a set of backup disks off-site if your company doesn't use Web-based storage.

There are various ways to back up computer files including floppy disks, tape backup, Zip® disks, Jaz®⁴ disks, Intranet, or Web-based drives (e.g., Xdrive.com, iDrive.com). Whatever your method, back up regularly. Performing regular backups can keep your business running smoothly through natural disasters, hack attacks, viruses, and disgruntled employee attacks.

Surge protectors can guard your systems from electrical surges. As you become more and more dependent on computer equipment, consider a backup plan for power outages. (In light of California's energy crisis and scheduled rolling blackouts, business owners across the country have to wonder what they would do if the power went out, whether the cause was human error or natural disaster.) During power outages, laptops can survive on battery packs. Desktop systems won't be so fortunate. Once the power goes, your computer equipment shuts down, and any unsaved information is gone. An uninterruptible power supply (UPS) can give you extra battery time for multiple devices and lets you log off properly during a power failure.

Some of you may have had the misfortune of losing equipment in airports, taxis, or hotels. Contact your company's insurance agent to see whether insurance is available to replace your computer after loss, theft, or disaster. If your business is home-based, review your home-owner's or renter's insurance policy to see whether your computer equipment is covered. Some PDA models come with insurance policies (for an additional fee, of course) that will replace a lost, stolen, or damaged handheld. (The policies don't cover the data, which must be—you guessed it—backed up regularly.)

Last, but certainly not least, let's talk about how your company can fend off the security risk known as the "hack attack." Most "hack attacks" in the headlines during the past few years have targeted Web sites of major government agencies, universities, and large corporations. These specific types of security breaches are technically referred to as "distributed denial of service" (DDoS) attacks and are caused when a trojan is used to flood a Web server with repeated information requests, blocking access to legitimate site visitors.

Hackers come in all forms—precocious teenagers, disgruntled employees, and malicious opportunistic thieves. There is actually an entire subculture of expert programmers and networking wizards who spend their time learning the nuances of computer systems—sometimes for good reasons (e.g., uncovering security holes in corporate networks). Some may view hack attacks as simple tricks of a few pranksters, but hacking is illegal and can cause major damage.

Hackers don't always target Web servers. In fact, a hacker can target any insecure networked computer system, including your home- or office-based computer that connects to the Internet. (Remember. The Internet is a network of computers.) Hacking wreaks havoc by blocking access to authorized users, permitting access to unauthorized users, downloading sensitive information (e.g., financial data, passwords, credit card numbers, databases containing client records), and exposing encoded information, among other things.

You can protect your company's computer system from hack attacks in the following ways:

- Use a personal or network *firewall* (a system that controls access to your company's computer network). The network firewall is configured by your company's network engineer or administrator to provide authorized access to specified persons and to protect the network against unauthorized server log-ins and access. (If you have DSL access to the Internet, your ISP may have provided you with a copy of a personal firewall to protect your system from unauthorized access while you're connected to the Internet.)

- Create unique passwords and never give password information of any kind to anyone outside of the company or to employees who have no need to access a specific system or server.
- Change passwords every so often.
- If you have a large company, enlist the services of a security expert. He or she will be familiar with the specific resources needed to protect your information and equipment.

No single solution is entirely foolproof. To be most effective, your security efforts should be combined. The biggest security concern for most businesses is people on the inside. Very little can protect you against employees who carelessly or purposefully provide outsiders with network access information, share infected disks, and don't back up computer files.

For more information on computer and Internet security, go to AntiOnline (www.antionline.com) or Hacker Whacker (www. hackerwhacker.com).

KEEPING UP WITH TECHNOLOGY DEVELOPMENTS

Now that you're up to speed on strategic technology integration, let's look at some ways to manage the plethora of technology information that bombards you daily, via TV, radio, magazines, and the Internet.

- Make every effort to establish a long-term relationship with your company's computer consultant, network administrator, and MIS Director. These people are vital to your company's technology plans, so do what you can to create and maintain open lines of communication. In Chapter 4, we will look at methods for attracting and retaining the best technology talent to support your business.
- Minimize your company's print technology subscriptions. Most of these magazines have more ads than content and will only serve to overwhelm you. Besides, more is not always better. (How many of you have piles and piles of magazines and newspapers strewn throughout your offices?) Focus more on technology product reviews in your own industry's publications. If you prefer a more mainstream technology publication, try *Small Office Computing*. For larger businesses, try *PC World* or *MacWorld* (depending on your operating system, of course). Hundreds of technology publications are available. If you hear about a publication that might seem beneficial,

check out the publication's Web site before investing in a subscription.

- Black Enterprise offers print and Web access to technology
  product forecasts, interviews of prominent African American
  technology entrepreneurs, and reviews of currently available
  devices.
- Limit your electronic mailing list subscriptions; especially
  limit lists that target serious geeks. First and foremost, the serious geeks might get ticked off at a "Newbie" who asks elementary questions. Second, a good number of these lists have major
  traffic (translation: dozens, if not 100+, messages each day).
- ZDNet's Anchordesk (www.anchordesk.com) provides a daily
  dose of technology industry information, distributed directly
  to your e-mail inbox. It is one of the most concise and useful
  services of its kind. Both the daily e-mail messages and the AnchorDesk Web site provide commentary on proposed technologies, interviews of high-profile tech industry personalities, and
  expert advice for selecting products and vendors. There is also
  a searchable archive on the site for info that isn't currently
  highlighted.
- Go straight to the source. Bookmark hardware and software
  manufacturer Web sites. Some manufacturers also provide
  regular e-mail announcements with product updates and
  helpful tips.

Throughout this chapter, I have listed a variety of Web sites that
can help you learn more about hardware, software, computer training,
viruses, and computer security. Be sure to bookmark these sites and
add other technology sites as you find them. The Web should definitely
be used to support your ongoing technology learning experience.

IN CASE OF EMERGENCY . . .

Unfortunately, bad things do happen to good people—and to their computer systems. It is best, as always, to be proactive versus reactive, so
prepare yourself by creating a contact list of technical support people.
This includes your computer consultant, network administrator, MIS
Director, ISP, software and hardware manufacturers, Webmaster, database developers, and programmers (for custom-developed software).

Photocopy the form on page 61, and keep it near your phone.

TECHNICAL SUPPORT				
COMPANY		PHONE	E-MAIL	NOTES
= SAMPLE = Internet consultant	Mary Johnson	(999) 999-9999 ext. 486	maryj@anyemail.com	Pager# (888) 888-8888
Network Administrator				
MIS Director				
Computer consultant				
ISP—Internet access				
ISP—Web site hosting				
Webmaster Software—OS				
Software—Office suite				
Software— Anti-virus				
Software—E-mail reader				
Software—Web browser				
Software—Utilities				
Software— Financial Manager				
Software—Fax				
Software—File compression				
Software—				
Software—				
PDA				
Hardware— Computer				
Hardware— Printer #1				
Hardware— Printer #2				
Hardware—Fax				
Hardware—				
Hardware—				

3

ACCESS ON-THE-GO

It's hard to go anywhere nowadays without seeing a PDA or laptop of some kind. For those still struggling to find the right mobile devices, there are plenty of choices. Nearly every major hardware manufacturer—including 3Com, Sony, Casio, Hewlett Packard, Compaq, IBM, Handspring, and Psion— has a version of a handheld PC. And laptops are going for as little as $700. With so many reasonably priced pagers, cell phones, laptops, PDAs, and two-way messaging available, staying plugged-in is not the issue. Creating seamless access to business information is what's most important. Mobile entrepreneurs must implement the right plan to create a truly efficient mobile office without going broke.

RULE 1. SIMPLIFY

If you're a person who just might need a special tool belt for all of your electronic and digital devices, a unified messaging system (UMS) is right up your alley. Unified messaging allows you to consolidate receipt of voice, fax, and regular text messages into a single mailbox that is accessible by e-mail or telephone. Incoming e-mail messages are saved as text and can be converted to audio files for phone access. Fax images can be saved or printed. Some unified messaging systems offer

---

WEBSEARCH

UNIFIED MESSAGING SYSTEMS

Captaris
www.captaris.com

J2 Global Communications, Inc. (formerly jFAX)
www.j2.com

OneBox
www.onebox.com

uReach
www.ureach.com

Virtual Office System
www.virtualofficesystem.com

---

additional services: phone conferencing, toll-free fax numbers, pager notification of incoming e-mail and voice mail messages, scheduling, broadcast fax, and wireless services.

RULE 2.   BACK UP, SYNC UP, AND CHARGE UP

In Chapter 2, I expressed the importance of backing up your computer's data. This advice goes for laptops as well as desktop computers. Because of the increased likelihood of losing equipment during travel, backing up data is especially important for mobile professionals. Keep floppies, Zip®, or Jaz® disks that contain backed up information separate from your computer; otherwise, they'll be lost or stolen right along with your equipment, and that would completely defeat the purpose of backing up. Also, if you have a PDA, be sure to regularly sync up your data with the Personal Information Manager (PIM) on your computer. Lastly, charge up your cell phone and laptop batteries, and make sure that you've got an extra set of batteries for your PDA and pager.

RULE 3.   CREATE A PLAN B

Heaven forbid, but if you forget one of your mobile devices at the office, or if your cell phone, laptop, or PDA is lost or stolen, you need to have a

Plan B for accessing important information. Stop for a moment, and think about the important numbers that are stored in your cell phone, or the dates and contact information that are stored in your handheld device. If you lose your cell phone, laptop, or PDA, do you have the stored information readily available in another format for safekeeping? If the odds are pretty high that you would need to start from scratch, which would mean gathering important data for input into another device, be proactive and minimize the effects of the crisis before it happens.

MOBILE OPTIONS

We are inundated with technological developments, and we have become so dependent on these devices that we expect our offices to travel with us when we're on the road. Luckily, plenty of options are available to maintain a connection with our offices and perform nearly all of our basic office duties virtually. Let's look at some of the options for entrepreneurs on-the-go.

Web-Based E-Mail

A good number of us have "@yahoo.com," "@blackplanet.com," and "@hotmail.com" addresses. Often, these are used as backup e-mail addresses, but, for some professionals, they are a primary means of sending and receiving e-mail. The benefits are obvious. Web-based e-mail accounts allow access to e-mail on the road or from someone else's Internet connection. Even if you don't have a Web-based e-mail account, you can access your POP-based e-mail account from any Internet connection. Most often, ISPs will allow access to your new e-mail messages from their Web site. You can also go to E-Mail Anywhere (www.e-mailanywhere.com) or WebMail (www.webmail.com), input your e-mail address and password, and gain access to your new messages. (Please note that some of these services are free; others may charge a nominal fee for excessive use.)

If you're traveling with a laptop and modem, and your ISP offers national or international access, you'll only need the local access number for your destination city and a phone adapter to access your e-mail.

To integrate mobile phone, text messaging, and PDA functionalities, a number of companies have developed *wireless messaging Internet appliances,* such as Motorola's Personal Interactive Communicator models (www.mot.com) and Research In Motion Ltd.'s Blackberry handheld device (www.blackberry.net). These appliances typically offer high-speed network connections for fast Internet access, global roaming, personal calendars, address books, colorful displays, keyboards, and ample memory. They can communicate with one-way and two-way pagers, and can even send faxes and sync up with your PC and some of the more popular Personal Information Managers (PIMs).

File Access and Storage

If your company does not use a network (LAN or WAN), consider using a Web-based file storage system so that you and your mobile staff members have continuous access to important company information. Companies like Xdrive (www.xdrive.com), SwapDrive (www.swapdrive.com), iBackup (www.ibackup.com), and Driveway (www.driveway.com) offer low-cost online file storage with enhanced security and remote access via the Web or a wireless handheld device.

Software programs such as Symantec's pcAnywhere (www. symantec.com) allow you to securely and remotely access your office computer. The primary drawback is that you have to leave your desktop computer on and connected to a modem while you're away, so it is susceptible to unauthorized access.

Intranets are also great file storage and management systems for your mobile workforce. Intranets are private networks that allow you to search for documents and share files with other authorized users. Often, they include a calendar, an e-mail client, and contact management features. In the heady days of dot-com fever, companies like Intranets.com (www.intranets.com), Punch Networks' WebGroups (www.punchnetworks.com), and Planet Intra (www.planet-intra.com) offered these services for free, but most of them now have low-cost solutions for personal or group usage.

A number of companies provide a combination of the above-referenced services; for example, TeamOn Systems (www.teamon .com) offers e-mail consolidation and access, file management, and contact management services.

Mobile Peripherals

If you travel frequently and need printing, scanning, and interactive presentation services, a number of manufacturers offer mobile devices that perform these functions. Typically, they're a lot smaller than usual and cost only a fraction of the cost for their larger counterparts. This may add a bit of weight to your luggage, but it may be worth the investment if you or your staff spend a lot of time and money at business and copy centers or are frequently renting expensive A/V equipment.

Remote Conferencing

This alternative not only minimizes office expenses during business trips, it can also reduce the need to travel. Why spend money on airfare, hotels, and cabs when you can meet with your out-of-area clients on the Web? Companies like Genesys (www.genesys.com) and Webex (www.webex.com) provide Web-based meeting capabilities for businesses of any size. Other services, like Microsoft's NetMeeting (www.microsoft.com/netmeeting/), include video and audio conferencing, chat, file transfer, a whiteboard to share graphic information, and security features to protect your conversations.

When selecting your mobile options for primary use or as a backup, go for the solution that consolidates the most tasks that apply to your immediate needs and any needs that you expect to have within the next six months.

OFFICE ANYWHERE

If there is no way to avoid making a business trip, a number of options can assist you while you're on the road.

- *Hotel centers.* Most international hotels with a three-star or higher rating have data ports for Internet access in guest rooms, and full-service business centers that provide computer and Internet access, copying, faxing, scanning, and printing services. Many luxury hotels have added high-speed access in guests' rooms. Check hotel Web sites, or call before you travel, to confirm the availability of these services.
- *Copy centers.* With nearly 1,000 locations around the world, Kinko's (www.kinkos.com) has cornered the market on mobile office services. In addition to printing, copying, binding, faxing, scanning, Internet access, and computer rental services, Kinko's also rents office space. A number of smaller, local copy centers in major metropolitan areas offer similar services. It's a good idea to check for locations before you go, just to be on the safe side. Most of the larger copy centers now have the capacity to receive job orders by e-mail, so you can reduce shipping costs by having large printing or binding jobs prepared locally.
- *Internet kiosks.* These publicly accessible stand-alone terminals, usually found in airports and business centers, are becoming more and more popular. Many of them now have the capacity to "beam" (wirelessly transmit) local information to PDAs.

- *Virtual offices.* If your company needs a satellite office without all of the expense, try using a virtual office, like those of Regus (www.regus.com) and HQ Global WorkPlaces (www.hq.com). For a nominal fee, you can use their private offices or conference rooms on an hourly basis. Virtual offices charge business customers a flat monthly fee for using their address to receive mail and for answering phone calls. Both Regus and HQ have offices all over the world and offer a variety of amenities (e.g., high-speed Internet access, small and large conference rooms, professionally answered telephones, and modern furnished office spaces). The cost of their services is based on the size of your company and the frequency of your needs.

- *Community technology centers* (CTCs), also referred to as "community access centers," are typically grassroots efforts to provide computer and Internet access to people in communities that would not otherwise have such access. In addition to providing access to computers, CTCs offer training for various computer skills and software programs. Some of the better funded CTCs offer small business services as well.

Here is a short list of CTCs around the country. They offer computer training as well as public access to computers and the Internet:

Breakaway Technologies
3417 West Jefferson Boulevard
Los Angeles, CA 90018
Phone: (323) 737-7677
Fax: (323) 737-7640
www.breakway.org

Computer Street Academy
2595 International Boulevard
Oakland, CA 94612
Phone: (510) 533-5815
Fax: (510) 533-5814
www.computerstreet.org

Fenway Community Development Corp. / Computer Learning Center
73 Hemenway Street #23
Boston, MA 02115
Phone: (617) 267-4637
Fax: (617) 267-8591
www.fenwaycdc.org

Charles River Public Internet Center
154 Moody Street
Waltham, MA 02453
Phone: (781) 891-9559
Fax: (781) 891-6535
www.crpic.org

Digital Access Organization
3228 22nd Avenue South
Minneapolis, MN 55407
Phone: (612) 724-9097
www.digitalaccess.org

Playing 2 Win
1330 Fifth Avenue
New York, NY 10026
Phone: (212) 369-4077
Fax: (212) 369-7046
www.playing2win.org

Wright Computer Connection
2530 Archwood Street
Dayton, OH 45406
Phone: (937) 274-6700
www.wrightcomputerconnection.org

Reboot Philly
1315 Spruce Street
Philadelphia, PA 19107
Phone: (215) 735-1151
Fax: (215) 735-3069
www.rebootphilly.org

Technology For All
109 North Post Oak, Suite 425
Houston, TX 77024
Phone: (713) 316-5761
Fax: (713) 316-5790
www.techforall.org

There are hundreds of CTCs around the world. To find one in your area or business destination city, go to the Community Technology Centers Network Web site at www.ctcnet.org. You can also contact your local library, Urban League office, or Chamber of Commerce and

---

WEBSEARCH

American Cyber Cafés
www.globalcomputing.com/cafes.html

Cybercafé Lists
www.indranet.com/potpourri/links/cybercafe.html

Cybercafé Search Engine
www.cybercaptive.com

HM USA Travel Guide—Cyber/Internet Cafés in the U.S.
and Canada
usa.dedas.com/cybcaf.html

Internet Café Guide
www.netcafeguide.com

Net Café Guide
www.netcafeguide.com

---

ask whether such services are offered or if one of their representatives can refer you to another organization.

Keep in mind that many of these centers need volunteers as well as equipment and financial donations.

- *Cybercafés.* Also referred to as "Internet cafés," these public access centers serve beverages and pastries to patrons who come to compute. Most of them are hip little stores with multiple multimedia stations (including PCs and Macs). There is usually a nominal fee to use the machines at your leisure.

A few cybercafé guidebooks list international locations. Many new cybercafés are opened each year, so it's probably best to check for locations on the Web prior to your travel.

A WIRELESS WORLD

What better way to be a mobile professional than to do business globally, with no strings attached? Wireless technology is expected to be the answer to myriad technology challenges facing growing businesses in countries around the world.

In actuality, we've been using wireless devices for quite some time. Simple household fixtures like radios, garage door openers, cordless telephones, baby monitors, and pagers all use wireless technology. Instead of wires or cables, wireless devices use electromagnetic waves to carry signals and transfer data. The renewed interest in wireless technology reflects developments that enhance data transfer, especially via Internet connectivity.

With technology developments to date, plus looming threats of convergence and all things wireless, we now have access to whenever–wherever communication. We no longer have to be "tied down" to our offices, or any other specific locations, to gain access to shared files or the Internet. The technology still has a long way to go; wireless Internet access is not always faster than high-speed, line-based connections, and coverage is not yet available everywhere. But, we can expect some great changes in the near future.

By 2002, Bluetooth™ technology (www.bluetooth.com) will be available in millions of devices worldwide. Bluetooth™ technology, a newly developed wireless standard, was collaboratively developed by a consortium of companies, including 3Com, Intel, Toshiba, Ericsson, IBM, Lucent, Microsoft, and Nokia. Its purpose is to simplify wireless connectivity and personal data networking by eliminating the need for cable attachments that connect computers, handheld devices, and phones. The technology, which actually revolves around a tiny microchip that's stored in digital devices, incorporates a radio transmitter that allows for globally compatible data transfer.

Here are some examples of what's to come from Bluetooth-enabled devices:

- *The three-in-one phone.* At home, your phone functions as a portable phone (fixed line charge). When you're on the move, it functions as a mobile phone (cellular charge). And when your phone comes within range of another mobile phone with built-in Bluetooth wireless technology, it functions as a walkie-talkie (no telephony charge).
- *The Internet bridge.* Use your mobile computer to surf the Internet wherever you are, regardless of whether you're cordlessly connected through a mobile phone (cellular) or through a wire-bound connection (e.g., ISDN, LAN, xDSL).
- *The interactive conference.* In meetings and conferences, you can instantly transfer specific documents to selected participants, and exchange electronic business cards automatically, without any wired connections.

- *The ultimate headset.* Connect your wireless headset to your mobile phone, mobile computer, or any wired connection. Keep your hands free for more important tasks when you're at the office or in your car.

Usage model: Automatic synchronizer.

- *The automatic synchronizer* does its job for your desktop, mobile computer, laptop, PDA, and mobile phone. For instance, as soon as you enter your office, the address list and calendar in your laptop will automatically be updated to agree with the one in your desktop, or vice versa.

From a business standpoint, wireless technology not only increases mobility; it can save companies lots of time and money. Employees will be able to access the Internet from their laptops at a client's office (or anywhere else, for that matter) without requiring cables or phone lines. Syncing up handheld devices won't be necessary; data will be transferred in real-time. Inventory management can be automated and remotely transmitted, so drive time for companies with numerous and widespread warehousing facilities and equipment is reduced. Equipment can be remotely diagnosed and repaired. It's too early to calculate the return on investment for wireless networks, but imagine the savings when you don't have to call a contractor every time your company needs to add one or more employee workstations. Without the cables, employees can change the physical layout of the office almost effortlessly, and new stations can be easily added. Troubleshooting time will also be minimized. Computer consultants can go directly to the problem, without having to check the connection between the server and each network node.

The primary shortcomings for wireless connectivity are capacity and security. Due to coverage issues and the fact that other appliances use similar frequencies, there may be conflicts and service interruptions. Also, network connectivity has to be closely monitored and

---

WEBSEARCH

WIRELESS ACCESS PROVIDERS

Captaris
www.captaris.com

iAnywhere Solutions, Inc.
www.ianywhere.com

MobileSys, Inc.
www.mobilesys.com

SmartServ
www.smartserv.com

Be sure to check with your current ISP for wireless Internet access.

---

managed so that visiting clients, vendors, former employees, and other unauthorized users cannot gain access to sensitive company information. If wireless-enabled equipment gets lost or stolen, an emergency plan needs to be in place to deactivate a user's access and/or to erase sensitive data.

M-COMMERCE

Just when you thought you were getting used to the notion of e-Commerce (electronic commerce), here comes m-Commerce (mobile commerce). Thanks to advances in wireless technology, advertisers are making every effort to keep up with mobile professionals. Corporations' efforts to wirelessly brand themselves are gaining momentum as I type. From the consumer side, your first thought is probably: "Great. Just what I needed; more ads." From a business perspective, m-Commerce spells potential opportunity.

Just think, as Bluetooth™ and other wireless technologies provide faster and more secure data transfer, we can expect more mobile professionals to trade stocks, access account information, pay bills, and make purchases on-the-go (no doubt, paving the way for even more new media terms, like "m-banking," "m-trading," etc.). Considering the amount of money that people invest in phones, pagers, PDAs, and other mobile devices, not only will your business become globally accessible because of your strategically planned and content-rich Internet presence, your company can actually follow clients and potential clients wherever they go. Talk about thinking outside of the box!

The cost of electronic billing is a fraction of what it costs to generate paper invoicing. Your company might consider implementing m-Commerce-enabled bill payment or using text messaging to send meeting announcements, marketing messages, or accounts payable reminders. These types of developments offer perfect opportunities for your business to save money *and* add value for clients, and these two goals should be the top priorities of your technology integration strategy.

KNOWING WHEN AND HOW TO DISCONNECT

Now that I've reviewed nearly every way in the world to stay connected, it's clear that connectivity is not a problem as much as the need to balance professional accessibility with free time away from clients and employees. The downside to *whenever, wherever* communication is that we can and do communicate anytime and anywhere. Contrary to the benefits of technology—namely, increased sales, productivity, and added value for clients—it can also create more stress, inefficiency, and burnout. Part of any company's technology plan should be a very clear set of expectations and ground rules for technology usage that applies to employees and clients.

As Internet and technology usage has grown, more and more people are spending less time enjoying themselves and more time in front of their computer screens—typing reports, troubleshooting software, surfing the Web, and answering e-mail. Time spent with friends and family is reduced to a few instant-message sessions over the course of a month, if we're lucky. Technology developments have contributed to a "do it now" expectation from business managers and clients alike. To maintain sanity, the cord must be cut.

Technology's pervasiveness calls for a few guidelines that will free you and your employees from its grasp, if only for a short while.

1. Set a specific response time (e.g., 24 hours, 48 hours) for e-mail messages, and let employees and clients know what to expect. Consider using your e-mail client's auto-response mechanism to remind clients of this.
2. Be sure to note how messages sent late on Friday, by management or clients, should be handled (e.g., respond by close of business on Monday, respond by Monday noon).
3. Create a disaster recovery plan ("Plan B") so that vacationing managers and employees don't have to be interrupted.

4. Set the right example. Managers should not develop a "Do as I say, not as I do" approach. Once you set the rules, you must follow them in order to create the right environment. If managers are setting an example, it will be much easier to reprimand employees who don't follow the rules.

5. Don't encourage employees who break these rules; it defeats the purpose of setting rules in the first place. We'd all love to have employees who happily work around the clock, but it is not good for morale, or for long-term productivity, to have employees who regularly burn the midnight oil.

6. Be clear about what constitutes the end of a business day. Is it 5:00 P.M. Eastern Standard Time, 7:00 P.M. Pacific Standard Time, or whatever time the employee leaves the office for the day? It's obviously more difficult to set a concrete time that applies to everyone, especially if you have a virtual office with employees in different time zones, so choose carefully. There are exceptions to every rule, and individual work preferences vary.

7. Create a regular monthly "tech-free" or "unplugged" time when employees can enjoy their spare time worry-free about receiving e-mail, two-way text messages, or phone calls about work-related material.

It will be difficult to create a universal rule for your company but, at the very least, having basic expectations set and understood by employees and clients will minimize the headaches and burnout. I've noted some additional e-mail communication tips in Appendix B.

4

HIRING AND PROMOTING TECHNOLOGY TALENT

It isn't difficult to figure out who's getting paid nowadays. Years ago, you'd hear parents talking about their kids' becoming doctors, lawyers, and educators. Now, all you hear is computers-this and Internet-that. This industry is still growing faster than the speed of light, and so are the bottom lines of people who are defying all of the old rules. Those rules—that you have to "pay your dues" by getting several degrees, and climbing the corporate ladder slowly and methodically— are all being shattered by new technology opportunities.

Young men and women who were college students only a few years ago are now boasting personal wealth in the tens of millions. People with little capital and less business experience have started part-time businesses out of their garages. In a few short years they have amassed wealth beyond anyone's wildest dreams. Bill Gates and his behemoth corporation are household names like no other CEO and business have ever been. Not a day goes by without our reading about another tech industry IPO, merger, or acquisition, despite the stock market's corrections and the dot-com meltdown.

Because of the growth of the Internet, technology jobs are being created faster than they can be filled.[1] In its annual IT staffing and compensation guide, The Meta Group, an international research and consulting firm, reported that U.S. companies are struggling to fill 600,000 IT positions, despite the recent dot-com bust.[2] While the unemployment gap is down from 1 million in 2000, the Meta Group predicts that overall demand will stay high for individuals with specialized talents.

In the midst of all this, many African American entrepreneurs claim that they are hard-pressed to find talented IT employees and vendors in the community. Major technology companies are saying the same thing; in fact, they have been arguing for years that American workers are not skilled enough to fill the hundreds of thousands of available IT positions. What's more, tech industry business leaders have been vehemently and successfully pushing for the government to lift immigration barriers so that they can hire more foreign workers through the H1-B[3] visa program.

The opposition, including the Coalition for Fair Employment in Silicon Valley, states that not enough outreach and training have taken place, and that the hiring of additional foreign workers will hurt America's long-term competitiveness. As far as these groups are concerned, tech firms have not attempted to tap all of their available resources, namely those of the African American community.

THE STATE OF TECHNOLOGY EMPLOYMENT FOR AFRICAN AMERICANS

So, who's to blame? Are American workers—most specifically, African American workers—truly lacking IT skills? Not necessarily. Many view the situation as a case of mutual responsibility. Deidre McIntyre, CEO of redIbis in New York, sees a lack of outreach on both sides. "Mainstream corporate leaders network with vendors they know. Unless African American IT professionals attend 'mainstream' technology events, then the heads of these corporations will not know African American vendors." While efforts like those of the Coalition for Fair Employment are needed, both the corporations and African American IT professionals have to do their part.

Antonio Cox, President of New York-based Kinetic Media, Inc., agrees with McIntyre. "I think mainstream firms seek to team with people and organizations they feel they can have good, profitable relationships with. This is typically done with people you know. If they do not know certain people, they will not seek to do business with them. If they think they have more of a chance to be profitable with Company A than Company B, they will deal with A. And realistically, if individuals that head these technology firms have no real relationships with African Americans, be they entrepreneurs, politicians, or neighbors, how will the good, profitable relationships develop?"

The Coalition for Fair Employment in Silicon Valley, mentioned earlier, is one of the efforts underway to increase minority representation in technology. An eight-month investigation by the *San Francisco Chronicle* in 1998 spawned the creation of the Coalition, which is actually an affiliation of three organizations: the Bay Area Black MBAs, Bay Area Black Data Processing Associates, and the Peninsula Area Black Personnel Administrators. The *Chronicle*'s findings showed that the presence of African Americans and Latinos in the tech industry is dismal, at best. Led by entrepreneur and author John Templeton, the Coalition's goal is to create more job opportunities at technology firms. The Coalition's summits have brought together Silicon Valley executives, the Department of Labor, and community groups to discuss solutions to the Digital Divide and IT training opportunities for domestic workers.

According to the Coalition, "Only discriminatory practices can explain the fact that there are more than 225,000 African American engineers, programmers and systems analysts,[4] yet there are only 1,688 black professional employees in Silicon Valley companies."[5] Wayne Hicks, President of the Cincinnati Chapter of the Black Data Processing Associates (BDPA), concurs: "In my view, major corporations haven't been serious about seeking diversity in their IT workforce. If corporations or entrepreneurs were serious . . . then they wouldn't continue to use failed methods of recruiting IT talent of color."

With an increasing number of tech industry layoffs and hiring freezes, Butch Wing, Director of the Rainbow PUSH Coalition Silicon Valley Project, feels that greater challenges are posed for these companies to rectify their hiring practices to include more people of color. "So, Rainbow/PUSH and community groups must work even harder to keep the issue of employment representation on the agenda of technology companies."

As the federal government, tech firms, and special-interest groups clash over who is responsible for educating American workers and increasing outreach to minority communities, African American entrepreneurs are still left seeking the technology support they need within the community. The question is: Does this serve to confirm the tech industry argument, or is something else going on?

With Digital Divide efforts increasing in the past few years, people like Anita Brown (aka "MissDC," founder of BlackGeeks); NetNoir's Malcolm Casselle and E. David Ellington; Willie Atterberry (founder and publisher of the Afronet Web site and print publication); Trish Millines Dziko (Technology Access Foundation founder and Executive Director); and Darien Dash (Chairman of DME Interactive Holdings and CEO of Places of Color) have practically become household names. (Other African American technology trailblazers are highlighted later in this chapter.) Their widening popularity and efforts serve not only to encourage tech firms to market to the African American community, but also to stimulate community interest in technology careers and businesses.

I know quite a few African American technology trailblazers—people who are building businesses as well as working in the trenches as programmers, analysts, engineers and designers. When this is the case, why are our own businesses having trouble finding talented, community-based technology vendors? Maybe African American entrepreneurs don't know where to look to find African American technology professionals. Maybe many of our technology pioneers are too preoccupied with their businesses and careers to expand their professional networks. Maybe they're purposefully keeping quiet so as not to become moving targets for criticism and other negativity. Or, maybe (and I use that term loosely), African American technology pioneers are simply being overlooked and overshadowed, not only by the New Boys' Club, but by our own community as well. To be perfectly honest, I think we're facing a combination of these problems.

FINDING AND SELECTING TECHNOLOGY EMPLOYEES AND VENDORS

When seeking new technology hires, most entrepreneurs and Human Resources (HR) managers use a variety of tactics, including classified ads, traditional placement agencies, industry-specific recruiters, Web-based career sites, and word of mouth—or, they hire internally.[6] Referral sources should also include local Black Business Associations, African American Chambers of Commerce, Urban League, community technology centers, and/or neighborhood churches. I have included a list of African American technology associations and career resources in Figure 4.1. Most of these resources are national in scope, so their representatives should be able to point you in the right direction. Wayne Hicks says, "You can't find a Chevy at a Ford dealership . . . and it is difficult to find African American IT professionals when you don't tap into the international network of BDPA. BDPA Information Technology Thought Leaders (www.bdpa.org) is a vibrant source of IT talent that has been untapped by Corporate America over the past 25 years."

Before setting out to hire technology professionals, you have to know what you're looking for and how to properly gauge the skill set of the candidates. Many entrepreneurs and business managers have no clue as to what types of skills and experiences IT employees and vendors should have. The usual factors still apply, with a few twists.

Figure 4.1   African American Technology
Associations and Career Sites

Black Data Processing Associates (BDPA) Phone: (800) 727-BDPA	www.bdpa.org
Black Equal Opportunity Employment Journal Magazine Phone: (800) 487-5099	www.blackeoejournal.com
Coalition for Fair Employment, Silicon Valley Phone: (415) 674-6961	www.blackmoney.com/coalition.html
Diversity Careers in Engineering and Information Technology	www.diversitycareers.com
Equal Opportunities Publications, Inc. Phone: (631) 421-9421	www.eop.com
Executive Leadership Council and Foundation Phone: (202) 298-8226	www.elcinfo.com
International Black Aerospace Council Phone: (812) 285-9855	www.BlackAerospace.com
Minorities Job Bank (aka IMDiversity.com or iminorities.com) Phone: (504) 523-0154	www.minorities-jb.com
Minority Internet and Technology Professionals	www.mitp.net
The Multicultural Advantage— Online Community for Professionals of Color Phone: (215) 849-0946	www.tmaonline.net
National Action Council for Minorities in Engineering Phone: (212) 279-2626	www.nacme.org
National Black Programmers Association	www.nbpainc.org
National Council of Black Engineers and Scientists Phone: (213) 896-9779	www.ncbes.org
National Society of Black Engineers Phone: (703) 549-2207	www.nsbe.org
The National Technical Association Inc. Phone: (757) 827-9280	www.ntaonline.org
US Black Engineer & IT Magazine Phone: (410) 244-7101	www.BlackEngineer.com

Education

Because of the growing number of billionaire college dropouts in the tech industry and the overwhelming demand for IT workers, some HR managers are willing to overlook the lack of a college degree in favor of an impressive amount of industry experience. It is up to you and your HR department to determine the importance of a new hire's college education. Rest assured, the more relevant the degree and the greater the amount of education, the more you will pay to retain the employee's services.

Butch Wing (Rainbow/PUSH) points out that there is a misconception that "one needs to be a computer scientist or math major to work in technology. Eighty percent of the jobs in any technology company do NOT require math or science backgrounds. For example, John Thompson and Robert Knowling, two of the leading African American CEOs of technology companies, do not have math or science degrees."

Whether or not the applicant's choice of a college major or completion of a college degree is relevant, continuing education is vital. If a person earned a Computer Science degree 10 years ago, what educational investments has he or she made since that time? Look for regular training courses and advanced certifications. Before your company invests in a potential employee's salary, you need to see how much that person has invested in himself or herself. Technology skills should remain current so that he or she can provide your business with the best possible technology solutions.

Industry Experience

How long has this person been in the industry? Naturally, because many developments in this industry are relatively new, it is absurd to expect many IT professionals to have 20 or 30 years of work experience. (I have actually seen Web development job descriptions requesting 10 years of industry experience!) If the person is relatively new in the industry, focus more on his or her education. The key is to find out how the described skills were acquired and how the person plans to maintain them. Request samples of earlier work, where applicable.

And don't be surprised to find quite a few resumes with dozens of positions listed, even for younger candidates. Due to the dot-com fallout, many IT professionals have moved from one company to another, often in a matter of months. Unlike previous generations, when job loyalty was assumed, IT professionals tend to go where the money and perks are.

Specialized Skills

Look for candidates and vendors who have specialized skill sets. Have you heard the old adage "Jack of all trades, master of none"? Beware of any IT professional who tries to assure you that he or she is a network administrator, security expert, Web site designer, and authority on database management and software development. It is quite possible for someone to have dabbled in all of these areas, but it's best to go with an expert. Dedication to one's field of interest is key.

Professional Affiliations

Another way to measure a person's commitment to a craft is to view his or her professional affiliations. The resume may indicate membership in industry organizations, or volunteer positions on committees or Boards of Directors. If it doesn't, query the applicant. Active participation in professional organizations may be beneficial to your business. Your employees' professional networks are extensions of your business contacts. Also, such extracurricular activities may provide visibility opportunities for your company for sales, hiring, or public relations (PR).

References

The best way to determine an applicant's level of professionalism, initiative, qualifications, and job performance is by checking references (e.g., previous employers, past and current clients, and so on). In the interest of saving your company time and money, it is your responsibility to properly screen any employee (before hiring) or vendor (before retaining its services). The goal is to establish a long-term, mutually beneficial relationship, so you will want to be sure that this person (or vendor) can provide the required services (or products) and that the style and work ethic of this new source fits easily into your corporate culture.

Wayne Hicks adds, "The bar is high for today's IT professional. It is no longer enough to simply know bits and bytes. Increasingly, we are learning that an IT professional must have other business skills. Technology is simply a tool. The well-rounded IT professional understands this fact and hones his or her skills in a wide range of areas, including finance, customer relationships, marketing, and so forth. It goes without saying that the top-rated IT professionals are constantly staying at the forefront of their industry with an ongoing education program. An IT professional that is not consistently learning new insights and technologies is rapidly becoming obsolete."

Two extremely important but commonly overlooked factors in IT hiring are: communication skills and attitude. IT people are notorious for bewildering managers, coworkers, and clients with industry jargon. A lot of companies have suffered because they hired an employee or consultant just because he or she talked a good game. There are plenty of IT people out there who are great at what they do, plus, they are able to communicate normally, without all the jargon. Entrepreneurs and venture capitalists alike have fallen victim to people who sounded as though they knew what they were talking about. In addition to the above gauges, make sure you hire someone you can understand.

Last, don't hire a skilled vendor or employee who has a bad attitude. This type of person has immobilized many a corporate computer system. These "geeks with attitude" are the kinds of people who disappear into the ethers just when you need them. They'll take your Web site hostage or they won't take the time to properly explain the issues and options at hand because they figure you "won't understand anyway." It is often difficult to measure this type of thinking during an interview or initial consultation, which is why it's important to check professional references. Also, try presenting a hypothetical problem during the interview and ask the applicant how he or she would solve it. Or, ask for a description of the most difficult problem the person ever had to explain to a client or former employer.

RETAINING IT PERSONNEL

Retention is a major problem in the tech industry, as I mentioned before. Consequently, a lot of companies are going out of their way to entice and keep good IT employees. Some of you may have been privy to the crazy perks that a lot of the dot-coms have doled out to retain staff—astronomical salaries, pricey vacations, obscene stock options, sign-on bonuses, top-of-the-line tech gadgets, office massages, expensive parties, high-priced furniture, and cars. Luckily, the meltdown has turned that around, to some degree. A lot of IT people nowadays are just happy to have a job with a stable company and a paycheck that doesn't bounce.

Traditional businesses can establish realistic budget figures for IT salaries by talking to corporate recruiters, checking job-posting sites on the Web (e.g., monster.com, diversityemployment.com, headhunter .net), reviewing the classified section of the newspaper, and getting referrals from colleagues. There are also numerous annual salary surveys[7] and reports on the Web. Tech Republic's 2000 Salary Survey is a pretty decent report targeted to larger businesses with dedicated IT departments. The problem with some surveys is that many of the salaries are inflated and misleading; hence the flood of people with little experience

---

WEBSEARCH

SALARY LINKS AND COMPENSATION RESOURCES

DICE.com Salary Query
marketing.dice.com/rateresults/conhr.asp

Information Week
www.informationweek.com/itsalaryadvisor

JobStar
www.jobstar.org

RealRates.com
www.realrates.com

SalariesReview.com
www.salariesreview.com

Wage Web
www.wageweb.com

ZDNet's Salary Zone
www.zdnet.com/enterprise/salaryzone/index.html

---

entering the tech industry. Often, these surveys don't account for the size of the company or the geographic location.

In addition to a competitive salary, the usual employee benefits are expected: healthcare, vacation time, overtime pay, mobility, and challenging projects. Additional leverage items include a 401(k) plan, profit sharing, bonus packages, paid training, extra vacation time, travel opportunities, flexible work schedules, and permission to dress casually. Keep in mind that there is no universally guaranteed method for retaining employees, especially when you're competing against companies with bigger budgets and better branding.

If you decide to outsource your company's IT projects, screen potential IT vendors just as closely as you would a potential salaried employee. Your focus should always remain on establishing a long-term relationship with the most capable and credible IT support network that your company can find.

AFRICAN AMERICAN TECHNOLOGY INNOVATORS

An innovator or pioneer is "one who leads" or "ventures into unknown or unclaimed territory." Many African American technology pioneers are not household names, but we have quite a few of them. These men and women have beaten the odds and are quietly leaving a legacy, not just for their own families, but for the entire community. I have selected a group of these entrepreneurial pioneers to highlight. Some are veterans; others are relatively new to IT. I have purposefully selected pioneers from different areas of technology and from different parts of the country, to show the wide range of achievements and opportunities that our fellow entrepreneurs are pursuing.

Only a small number of African American dot-coms get press, but there are actually quite a few successful African American-owned technology businesses. Among them are: EasyWeb Inc. of Research Triangle Park, North Carolina (www.easywebinc.com); NiaOnline of Chicago, IL (www.niaonline.com); Imporito Networks of Santa Clara, CA; Network Commerce, Inc. of Seattle, WA (www.networkcommerce.com); SongPro Inc. of Beverly Hills, California (www.songpro.com); TechnikOne of Gaffney, South Carolina (www.technikone.com); Cyber Group Network, Inc., of San Bernadino, California (www.cybergroupnetwork.com); and The GilWil Group of Atlanta, Georgia (www.gilwilgroup.com). (You will find a list of additional African American-owned technology businesses in the Networking Directory of this book.) Each year, blackmoney.com publishes a list of the 50 most important African Americans in technology. This list includes high-ranking African Americans in government; private industry; the fields of science, computing, and engineering; as well as technology entrepreneurs.

I encourage African American trailblazers to speak out, stand up, and be counted. African American youth need to see these talented people and know that sports and entertainment are not the only roads to success. Also, mainstream America and tech businesses need a tap on the shoulder to remind them of our past contributions and current capabilities.

Dr. Michael Batie
Founder and CEO
SuccessNet

Location: Los Angeles, CA

Web Site: www.successnet.net

Dr. Michael Batie has been involved in Information Technology since 1977 when, as an undergraduate physics student, he used the Internet to exchange data with colleagues at other universities. He is currently the CEO of SuccessNet, a privately owned Internet Service Provider based in Los Angeles, California. The five-year-old company provides Internet access, Web hosting, and training for businesses and nonprofit organizations. Dial-up Internet access is available throughout California, Michigan, New Hampshire, and Rhode Island, and in Denver, New York, Chicago, Dallas, and Washington D.C., for as low as $10 per month. SuccessNet has eight employees and boasts several thousand customers.

Over the years, Dr. Batie has been involved in various leading-edge online ventures, the earliest of which was Personal Computer Engineers (PCE). Partnered with Laurence Rozier and Kevin Martin, PCE created the National Black Computer Network (NBCN), the first black-owned international computer network. PCE was also among the first software companies to offer product support and upgrades online via the Engineers WorkBench Network (EWBNet). This network was accessed via the Ziff-Davis online service called BIX (Byte Information Exchange). In addition, PCE marketed and sold expert systems shells, using off-the-shelf database products.

Dr. Batie's experience also includes working as a technician and engineer at TRW and Hughes Aircraft; serving as an elementary school teacher in South Central Los Angeles; working as an Assistant Professor of Education at California State University Los Angeles (CSULA) in the Charter College of Education and as a Lecturer in the CSULA School of Engineering.

Dr. Batie holds a BS in Physics and an MA in Education, both conferred by California State University at Los Angeles, and California State Teaching Credentials in Adult Education, Vocational Education, and Elementary Education. In 2001, Dr. Batie completed his dissertation for the PhD in Education, with an emphasis on Organizational Theory, at the University of California at Riverside.

As if that's not enough, Dr. Batie helped to start an Inglewood, California-based cybercafé, Café Future and Gallery (www.cafefutureandgallery.com). He also created the Math Literacy Across America 2001 program (www.acrossamerica2001 .com), a cross-country bicycle ride to facilitate community awareness about math literacy for inner-city students, and he spearheaded the development of three charter schools in the Los Angeles area.

Dr. Batie's awards and affiliations include:

M. W. White Award from The American Society of Physics Students

Achievement Award, Los Angeles Council of Black Professional Engineers

Listing in Marquis International Who's Who in Optical Science and Engineering

Superior Performer Award, Hughes Aircraft Company

Outstanding Alumni Award, CSULA/CBEMSS

Service Award, Los Angeles Urban League Independent Living Program

California State University Doctoral Incentive Award

Committee Chairman, Los Angeles Council of Black Professional Engineers

Committee Chairman, Engineering Student Council, CSULA

Committee Chairman, Inner City School District Association

President, Physics Club, CSULA

President, Council of Black Engineering and Science Students, CSULA

Member, Physics Honor Society

Member, Corporate Advisory Board CSULA Minority Engineering Program

University of California Research Fellowship, California Educational Research Cooperative at the University of California, Riverside

Donna Auguste
Cofounder
Freshwater Software, Inc.
Founder, CEO, and President
Leave A Little Room Foundation

Location: Boulder, CO

Web Site: www.leavealittleroom.org; www.freshtech.com

Donna Auguste is truly a "wonder woman." In the past 20 years, she has quietly established herself as a leader in the IT industry. Her entire career is filled with achievements, the most recent of which was the founding of her own private nonprofit, the Leave A Little Room Foundation. Her vision for the foundation is to encourage people to share their gifts and talents with each other. The two primary areas of focus are a global gospel music ministry and a technology-based global outreach ministry in Africa. For the past few years, Auguste has been leading an effort to bring solar-powered electricity and e-mail communication to schools and hospital clinics in remote villages in Tanzania.

Auguste serves as President and CEO of the Leave A Little Room Foundation, and she manages five employees in two U.S. locations.

The company that she cofounded in February 1996, Freshwater Software, Inc., was acquired by Mercury Interactive Corporation in May 2001. Mercury Interactive paid $147 million in cash and assumed Freshwater's stock option plan. Freshwater Software continues to operate as a wholly owned subsidiary under Mercury Interactive's Application Performance Management (APM) business unit. After a short transition period, Auguste chose to leave the company to pursue the management of Leave A Little Room and her other philanthropic interests.

Freshwater Software provides software development for Web server and monitoring applications. The company designs and delivers tools that help Web administrators achieve and maintain control over rapidly changing corporate Web sites. Freshwater's solutions enable e-business growth and ensure that Web sites are available 24 hours a day, 7 days a week. Products include SiteScope (a real-time solution for internal Web server performance monitoring), SiteSeer (remote Web server monitoring), and Global SiteReliance (an annual subscription service that offers complete Web server management at the network, server, and application levels).

In May 2000, Freshwater was ranked as the second-fastest-growing private company in the Denver area. Freshwater's 1999 revenues reached $2.8 million, and first-quarter 2000 revenues were $1.7 million. Total revenues for 2000 exceeded $15 million. In five short years, the Boulder, Colorado-based company has acquired over 3,000 domestic and international clients, including CNET, Intel Online Services (an Intel Corporation company), Motley Fool, Alta Vista, Microsoft, America Online, Lycos, Merrill Lynch, GO.com, and Barnesandnoble.com. In 2000, the 64-employee company opened an office in London to serve its growing international client base.

Prior to founding Freshwater Software Inc., Auguste was senior director for US West Advanced Technologies. She built and led an engineering team assigned to developing the architecture for interactive television applications for US West's fiber-optic broadband network. Before joining US West, she was a key engineering manager for the landmark Newton Personal Digital Assistant product family at Apple Computer, a product achievement noted for its "intelligent" user interfaces and engineering innovations, which made possible its small form factor. Prior to joining Apple, Auguste spent six years at

IntelliCorp as a member of the engineering team that introduced some of the world's first commercial artificial intelligence knowledge engineering technology products.

For her innovative engineering work on the Apple Newton Personal Digital Assistant, Auguste was awarded four patents by the U.S. Patent and Trademark Office. She is a member of the IEEE Internet Computing Editorial Board and is a Commissioner for the Colorado Commission on Science and Technology. She is also editor of a bimonthly business newsletter, WomenCompute.com.

Auguste holds a bachelor's degree in electrical engineering and computer science from the University of California, Berkeley. She completed her graduate studies in Computer Science at Carnegie-Mellon University.

During her career, Auguste has received the following awards and affiliations:

- Inducted as a member of the Young Presidents' Organization, the leading international alliance for young global leaders.
- Named to the Colorado Commission on Science and Technology, a state panel of industry leaders that advises the governor on technology issues.
- Named one of the Top 25 Women in Small Business by *FORTUNE* Business, 2001.
- Received the Golden Torch 2001 Outstanding Woman in Technology award from the National Society of Black Engineers.
- Named one of the Top 25 Women on the Web by *Family Money* Magazine, 2000.
- Received the *Denver Business Journal*'s Outstanding Women in Business Award, 2000.
- Received, in 2000, the Colorado Women in Technology Lifetime Contribution award.
- Honored as the Delta Woman of the Year, 2000.
- Member, Aspen Institute Henry Crown Fellowship Program.
- Voted one of 1997's "Most Influential Women on the Web."
- Honored by the Women in Technology International Hall of Fame.

Her affiliations include National Society of Black Engineers, Forum for Women Entrepreneurs, and Gospel Music Workshop of America. She regards Jesus Christ as her mentor and inspiration.

Ken Granderson
Founder, President, and CEO
Inner-City Software

Location: Boston, MA

Web Site: www.innercity.com

A self-proclaimed "technology evangelist," Ken Granderson preaches the message of technology as a tool to uplift communities of color both locally and nationally. He has addressed national audiences at Congressional Black Caucus Foundation and National Society of Black Engineers (NSBE) conventions, as well as the Schomburg Center for Research in Black Culture, in New York. Granderson also makes technology presentations at local schools and on the Boston media on a regular basis. He has been quoted and featured in *Black Enterprise, Emerge,* and *Ebony Man* magazines, in addition to the *New York Times.*

Granderson is a 1997–1998 MIT Community Fellow as well as a 1985 MIT graduate in electrical engineering. He has 13 years of work experience in the IT industry and, for the past nine years, has been President and CEO of Inner City Software (ICS), a Web development, desktop development, IT consulting, and Web hosting company that he founded.

ICS was a charter contributor to the first forum on a major online service established by and for people of color, the CompuServe Afro-American Culture Forum (AACF), where Granderson was the Section Leader of the Software Development area.

ICS has been developing Internet-based solutions since 1995. ICS's three employees specialize in delivering cost-effective and robust solutions for the desktop, enterprises and the Web, using Microsoft technologies such as Visual Basic, Access, Visual C++, SQL Server, FrontPage, Active Server Pages, Office, and Exchange. With high proficiency in the C++ and Visual Basic programming languages, ICS has produced a wide variety of products, such as contact management applications, accounting systems, electronic books, multimedia CD-ROMs, component software for multimedia authors, and World Wide Web sites. ICS's database expertise has resulted in online products such as Black Facts Online (an online Black History search engine). ICS's customer base spans the globe, and its technology has shipped on thousands of computers by IBM, Compaq, and NEC. ICS's Web business consists primarily of clients in the Boston area, but businesses in New York, Washington, DC, and Baltimore have benefited from ICS's Web expertise.

Achievements and Community Technology Initiatives:

- ICS is opening the first 100 percent black-owned, -operated, and -programmed targeted Internet portal at www.blackpeople.com.

- ICS manages the "Black Developer's List," an electronic forum of 150 black computer science students and computer professionals across the United States. In this online discussion group, people share technical tips and solutions, and discuss issues concerning technology and society.

- ICS 's projects and its efforts to connect communities of color with the technology of the future have been featured in local and national media of all forms since 1995. Print media coverage includes the *New York Times,* the *Washington Post, Black Enterprise* , the *Bay State Banner, Commonwealth* Magazine, *Ebony Man,* the *Taunton Daily Gazette,* and the *Boston Herald.*

- ICS published the entire 600+ business listings of the New England Black Pages on the Web, via a database-driven Web site that allows visitors to locate black businesses in the New England area.

- ICS designed and built Black Facts Online (www.blackfactsonline.com), an online search engine of Black History facts that currently boasts over 1,750 research associates around the globe, who keep the database relevant and current. Black Facts Online is a popular site with many schools, and has received over a half million hits in a month.

- ICS created Boston Blacks Online (BBO), an e-mail-based online discussion group designed to provide a place for people of color to share viewpoints and other information via the Internet. BBO is a completely free resource that currently connects over 700 members throughout the Boston area, the United States, and several other countries.

- In 1996, ICS organized the Inner City Access Web Site Project, a collaborative effort of a dozen local technology professionals of color to build informational Web sites for Boston's communities of color.

- In 1995, ICS designed and developed the only multimedia CD-ROM ever produced to feature the history of Boston's black community, and made it available to the public for free via touch-screen kiosks in several Boston area locations.

In addition to an extensive list of public speaking engagements and management of his business, Granderson supports the community with his involvement as a board member of several local organizations.

- Granderson serves as Chairman of the Board of Virtually Wired, a well-known Boston-based public Internet access center.

- He is an active board member of Freedom House (Roxbury, MA), helping to implement the new technology strategy of this community icon.

- Granderson is an active board member of the Urban League of Eastern Massachusetts (Roxbury, MA). He assisted the Urban League in the design and implementation of a new technology infrastructure.

- He is a board member of the Roxbury Entrepreneurs' Club (Roxbury, MA). Granderson is one of the senior members of this local organization that supports grassroots community entrepreneurs.

Granderson's awards and affiliations include:

May 1999: Honorary Doctorate Degree, Salem State College

August 1998: Minority Business Entrepreneur of the Year Award, given by the Minority Business Assistance Center of the College of Management of the University of Massachusetts/ Boston Small Business Development Center

April 1998: Black & White Boston Award

1997: Microsoft Most Valued Professional Award

Vercell Vance
Founder and CEO
Alpha Data Corporation

Location: Fort Walton Beach, FL

Web Site: www.alphadata.com

Vercell Vance is Founder and CEO of 12-year-old Alpha Data Corporation, a Florida-based IT solutions company headquartered in Fort Walton Beach. Alpha Data offers software and hardware engineering for computer, data communications, telecommunications, and network systems services. The company is 8A Certified by the U.S. Small Business Administration and currently boasts 107 employees. Its out-of-state locations are in New Orleans, Louisiana; Huntsville, Alabama; Warner Robins, Georgia; Jackson, Mississippi; Vicksburg, Mississippi; and Washington, DC.

Vance expects to open four additional locations and to hire 95 new employees by year-end 2001. Year 2000 revenues totaled $8 million. Alpha Data is on course to bring in $15 million for 2001, and Vance projects that revenues will exceed $25 million in 2002. Alpha Data is a participant in the U.S. Small Business Administration's Mentor Protégé Program, as a protégé to Adroit Systems, Inc. Alpha Data is also set to achieve ISO 9000/9001 Certification by the end of 2001, and Software Engineering Institute Capability Maturity Model (SEI/CMM) Level 3 Certification by Spring 2002.

Vance has 28 years of experience in the IT industry. He is a graduate of Jackson State University, in Jackson, Mississippi, with a Bachelor of Science degree in Computer Science. He is currently completing a master's degree in Business Administration and Technology Management at the University of Phoenix.

In recognition of his commitment to the community, Vance has received numerous board elections and service awards, including:

- 2001: Kappa Alpha Psi Citizen of the Year Award
- 2000: NAACP Nathaniel Harris Striving for Excellence Award
- 2000–2001: State of Florida Small Business Advisory Board
- 2001–2006: YMCA Emerald Coast Board of Directors
- 2000–2003: Bridgeway Center Inc. Board of Directors

For its service and fast-track status, Vance's Alpha Data Corporation has also been recognized with the following awards and acknowledgments:

- 2001: SBA National Prime Contractor of the Year

  SBA Region IV Prime Contractor of the Year

  SBA Administrator's Award for Excellence

  Florida 100 Fastest Growing Privately Held Businesses (#46)

- 2000: *Inc.* 500's American Fastest Growing Privately Held Companies (#263)

  Winner of the *Inc.* 500 Magazine Award of Excellence

  SBA Administrator's Award for Excellence

  Diversity 2000's list of the Top 50 Minority and Women-Owned Businesses in Florida (#14)

  Nominated for the SBA National Prime Contractor of the Year Award

  Top 100 Florida Privately Held Corporations (#46)

Okaloosa County Economic Development Council, Industry Appreciation Winner

- 1999: *Inc.*'s 500 American Fastest Growing Privately Held Companies (#313)

  SBA Minority Small Business Person of the Year for North Florida

  Nominated for the SBA National Prime Contractor of the Year Award

  SBA Administrator's Award for Excellence

- 1998: Nominated for the SBA National Subcontractor of the Year Award

  SBA Administrator's Award for Excellence

- 1997: Northrup-Grumman's International Team Recognition Award of Excellence

Angela Walton
President/CEO
Melador Technologies, Inc.

Locations: Carson, CA and Baltimore, MD

Web Site: www.melador.com

Angela Walton is President and CEO of Melador Technologies, Inc., based in Carson, California, and Baltimore, Maryland. A high-technology company, Melador provides end-to-end e-business solutions and infrastructure with expertise in data warehousing, data-based management and design, IT consulting, and project management.

Melador Technologies, Inc. grossed $9.5 million in sales for 2000 and $21 million in projected sales for 2001. Fortified with confidence and a desire to involve African Americans in the computer industry, Walton established her own business in 1985. She has been in the IT industry for 20 years and has owned her own business for 16 years. Melador's headquarters, in Carson, California, employs 16 employees. Through strategic alliances, the company employs over 2,100 consultants in 27 offices nationwide.

Walton is a graduate of Xavier University and holds a B.A. in Business Management. She is a proud member of the Black Business Association, the National Association of Women Business Owners (NAWBO), the National Association for the Advancement of Colored People (NAACP), Black Women's

Network, the National Association of Women Entrepreneurs, the Association of Black Women Entrepreneurs, the Los Angeles Chamber of Commerce, and Operation Hope. Walton also sits on the Board of Directors for Mount Moriah Housing Development Corporation, and is a member of Beta Pi Sigma Sorority—Alpha Gamma Chapter of Carson, California.

Walton has received numerous awards, including the Entrepreneurial Excellence Award from the Southern California Regional Purchasing Council, Inc. and PG&E, and the World Class Team Recognition Award from Northrop Grumman. She was selected as one of the Outstanding African American Women in Business from Black Entrepreneurs. In 1987, Walton was featured on "Making It: Minority Success Stories." She has been featured in the *Los Angeles Times* Business Section and on NBC's *Morning News,* addressing, in each case, African American female entrepreneurial issues.

Walton plans to open a third office in Atlanta, Georgia, by the first quarter of 2002. She continues to empower the youth of Los Angeles through the **Melador Foundation,** a nonprofit organization dedicated to bringing information technologies to the inner city. The Melador Foundation provides annual scholarships to well-deserving youth who are seeking educational resources in the computer/technology field; grants computer hardware and software to other nonprofit agencies, economically disadvantaged families, and/or individuals; and provides mentors for youth and welfare-to-work participants.

Tyrone Taborn
Chairman & CEO
Career Communications Group
Publisher, *US Black Engineer & Information Technology* and *Hispanic Engineer & Information Technology* (magazines)

Location: Baltimore, MD

Web Site: www.ccgmag.com

Tyrone D. Taborn, Chairman and CEO of Career Communications Group, Inc. (CCG), is the publisher and editor-in-chief of *US Black Engineer & Information Technology,* the nation's only general-interest technology magazine for the African American community. Mr. Taborn is also the producer of the

award-winning syndicated TV show "Success Through Education." In addition to *US Black Engineer & Information Technology,* CCG, a multimillion-dollar company, publishes *Hispanic
Engineer & Information Technology* magazine.

Mr. Taborn has been a guest editorial writer for the Baltimore Sun and has been a panelist on the television program
"Square Off" at WJZ-TV, the CBS affiliate in Baltimore, Maryland. He now writes a national technology column that appears
in newspapers, magazines, and on Web sites and is currently a
member of The National Association of Hispanic Journalists.
Taborn has been a member of the Baltimore Engineering Society and has served on the boards of the Afro-American Newspaper Company, the Baltimore Urban League, and the Granville
Academy.

His other current and past board positions include Centro
de la Comunidad, Inc., Baltimore Area Council Boy Scouts of
America, the Montessori School in Baltimore County, Maryland, Afro-American Newspapers, the Executive Board of the
Morgan State University Foundation, and the Board of Trustees
of The Baltimore Educational Scholarship Trust. In 1992, Mr.
Taborn was elected into The Presidents' Roundtable; he now
holds the position of first vice-president.

Taborn is the founder of Black Family Technology Aware-
ness Week program, which is sponsored by IBM Corporation,
Microsoft and Sun Microsystems. He is also the founder of
LaFamilia Technology Awareness Week.

Mr. Taborn was recently selected as one of only nine
Internet and Technology leaders honored by Sprint and MOBE
IT, which recognizes African-Minority leaders and geniuses
in technology, and was also named as one of the "50 Most Important African Americans in Technology" by the editors of
Blackmoney.com and souloftechnology.net, which sponsors the
awards to demonstrate the critical role that Blacks play in the
growth of cutting edge industries.

An Afro-Latino who grew up in Los Angeles, California,
Mr. Taborn attended college at Cornell University in Ithaca,
New York. At Cornell, Mr. Taborn majored in government. He
also held membership in the Senior Honor Society "Quill and
Dagger" and was one of 32 academic scholars honored with
membership in the prestigious Telluride Association. In 1978,
Mr. Taborn was selected the first LBJ Intern in the office of
late Congressman Julian C. Dixon.

Joseph Mouzon
CEO
MusicTabs.com/Imhotech, Inc.

Location: San Francisco, CA

Web Site: www.imhotech.com

Mouzon cofounded Bay Area, California-based Imhotech, Inc. (now BayView Systems) with Ron Cadet. Imhotech was founded as a new media software, design and content company that delivers products via the Internet for the entertainment industry. The core product is MusicTabs, the first business-to-business Web based application providing a complete environment for record company promotions to conventional and online radio and retail outlets. MusicTabs improves the process that record labels use to market new music to radio stations and retail stores. Mouzon served as Imhotech's CEO until May 2001.

Imhotech's overall strategy is based on the integration of technology with urban culture and the entertainment industry—driven by a belief in the powerful synergy between technology, the entertainment industries, and urban culture. To this end, the management team's business goals are fueled by a strong commitment to provide quality jobs and economic opportunity to African American young people who have experienced barriers to economic and professional growth.

Imhotech's primary accomplishments to date include a successful seed round of financing from Silicon Valley Community Ventures, a strategic alliance with EMI, the development of the MusicTabs demo and the initial launch of MusicTabs.

As cofounder of *The Conduit*—the definitive technological guide for the African in America—and Imhotech's first product, Mouzon contributes articles and conducts interviews. This quarterly newsletter and Web site (www.theconduit.com) keep readers current on the latest issues concerning technology and the African American community. Mouzon is also a technology pundit for the Tech TV™ Silicon Spin television show and often speaks at technology- and entertainment-focused conferences.

Mouzon serves as the Executive Director of the Rhythm of Life Organization (ROLO—www.rolo.org). ROLO, headquartered in San Francisco, was founded in 1996 by Herbie Hancock. The organization's charter is two-fold: (1) to help reduce the gap between technology haves and have-nots and (2) to use technology to improve humanity. Mouzon oversees the entire development process currently underway to bring ROLO to fruition.

Mouzon assists Mr. Hancock with achieving the goals of ROLO by establishing strategic partnerships with "like-minded" organizations; informing Mr. Hancock of synergistic opportunities; and offering consulting services to the Bayview Center For Arts and Technology (BAYCAT) in San Francisco.

Previously, Mouzon was the Vice President of Sales and Marketing for NetNoir Online. His responsibilities included generating revenue for NetNoir through strategic alliances, sponsorship opportunities, advertising sales, and directory listings. Mouzon also directed NetNoir's advertising and marketing communications, media, and press kit development. In addition, he reported on high-tech and business issues for Soul Beat (an East Bay cable television station serving 100,000 homes) and WRKS-FM radio in New York City.

Before joining NetNoir Online, Mouzon was employed by Working Assets Long Distance as a Director of Business Services. Under his leadership, Working Assets Business Long Distance grew 99 percent in his first year and 33 percent in his second. Mouzon's responsibilities included the overall rebuilding, managing, and developing of the business services division, including leading 20 staff members working in sales, marketing, customer service, project management, financial reporting, and systems.

Mouzon held several other key management positions for Working Assets Long Distance. He was concerned with new product development, billing enhancements, and cost reductions during a five-year period in which overall company revenues grew from $2 million to $100 million.

Mouzon currently serves on three advisory boards: IT Pathways—connecting kids with careers in high technology; Marketing Opportunities for Business and Entertainment (MOBE)—connecting African Americans with business (marketing/entertainment) opportunities; and The Acapulco Black Film Festival—integrating black cinema and technology.

Mouzon received his bachelor's degree in Accounting from the University of San Francisco.

Shirley F. Moulton
President & Cofounder
Universal Solutions Inc.

Location: Southfield, MI

Web Site: www.usi-online.com

Shirley F. Moulton is cofounder and President of Universal Solutions, Inc. (USI), a full service national IT consulting. USI has been supporting the IT needs of diverse businesses since 1983. The company's sole purpose is to help its clients more effectively and efficiently run their businesses by optimizing the use of advanced technology. Proven methodologies USI has developed over the years, under Moulton's direction, ensure the best practice solutions and timely implementation that help clients be more efficient, competitive, and profitable.

Moulton has a Bachelor of Arts in Business Administration from Lincoln University and a Masters in Business Administration in Finance from Philadelphia's Temple University. She also holds a Minority Business Executive Program certificate from the University of Wisconsin-Madison.

Moulton began her career with Atlantic Richfield Corporation in Philadelphia in 1977 as a Staff Auditor in the area of Corporate Finance and Accounting. In 1979, she joined Sun Oil Company in Philadelphia where she was a senior financial analyst in the Corporate Finance division. After leaving Sun Oil Co., Moulton collaborated with members of her family in 1983 to establish USI. Two weeks after opening the doors, participation in their first computer trade show in Detroit landed their first million-dollar account with General Motors. Since then, Moulton's leadership and vision has lead USI to recognize the importance and benefits of emerging computer technologies, which has made USI a leader in the industry.

Moulton's business honors and media recognitions include:

- Entrepreneur of the Year Finalist, Ernst & Young—1999, 2000, and 2001.
- American Dreamer Award, Crain's Detroit Business—1999.
- Detroit's 100 Most Influential Women, Crain's Detroit Business—1997.
- Minority—Business Maven, Corporate Detroit—1996.
- USI listed as one of the Top 100 Systems Integrator in Document Management; Crain's Detroit Business—1994 and 1993.
- 1990 Recipient for Vendor of the Year Award, presented by the Michigan Minority Business Development Council (MMBDC) and Nominee for 2000.
- Carib News, Marcus Garvey Award, for a Bridge Builder in the Diaspora—2001.
- Listed in Crain's Detroit Business Top 100 List of Black Owned Firms, 1989—2000.
- Minorities and Women in Business Magazine, Company Profile, Cover Story—1999.

- Black Enterprise Magazine, Company Profile, October 2000.
- MOBE Influencers and Innovator of the Internet and Technology Award—2001.
- Temple Review, Alumnus Profile, March 2001.
- Minority Business and Professional Network (MBPN), 2001 Fifty Influential Minorities in Business.
- Member of the Kodak VAR Council—2001.

Her board affiliation and memberships include:

- Member of Northwest Airlines WorldPerks Elite Advisory Council.
- Detroit Area Pre-College Engineering Program (DAPCEP) Steering Committee.
- Board of Trustees of Marygrove College—Chairman.
- Board of Trustees of the Detroit Medical Center-Adult Clinical Services.
- Advisory Board Chair of the Golightly Academy of Information Technology.
- Board Member of the American Foundation for the University of the West Indies.
- Member of National Organization of Women Business Owners.
- Alpha Kappa Alpha Sorority.

Kim T. Folsom
Founder, President, and Chairman
SeminarSource

SeminarSource, a leading online software application service provider to the association and meetings industry, was founded in 1998 to provide an efficient means for associations and conference providers to extend the life of their meetings by providing innovative enabling technology to allow persons to obtain best practice and continuing education online.

The company has had more than 100 clients utilize its technology since its inception. SeminarSource's staff has included more than 60 people, with offices in Chicago, New York, San Diego, and Washington DC. Folsom has secured more than $12 million in equity financing from angel, strategic corporate, and venture capital investment.

When Folsom started the business, the signature product was SeminarCast™, a Web-based, automated evaluation, testing and certification tool. Using this tool, individuals from professional societies, trade associations and Fortune 1000 organizations can attend continuing education presentations and professional development seminars, take tests and receive certifications from the comfort of their home or office. SeminarSource also provides other Web-based software to assist organizations with managing their conferences on line.

In April 2001, SeminarSource launched its latest phase of software products, the Evance Association Suite. This new technology is based on a patent pending, integrated services delivery platform. It allows organizations to streamline the delivery of meeting-related and membership-oriented services by offering them in a "self service" method over the Internet.

SeminarSource's clients include Prudential Securities, Black Enterprise, Les Brown Ltd., African American Women on Tour, the American Bar Association, the American Marketing Association, and the American Diabetes Association.

Prior to founding SeminarSource, in 1995, Folsom founded a Web development and e-commerce software firm called The Business Source that provided comprehensive services to e-tailing small and medium sized businesses. The Business Source was merged into SeminarSource.

Before starting The Business Source, Folsom held senior management positions in the area of business development, operations, and MIS with several Fortune 1000 corporations. She is an accomplished business executive with over 15 years of experience developing, implementing and managing strategic relationships which provided positive contributions for revenue growth, technology innovation, and business operations efficiencies for major US.-based corporations. She was instrumental in the implementation of strategic initiatives for Central Federal Savings, Great American Bank, Advanta Mortgage Corp., Alltel Communications, The National Dispatch Center and the law firm of Luce, Forward, Hamilton and Scripps.

Folsom holds a Bachelors of Science degree in Information Systems from San Diego State University. She also holds a teaching credential from the San Diego Community College, where she was an Adjunct Professor of Computer Technology. She is an M.B.A. candidate at the University of Pepperdine.

Folsom has been recognized in the Who's Who of Young American Executives in 1998 and most recently was selected as a semi-finalist in the 2001 Ernest and Young Entrepreneur of the Year Award.

5

IMPROVING YOUR COMPANY'S INTERNET RETURN ON INVESTMENT

It's time to rethink your company's business model. Businesses are now operating in environments of much greater and much faster change than ever in history. New technology is often complicating and quickly morphing many of the old-school business models. It has transformed competitive methods, simplified the means of creating value for clients, and automated nearly every facet of the day-to-day business process. With hordes of competitors unleashed onto a global market, all businesses must now look more closely at every opportunity as a learning experience, and they must adjust their strategies accordingly.

Entrepreneurs are also finding that the old rules of doing business don't always apply. New forms of customer interaction have emerged, and companies, from sole proprietorships to large conglomerates, are adopting radical new ways of getting in front of a global audience. Although many of the dot-commers have come and gone, they've left behind a resurgence of discussions around the frequently misunderstood aspect of the corporate business model, especially as it relates to e-business.

So, what is a business model and which is the right one if your company hopes to make money on the Internet? A business model is essentially the way that a company attracts and retains customers. It clearly spells out how your company generates revenue and provides value to its customer base. Many of the proposed Web-based business models are not as bad as observers had originally predicted. The core problem with many of the now-defunct dot-coms was that the involved parties seemed to have forgotten that growing too quickly can kill a business much faster than being undercapitalized. These business managers expected to ramp up quickly without investing the time to break even or prove that their models were solid. Rapid growth with red ink all over one's financial statements does not make for a solid business, even if venture capital is readily available.

Another reason that a lot of these dot-bombs took place was a lack of balance in emphasizing the technology versus assuaging customers' fears about this new way of communicating. It's okay to be excited about technology, but reality has to step in at some point. For us to live in a high-tech world, our customers have to be ready, willing, and able to make the transition. Rather than focusing their efforts on educating the marketplace to facilitate the needed shift in mindset, these companies' business models focused solely on the technology architecture that streamlined the business or communication process. Customer retention and service took a back seat. Companies adopting this technology-focused business model were the first to go in the fallout.

Customer acquisition, these corporate managers thought, resulted from what I call "Superbowl" marketing efforts. Armed with millions in venture capital, many dot-coms focused on creating a quick brand rather than segmenting the market and strategically targeting their goods. Many of you witnessed the proliferation of dot-com commercials during the past few Superbowls. Some of these companies actually poured up to 50 percent of their invested capital into these commercials, and they were out of business within months after the game.

And it's not just the dot-coms that are at fault. A lot of traditional businesses have suffered because of the proliferation of new technological developments and misjudgments about online branding. Time and time again, we have seen many of the older, more established brands struggling to make their online ventures worthwhile. A lot of Fortune 1000 corporations have either reduced or completely dismantled their newly developed interactive divisions because their Web sites didn't perform nearly as well as expected. Corporate managers assumed that traditional brands would have no trouble making a smooth transition into the virtual marketplace and would generate lots of traffic and revenue. They took for granted that their off-line efforts would translate into immediate online revenue based on name only. Obviously, that wasn't the case. In virtual space, consumers have a wider variety of options, and they don't have to leave their homes or offices to get what they need. Even if a business has created an extremely successful brand off-line, it needs to prove itself against its new and nimble virtual competitors.

Take, for instance, the ongoing battle between Amazon.com and BarnesAndNoble.com. Rest assured that Barnes & Noble's corporate managers never figured that Jeff Bezos, an unknown upstart, would give them a run for their money. Bezos took the entire retail industry by surprise by using his understanding of the virtual consumer, forming strategic alliances to cut costs, remaining flexible, and parlaying all this into a multibillion-dollar empire in just a few years. Today, Amazon.com is one of the most widely recognized online brands in the world, right along with Yahoo! and eBay.

Branding, whether online or traditional, requires a financial investment but, more importantly, it takes time and effort. A solid business model needs to account for the target audience's available options and potential apprehension about purchasing the proposed product or service. Whether your business is brick-and-mortar, click-and-mortar, or strictly virtual, your business model should be carefully selected.

CHOOSING THE RIGHT WEB-BASED BUSINESS MODEL

A business model can be quite simple. A company that uses a common retail business model produces a product or service, sells it to the targeted audience, and, if revenues exceed expenses, turns a profit. Other traditional business models include manufacturing, distributing, and service. Some companies, depending on their size and the variety of products and services they offer, may utilize a combination of interwoven business models. Thanks to the Web, a number of new models have originated. The Web is also breathing new life into some of the old models.

Some of the more popular Web-based business models include:

1. Content Delivery.
2. Sales/Merchant.
3. Marketplace.
4. Advertising.
5. Pay-for-Access.

6. Auction.

7. Affiliate.

The broadest category of Web-based business models is *Content Delivery*. This refers to sites that provide information about a specific topic, industry, person, or product. The most popular Content Delivery sites are online brochures (aka "e-brochures"). Online brochures provide product, service, and general company information. They are relatively simple to maintain and they provide a company with a global image that can save money on printing and postage. Costs include domain name registration, site development, hosting, and maintenance. The primary drawback for this conservative model is that market penetration can be expensive and difficult. This model is often based on the "build it and they will come" stance. Entrepreneurs who choose this Web-based business model should accept that their site will primarily serve to support off-line collateral pieces unless they employ an aggressive marketing campaign to generate online interest in their products and services.

A more aggressive Content Delivery strategy involves promoting a company's product or service by offering related information at no charge. E-commerce functions are typically not included in this model, but site content has to be maintained regularly and it needs to be interesting enough to keep people coming back. An example would be an event management company that offers meeting planner tips and links to venue and conference sites on the Web. The potential of this model is moderate; it has advertising potential and may generate word-of-mouth traffic.

Specialized search agent sites are yet another form of Content Delivery. These include electronic clearinghouses that provide site visitors with very specific or hard-to-find information (monster.com). MySimon.com and Price.com are examples of specialized search agent sites that provide comparative prices for goods and services.

The *Sales/Merchant* model offers product information (e.g., photos, descriptions, prices) and incorporates e-commerce for online transactions. It is usually based on the fulfillment of a physical product (e.g., books) or a service (e.g., unified messaging) that can be delivered electronically. Brick-and-mortar retail businesses transform themselves into click-and-mortar businesses with this model. Sales/Merchant sites lower overhead costs for virtual storefront businesses. A business can then expand its market geographically, but the expansion will require aggressive and integrated marketing efforts. Costs include providing a secure server and an electronic gateway for online transactions; merchant fees; and fulfillment-related expenses. Fulfillment costs, especially shipping, increase as the audience broadens geographically, thus reducing profit margin. Whether a business is a brick-and-mortar establishment or a virtual storefront, successfully building a retail brand online can cost a fortune. Typically, businesses targeting tech-savvy customers will have a better chance at success with this business model.

Other versions of Sales/Merchant sites include corporate retail and wholesale catalog sites, discount sites (Buy.com), "name your price" sites (Priceline.com), and traditional B2B and B2C e-commerce Web sites. General travel and financial sites (e.g., E*Trade, Expedia) also fit within this category because they are providing a service in exchange for the cost of the service plus a transaction fee.

Marketplaces, sometimes called "transaction broker" sites, bring buyers and sellers together. These sites include online shopping malls, market exchanges (where the seller is charged based on the value of sales generated), and aggregators (sites that bring individuals together to make purchases as a group, in order to get discounted rates). Distributor sites are also commonly categorized as Marketplaces. Examples of Marketplaces are StoreRunner.com, the African American Cyber MarketPlace (www.aacmp.com) and ShopMidCities.com. Marketplaces often include e-commerce features that accommodate online transactions and offer additional marketing opportunities for their community of sellers. Sellers' costs may include a set-up charge, a monthly fee, and/or a per-transaction fee for all sales generated through the marketplace. Many online marketplaces found it difficult to market the virtual "mall" concept and quickly fell out of favor with Web surfers who were seeking the unlimited options afforded them in virtual space.

An *Advertising* model offers a free service or product, or free information, to attract a high volume of traffic to a particular Web site. A number of companies that once focused primarily on an Advertising-based business model have changed their tunes. Web-based ad models have a long way to go before they can prove themselves and elicit a similar (or even substantial) return on investment that compares with traditional media. Portals, general subject search engines, and community sites use an ad-based business model that requires significant traffic and constant analysis of both the traffic and the audience. This model is better for sites that target a specific, identifiable demographic. The big mistake made by the original online media sellers was their overestimation of their targeted audience's size and the value of the advertising inventory. Another self-inflicted challenge is that the ads take the site's target audience away from the content that is provided. Sites like BlueMountain.com, and formerly free service-oriented sites like NetZero and Intranets.com, are based on an Advertising model. The ad-based business model is undergoing a major transition, but it will not go away.

Loyalty-based or incentive sites such as MyPoints.com, Beenz.com, and CyberGold.com represent modified versions of an advertising-based business model. Web surfers receive cash, points, or coupons for visiting advertisers' sites or following links sent to them via e-mail.

At *Pay-for-Access* sites, surfers must pay for access to content or enhanced site features, or they are charged per document viewed or per subscription. This model is typically used by brick-and-mortar newspapers and magazines that move into virtual space (e.g., the *Wall Street Journal:* wsj.com). Some sites offer a limited amount of content for free, to whet site visitors' appetites. Additional content is available only by registering, paying required fees, or subscribing to the print publication.

The concept of freely available information on the Internet has caused problems with a subscription-based business model. This model tends to work best for publications with specialized or hard-to-find content.

Another version of the Pay-for-Access site is the "knowledge network" group. These sites require a one-time or pay-per-request fee in exchange for expert consultation (AllExpert.com, Guru.com, and Exp.com). There's also a "free, with strings attached" version. Companies employing this business model offer a free or inexpensive product or service, as long as the customer buys a long-term subscription or maintenance contract. An example is a free computer offer, as long as you purchase a three-year Internet access subscription.

Auctions, also known as virtual trading communities or intermediaries, have been all but reinvented with new technologies. The success of eBay has broadened the appeal of this model and has expanded Auctions to include products and services never before considered for this model. Auctions, like marketplaces, bring buyers and sellers together. The buyers and sellers may be businesses or consumers. Typically, the seller is charged a fee and the auctioned product or service is sold to the highest bidder above an established price. Quite a few of the more popular and heavily trafficked sites, such as Yahoo! and Amazon.com, now include their own branded Auctions.

Affiliate sites are based on a "Get 'em where they surf" model. Instead of requiring Web surfers to leave the currently viewed site to see more about a product or service, a button or banner provides the sales opportunities wherever the site visitor happens to be surfing. The Affiliate model, also referred to as a "revenue sharing program," pays the merchant for performance only. In other words, the merchant makes an established fee, or a percentage, of the sales generated on their site. This model is quite popular and has contributed to the evolution of companies like Commission Junction (www.cj.com) and Be Free (www.befree.com), which are classified as revenue-sharing networks. Amazon.com and BarnesAndNoble.com have two of the more popular Affiliate programs. We'll take a closer look at affiliate programs in Chapter 6.

The lines are blurred for several of these models. A Content Delivery site could very easily morph itself into an Advertising or Merchant site. A portal site could very easily utilize an Auction model as one of its many elements, and a manufacturer's Web site could just as easily be considered a Content Delivery site or a Merchant site. The key factor is to clarify, in advance, how your company will attract and maintain its customer base in virtual space. Each Web-based business model requires a specific set of costs, skills, and responsibilities. Each will also have a different source of profit. You will need to work closely with your Marketing Director and tech support team to establish the Web functionalities required for a reliable estimate of your associated costs and return on investment.

This list is by no means exhaustive. There's no doubt in my mind that new business models will have evolved before this book goes to print. Creativity and new technology are great assets for nimble and

Figure 5.1   Employing Web-Based Business Models

Sample Company (Service):   Williams, King & Kimbrough, LLP, Attorneys at Law

Business Description: Full-service business law firm serving small to mid-size businesses and self-employed individuals.

Content Delivery: Establish an e-brochure site that includes the firm's history, partners' biographies, contact information, services list, client list, and monthly articles written by the firm's attorneys. Articles are archived and searchable on the Web site.

Sales/Merchant: Incorporate e-commerce to sell books or law journal articles written by the partners.

Marketplace: Create an online marketplace called "Cyber Law Center" for a limited number of legal colleagues who offer complementary services. Charge the colleagues a monthly fee for inclusion in the Marketplace.

Advertising: Sell banner and button ads to legal colleagues who can offer complementary services (e.g., tax law, civil litigation, etc.). Drive traffic by providing up-to-the-minute results of high-profile court cases around the world. Create a forum where site visitors can offer their opinions about case outcomes.

Pay-for-Access: Incorporate e-commerce to offer expert assistance on a pay-per-access basis. Upon payment, site visitors can submit a question to one or all of the law partners and receive a telephone or e-mail response within 24 hours.

---

radical-thinking entrepreneurs, so look for some new and interesting variations of Web-based and traditional business models in the very near future.

One last point if you plan to employ entrepreneurial creativity to develop new Web-based business models: Be sure to discuss your ideas with your attorney before you move forward. Companies like Amazon.com and CyberGold have patented their Web-based business models, so tread carefully to avoid litigation.

I have included two sample companies (Figures 5.1 and 5.2) to show how the above-referenced business models can be utilized by product- and service-based businesses.

Figure 5.2   Employing Web-Based Business Models

Sample Company (Product): S&S Gift Baskets

Business description: Specialty gift basket service offering custom, hand-woven, and hand-decorated baskets of gourmet food, wine, chocolate, cigars, and more for corporate and personal occasions.

Content Delivery: Offer an e-brochure site that lists services, displays photos of products, client testimonials, list of most popular basket products, product and shipping costs, a custom-basket request form and sales information. Also include theme-based "virtual gift baskets" that site visitors can send to friends via e-mail with a personalized message. Incorporate an annual calendar of national events with an e-mail reminder service for regular site visitors and customers.

Sales/Merchant: Incorporate e-commerce to provide on-site product sales. Offer product coupons and provide e-mail gift suggestions to opt-in customers with a link back to a specific product on the Web site.

Marketplace: Create an online Marketplace called Corporate Gift Central, where a collection of concierge and event planning companies sell a variety of services, promotional items, and specialty/one-of-a-kind gifts. Participants pay a $100 set-up fee for a virtual storefront in the Corporate Gift Central Marketplace, and a 2.5 percent transaction fee. (The Marketplace is e-commerce-enabled, so all merchant transactions go through a single gateway.)

Auction: Create a Gift Basket Auction targeted to the affluent market and last-minute shoppers. Select specialty/one-of-a-kind, and collectible items that can be linked to events, holidays, and unique themes.

Affiliate: Create an S&S Gift Baskets Affiliate program that establishes a company presence (via button ads) on portal and vortal sites targeting mid- and upper-level management executives. Pay up to 3 percent per sale generated by each site owner.

DEVELOPING AN INTERNET STRATEGY

After you've carefully selected or revised your business model (which is, in essence, the foundation of your business), it's time to focus on your Internet strategy, which should encompass the specific details for reaching your targeted market and achieving your goals. Whether you're developing a new Internet presence or renovating an old one, strategy is the key to profitability online. Your company might have to spend a lot of time, energy, and money to become successful online; the time needed to build a proper Internet presence has been grossly underestimated. And, there are no guarantees.

By developing a complete Internet strategy for your company, you prepare for success. Without a strategy, how will you know whether your Internet presence has provided a return on your investment? Remember: "Those who fail to plan, plan to fail."

The initial Web efforts of many companies, large and small, involved retaining the services of a Webmaster (or encouraging an employee to learn HTML), passing along some print collateral pieces, and "*Voilá!*"—a Web site was born! In the beginning, most entrepreneurs simply didn't know any better. They were inspired by the gloss of new technology, the hype of being able to market their businesses globally, and the possibility of making a lot of money from a small investment. Problems quickly evolved when sites didn't get traffic or failed to generate the vast amounts of revenue projected in this newfound space.

These "Version 1.0" sites, as I endearingly call them, are easy to spot. Often, their look and feel are completely different from the companies' print materials. In their efforts to create additional revenue streams, these site owners tend to clutter their sites with affiliate program buttons and ad banners. Many Version 1.0 sites haven't been maintained or upgraded because business owners and managers are still trying to figure out how to create and implement effective Internet strategies.

A basic Internet strategy includes the following tasks:

1. Clarify your company's online target markets.
2. Check out your competitors' Web sites.
3. Prepare yourself and your staff for some extra work.
4. Review your budget regularly.
5. Create specific goals for your company's Internet presence.
6. Develop an integrated marketing plan.

Let's take a closer look at each step to see how your company can benefit from a sound Internet strategy.

1. *Clarify your company's online target markets.* Some businesses use the Web to target new or slightly different audiences for their products and services. Whether you target the same customers online and off-line or choose to pursue a different audience in virtual space, you need to truly understand who your clients are. Do your company's products or services target consumers? Businesses? Government agencies? Universities or nonprofit organizations? If your clients are consumers, are they affluent or middle class? Are your customers African American, Hispanic, Caucasian, or Asian? Are they male or female, young people or seniors, baby boomers, Gen X or Gen Y? Where do they live? What do they do for a living? How do they spend their spare time? Among your corporate clients, what is the average number of employees? How long have the corporations been in business? What average annual revenues are generated by your corporate clients? What services or products do they provide?

Many small business owners take the easy way out and make a general guess about their target market. A clothing company owner might say, "My business targets women." Well, what kind of women—petite, plus-size, mature, Gen Y, tall, women entrepreneurs? When marketing your business, traditionally or online, don't try to be all things to all people (or all companies, for that matter). It's far too expensive. The Internet has opened up global possibilities, but you have to be strategic if you hope to be profitable.

The more detailed your client profile is, the easier it will be to effectively market your company online. You will know immediately whether it is better to advertise on a particular Web site or to provide content on another. You will have a better idea of where to direct your online press releases and which electronic mailing lists are worth participating in. If your company targets more than one market, you need to create a profile for each of your markets.

Remember to review your target audience occasionally. It is likely to change based on product and service development, marketing campaigns, and other factors.

2. *Check out your competitors' Web sites.* Track down your local and national competitors. Surfing competitors' sites may give you ideas for your own site. It will also tell you what type of value your competitors are adding to their client services. If possible, find out how much traffic they are getting, who's advertising on their sites, and who's linking to their sites.

When you are performing research online, be sure to run general searches for competitors by company name, product, service, and industry. (Appendix B offers surf tips and search basics to help you with online research.)

And lastly, do not believe for a minute that your business does not have competitors! Your direct competitors are selling the same types of products and often are targeting the same audience. A lot of companies have indirect competitors. Even if you have secured a patent on a brand new product, there is someone, somewhere, who would claim to have something similar or better. If your product is an enhancement of something that has already been developed, find out how your competitors brand their product; then clearly differentiate your product from theirs.

3. *Prepare yourself and your staff for some extra work.* The most successful online companies are those that offer valuable information in an interactive and constantly changing environment. How much time and energy are you willing to spend on your Internet presence? Do you, or members of your staff, have time to answer e-mail queries and make regular updates to your organization's Web site? Who will develop and implement your marketing methods?

Customer service on the Web is lacking, for large *and* small companies. Naturally, this hinders online sales. I have personally sent messages to several Fortune 500 corporations and never received a response. I also recall sending an information request via e-mail to a fellow entrepreneur after meeting her at a conference. She responded (literally) one year later! Good customer service must be an integral part of your Internet strategy if you plan to be successful in virtual space. Incoming e-mail should be answered as quickly as humanly possible, and online product requests should be fulfilled immediately. (More about that later.)

Company e-mail should be checked regularly—daily, if possible. Entertainment, news, and portal Web site owners should set a schedule for changing content regularly. Web site links and contact forms should be checked on a regular basis to ensure appropriate distribution of information. It should be clearly established who is responsible for content collection, site updates, product fulfillment, and e-mail response.

4. *Review your budget regularly.* As with hardware and software upgrades, you should perform a cost analysis before developing or renovating an Internet presence for your organization. Developing an Internet presence can add anywhere from a few hundred dollars to tens of thousands of dollars in expenses to your budget. Table 5.1 shows some of the expenses that you will incur in the development of your company's Internet presence.

5. *Create specific goals for your company's Internet presence.* If you don't set measurable goals for your Internet presence, you will never

Table 5.1 Internet Presence Expenses

Expense	Cost (Range)	Options	Notes
E-mail and Internet access[a]	FREE or up to $50 per month per employee	• Dial-up • ISDN • DSL • Cable • Wireless • T-1 • T-3	While you will be hard-pressed to find totally free e-mail and Internet access for your business, there may be programs available for free personal Internet access (e.g., Juno (www.juno.com)).
Domain name registration (e.g., www.yourcompany.com, www.yourcompany.net, www.yourcompany.org)	$10 to 35 per name, per year	Previously, commercial entities were only allowed to register ".com" domains. Now, your business is welcome to register ".com," ".net," and ".org" addresses, in addition to a variety of newly approved top-level domains (e.g., .tv, .info, .biz, .ws)	The premier domain registrar is Network Solutions. Since 1999, many other organizations have been granted the right to register Internet domain names. To find a list of accredited registrars, go to www.icann.org.
Web site design[b]	FREE to hundreds of thousands of dollars; average range: $500 to $5,000	• Low-cost, do-it-yourself (Microsoft's bCentral, BigStep, Image Café, Yahoo! Store) • Internal staff • Outsource to a freelance Web designer • Outsource to a full-service Web design firm	Web site design is never truly free because it requires, at a minimum, an investment of time to gather materials, create content, and upload site files. Additional costs may include development software (e.g., FrontPage, Dreamweaver) and an FTP client (e.g., CuteFTP, WS_FTP).

Web site maintenance	$10 to $200 per hour	• Internal staff • Outsource to a freelance Web designer • Outsource to a full-service Web design firm	Maintenance includes updating site content and images, analyzing Web site statistics, managing the hosting server, and handling any error messages or design-related problems that arise.
Web site hosting	$10 to hundreds of dollars per month	• Virtual/shared server • Dedicated server • Co-located server • In-house Web server	Hosting costs increase based on Web site size, data transfer allowance, and enhanced features (e.g., e-commerce, database, chat, streaming). Also, dedicated, co-located, and in-house Web servers require substantial costs (including hardware, software, maintenance, and monthly fees) above those of virtual servers.

(continued)

Table 5.1 (Continued)

Expense	Cost (Range)	Options	Notes
e-Commerce	• Set-up costs (\$0 to \$1,000) • e-Commerce gateway • Per-transaction fees (1.5% to 5% of the sale plus \$0.15 to \$1) • Software (shopping cart and inventory tracking) • Hardware (POS terminal: \$30 to \$50 monthly lease fee or \$300 to \$1,000; one-time) • Fulfillment	• Traditional bank merchant account • Online merchant account (e.g., Charge.com, e-Commerce Exchange, etc.) • Electronic payment services like PayPal.com, Checkspace.com, and Propay.com	• Many hosting companies provide shopping cart software for free. • Electronic payment services alleviate the need for merchant accounts, but transaction fees may be slightly higher. • Additional fees may apply for chargebacks and monthly processing (\$15 to \$75). • Fulfillment includes product shipping and storage.

[a] There may be additional hardware costs (e.g., hubs, routers) for larger companies providing "wired" (versus wireless) e-mail and Internet access to employees via a network.

[b] Web site design and maintenance costs increase, depending on the size and enhanced features of your company's Web site, which may include database development and integration, e-commerce, interactive elements, streaming media, dynamic content generation, and advertising.

know whether or when your company is successful online. Before you begin to discuss Web site renovations or search engine listings, decide whether your company is trying to:

- Save money on operational costs.
- Expand your market share regionally, nationally, or internationally.
- Enter a brand new market.
- Reduce customer service costs.
- Create an additional revenue stream.
- Support existing marketing and advertising efforts.
- Distribute a new Internet-enabled product or service.
- Provide information to a specific market.
- Add value for your company's clients.

There are as many reasons for creating an Internet presence as there are businesses. Your company's Internet strategy may even include two or more goals. The point is: Be very specific. How much traffic do you want to generate—5,000 page views per month, 1 million page views in a year? By what percentage would you like to increase sales—10 percent, 200 percent? How much money do you want to save? Over what period of time? Will this money be saved in a specific budget area, such as printing, postage, or graphic design?

These goals, along with your clearly profiled target markets, will affect your entire Internet presence. You also have to realize that your goals must be realistic. The more goals you set, and the higher the numbers (for revenue, site traffic, and so on), the more time, money, and effort will be required to achieve success.

6. *Develop an integrated marketing plan.* It is not enough to put up a Web site and send out a few sporadic e-mails. Without marketing, how will your customers and potential customers know that you exist? Even more important, your online marketing efforts should be combined with your traditional marketing efforts to achieve the greatest success.

Developing an integrated marketing plan will help to answer key questions: Is your company's online target audience the same as your off-line target market? Are you planning to use your Internet presence to widen your market or to provide convenience for your current customers? How do your online marketing efforts support your company's marketing goals overall?

As you review online marketing options, it is advisable to focus first on saving money for your business. Next, focus on adding value to your products and services for your company's existing client base. Additional focal points include creating new revenue streams and testing new products and markets.

Your company's Marketing Director and PR Manager should play fundamental roles in the development of your integrated plan. Once you are all on the same page regarding goals and resources, it will be easier to select the most appropriate avenues for your marketing efforts. And, most importantly, you increase the likelihood of reaching your goals.

Many entrepreneurs make the mistake of starting or trying to grow their businesses by only focusing on Internet marketing options (versus integrating Internet and traditional efforts). A lot of business owners still want to believe that their Web efforts will take care of themselves, and that the Web requires a minimal time and dollar investment to achieve success. One extremely overlooked fact is that as barriers to entry are lowered, the threat of competition increases; therefore, there's more work to be done to set your company apart from the crowd.

We'll discuss how to build a successful virtual brand in the next chapter. For now, it is important to note that your traditional marketing efforts are vital to the life and success of your company's Internet presence. (It goes without saying that e-mail and Web site addresses should be added to all print collateral pieces. If your company advertises via TV or radio, make sure that your Web site address is always mentioned.)

BUILDING A SUCCESSFUL WEB SITE

I would venture to say that 50 to 60 percent of the Web sites that I have seen are unattractive. But, an unattractive site doesn't bother me nearly as much as a Web site with little or no meaningful content and bad navigation. I'm sure you've seen plenty of these—sites without contact information; sites with a different top-level menu on each page; sites with bad links; or sites that require you to click at least 10 different links before you get to any real information. Attractiveness is relative, but form and function go a much longer way toward affecting the success of a Web site.

Media-reported and well-hyped sites are deemed successful if they generate heavy traffic (millions of page views per month) and millions of dollars in annual revenue. As a result, a lot of business owners judge their sites by the same yardstick. In actuality, a site's success is determined by a company's specific goals, which may or may not be related to traffic or revenue. (Remember Step 5 of "Developing an Internet Strategy" earlier in this chapter.) For instance, the owner of a consulting business may set a goal for his or her Web site to save the company 25 percent in printing costs within one year. If, by the end of the following year, the company has saved 25 percent or more in printing costs by delivering information via e-mail and the Web site, that company's site is indeed successful.

Naturally, businesses exist to make money, so the vast majority of companies on the Web want to attract new customers and generate revenue. But not all businesses are immediately using their sites to make money. Some businesses simply don't have the resources in place to aggressively market themselves and generate millions, or even hundreds of thousands, of dollars in online revenue. Other site owners are happy if their sites pay for themselves. The only way to determine whether your company's Web site is successful is to set specific goals and regularly analyze your site's performance. Your company's Web development should be directly connected with your Internet strategy.

We tackled the method for developing an Internet strategy earlier in the chapter, so you are now ready to roll up your sleeves. Here's your action list for developing (or renovating) your company's Web site:

1. Register one or more Web site addresses.
2. Secure your Web design team.
3. Plan your site carefully.
4. Assign staff duties.
5. Compile the site's content.
6. Select a hosting service.
7. Incorporate e-commerce (if necessary).
8. Analyze your Web site traffic and audience.

REGISTER ONE OR MORE WEB SITE ADDRESSES

What's in a name? Actually, quite a lot. Your company's Web site address (aka "domain name" or "URL") tells your customers how to find you in virtual space. A hard-to-spell, unrecognizable, or very long Web site address does not encourage traffic or help to positively brand your company. You may think a name is cute or catchy, but that doesn't mean your clients will. It is vital that you carefully select a memorable, easy-to-spell Web site address. Typically, you would choose something like "yourcompany.com," "yourproduct.com," or "yourservice.com," but with tens of thousands of Web site addresses being sold each day, the odds are pretty high that your first dot-com choice has been taken.

Initially, ".com" domains were reserved for sites offering products or services, ".org" was reserved for nonprofit organizations, and ".net" was reserved for networks. Due to domain name popularity and the often blurred differentiation between the original top-level domains,[1] commercial businesses are now allowed to reserve .com, .net, and .org addresses. The Internet Corporation for Assigned Names and Numbers (www.icann.org) has since approved the use of several additional top-level domains, including .tv, .ws, .cc, .biz, and .info. Despite this expansion, the dot-coms are still the most popular domains in the world. It will take some time for the other domains to catch on, so focus your initial attention on securing the .com, .net, and/or .org domains. If you feel that it is strategically important for your business to have every top-level domain registered, then, by all means, go for it! There is no limit on the number of Web site addresses that you can purchase. Just make sure that your address is catchy, easy to spell, and simple to read.

If you expect a lot of traffic to your Web site, definitely consider registering all domain extensions for your site. Often, highly trafficked sites fall victim to competitors or adult-oriented Web sites that choose similar domain names or other top-level domain extensions for the same address. In other words, if your site is www.successfulbiz.net, another company may try to benefit on those site visitors who incorrectly type www.successfulbiz.com into their Web browsers.

You can check for Web site address availability on nearly any portal, ISP Web site, or on the Web site of a domain registrar. Network Solutions[2] (www.networksolutions.com), the premier domain registrar, has a free service called NameFetcher that will help you to find available domain names based on keywords that you input.

When selecting a Web site address, try to come up with at least three alternates, just in case your first choice is not available. If your company name is unavailable or hard to spell, consider using an acronym or a name that describes your product or service. If your preferred domain is a generic word that is often misspelled, consider registering the misspelled versions of the word. For example, if you have a catering company called "Hors d'oeuvres, Etc." and your Web site address is www.horsdoeuvresetc.com, you might also register www.hordervesetc.com, www.ordurvesetc.com, and similar versions.

Tens of thousands of Web addresses are sold each day. If you find that your preferred Web site address is unavailable (using one or more of the approved top-level domains), you can offer to buy the address from the current registrant or utilize the services of an Internet broker, such as Great Domains (www.greatdomains.com). If your preferred Web address is a generic word or a popular name, the asking price may be quite expensive. Thanks to cybersquatters, domain names have been sold for amounts in excess of $1 million (e.g., business.com), even though the actual cost of a domain name is only $10 to $35 per year. Cybersquatters are people who register popular domains, including celebrity, corporate, and trademarked names, for the sole purpose of selling them off to the highest bidder. A few celebrities and companies have been successful in recovering their names, but others have paid steep fees (up to $1 million) to get the right name for their Web site. (The American Cybersquatting Protection Act, signed into law by President Bill Clinton in 1999, provides civil liability for the bad faith registration or use of a trademark or service mark of another as a domain name.)

Another important note: Many Web site hosts will allow you to "point" or redirect one address to another. For example, if your company's Web site address is www.xyzcorporation.com and you have purchased www.xyzcorporation.net, www.xyzcorporation.org, www.xyzcorporation.biz and www.xyzcorporation.info, your Web site host can set the other registered domains to lead to www.xyzcorporation.com. If a site visitor types in www.xyzcorporation.com or www.xyzcorporation.biz, he or she will be directed to the same site. You can also use pointers to lead to other pages within your primary Web site.

```
www.xyzcorporation.net              www.xyzcorporation.org
                    ↘            ↙
              www.xyzcorporation.com
                    ↗            ↖
www.xyzcorporation.biz              www.xyzcorporation.info
```

SECURE YOUR WEB DESIGN TEAM

The Web site design market is excruciatingly competitive, to say the least. Users' awareness has grown right along with the industry, and many of us understand basic HTML commands. Actually, there are plenty of nine-year-olds who have a decent grasp of creating a basic Web page. That said, an unfortunately high number of people consider themselves "Webmasters" or "Web site designers."

The American Heritage Dictionary defines "master" as "one highly skilled, as in a trade." Without stringent licensing requirements, this designation has unfortunately been applied to many people who are barely adept at surfing the Web, let alone capable of creating a global image for a business. Rarely does a day go by when I don't see a Web site with misspellings, incorrect grammar, poor navigation, broken links, or just plain bad design. And it doesn't help that there are no pricing or salary standards in the industry. Development bids for the same Web site could range as much as 1,000 percent. (Imagine paying an exorbitant amount for an ineffective, unattractive, unsuccessful site!)

With all this in mind, choosing your Web design team is definitely not an easy task. Naturally, the biggest issue will be your budget. Salaried Web designers have been known to command annual rates in excess of $100,000. The average Web designer's salary falls in the $40,000 to $60,000 range. Hourly freelance Web designers charge anywhere from $25 to $200 per hour. The cost for most small Web sites is in the $500 to $5,000 range, and larger sites can cost anywhere from $10,000 to $250,000. In the midst of the initial Web rush in the late 1990s, there were reports of Web sites that cost over $1 million!

How much should *you* pay for a Web site? If only there was a simple answer. An infinite number of options are available, but there are few standards. You could:

- Use a service like Microsoft's bCentral (www.bcentral.com) or BigStep (www.bigstep.com), which allows you to create your own Web site at no cost. These types of services host your Web site for a nominal monthly fee. Domain name registration fees are additional.

- Use a template service, like that of ImageCafé (which was created by two very talented African American entrepreneurs, Clarence Wooten and Andre Ford). ImageCafé, now owned by Verisign, sells template-designed Web sites for a one-time fee of $99 to $200. After you purchase the template of your choice, you can upload your own text and additional images. Domain name registration and hosting costs are additional.

- Select one or more staff members to take a few basic Web design courses and then develop your company's Web site. Your costs will include staff training, graphics development (if needed), and payroll expenses for the amount of time it takes to create and maintain the site.

- Hire your ISP, or a large firm like IBM, to provide a small business Web site for under $1,000. Packages like these often include at least one year of hosting as part of the Web design package.

- Hire a freelance Web designer to create a small packaged site for $500 to $1,500. An endless number of freelancers charge bargain-basement prices, so if cheap is what you're looking for, a freelancer won't be hard to find. The important issue is to keep quality work and good customer service at the top of your priority list.

- Hire a Web design firm to create a fully customized site. The price range for customized sites is $2,000 to "the sky's the limit."

Large Web design firms have to set their rates to cover overhead costs. Freelance Web designers can afford to charge lower rates. By the same token, freelance designers may sometimes have difficulty providing support services after the site is developed. Large Web design firms typically have plenty of support staff available if the site has problems, or needs to be updated regularly. Also, larger firms are better equipped for one-stop shopping. Many offer hosting, marketing, and graphic design services, in addition to their multimedia development services.

Whichever option you choose, the more pages and features your site has (e.g., database functionalities, audio, video, interaction with back-end software systems, real-time e-commerce transactions, enhanced security features), the more it will cost. The more technologically elaborate and tailor-made you want the site to be, the more you can expect to pay. Fees also depend on the geographic location and the experience of the designer or firm. Naturally, the fees of designers and firms based in high-tech corridors like New York, San Francisco, Washington, DC, or Los Angeles will be higher than the fees of designers and firms in Juneau, Alaska, or Des Moines, Iowa.

Another important factor to keep in mind is that Web design fees can change, not only from freelancer to firm, but from client to client. If your company is "high maintenance" and requires constant attention—phone conferences, meetings, training, technical and other support services—expect to pay more money.

When you've reached the point of selecting your Web design team, your budget should be in place. You may need to revisit your budget and/or your expectations, based on the Web development proposals you receive. It is not uncommon for Web design customers to have grandiose ideas for their corporate Web sites and then change their tunes when they see Web design rate cards or customized proposals. I would recommend getting three to five bids before you make your final decision. If available, ask for a breakdown of rates for specific Web site bells and whistles. (Please note that not all designers or firms will have rate cards. Many freelancers and design firms charge flat fees based on the number of pages or packaged features.) Don't be surprised to see a wide range of varying rates from one freelancer or firm to another.

I vehemently recommend against letting just anyone who claims to be a Webmaster create your company's online image. Web site design involves a lot more than simply understanding a few HTML commands. It requires creativity, programming, graphic design, project management, marketing, and good communication skills.

The World Organization of Webmasters (www.joinwow.org) defines a "Webmaster" as:

> One person interfacing with Net-based communication, back-end technology, and business management. A Webmaster is the general contractor/team leader for the creation and management of Web sites.

Most Webmasters would certainly claim that they fit within this definition. The problem is that most entrepreneurs don't know enough about the industry or the position to truthfully determine the level of a Webmaster's skills. To effectively choose from among the thousands of self-proclaimed Web designers, ask colleagues and associates for leads. Look at Webmaster credits on well-designed Web sites. (We'll talk more about the elements of good design in the next section.) Be careful not to immediately choose the first or the cheapest designer or firm. Remember, you often get what you pay for. When you "interview" Web designers, ask for references and samples of their work. Clarify what you'll be paying for. Some designers charge hourly; others provide "packaged deals," depending on the size and features of your desired site. Others will develop a customized proposal specifically suited to your desired elements and features.

Before signing a contract, make sure you know how maintenance fees will be charged, and whether maintenance is included in the initial Web development proposal.

Don't be fooled by the flash! A lot of Webmasters have attracted clients because they created sites with bright-colored backgrounds, lots of motion, rotating images, looping music files, and needless amounts of high-end programming. More is not always better. Your company's Web site should be consistent with your off-line brand. Ask what the development process will be. If the designer doesn't mention your target audience or online goals, take your business elsewhere.

Look for someone who has good knowledge of the Web environment, customized design skills, good customer service, good communication skills, marketing savvy, and an expressed interest in the process of delivering your goods and services to your clients. A Webmaster should be thorough. He or she should test your site's design on a variety of browsers and Internet access speeds (for load time) and should check site map links and all outgoing links to make sure that they're not broken.[3] He or she should assist with the creation of content for the site (which should be spell- and grammar-checked before uploading!) and should design your site to achieve specific goals and to target a specific audience. A good Webmaster is someone who wants—and

Figure 5.3   Web Relationships

As you develop your Internet presence, you may find yourself working with several firms or consultants, including:

1. An Internet Service Provider (ISP) for e-mail and Internet access.

2. A Webmaster or a Web site design firm (for design and maintenance).

3. A Web hosting service (may be same as e-mail and Internet access ISP).

4. A database developer.

5. An Internet consultant (for marketing assistance and search engine submissions).

6. A media buyer (for online advertising).

Many times, you will be able to find a company that offers a combination of these services. When you are selecting an Internet vendor, be sure to ask what the fee structure includes.

needs—to understand your business products, services, and marketing methods before setting off to create your global image.

Lastly, you must hold a Webmaster, whether salaried or freelance, to the same standard to which you hold your attorney, CPA, or auto mechanic. You may not understand the intricacies of their professions, but you must clarify the desired project outcome and ask questions along the way to educate yourself and minimize detrimental situations in the future. If you hire someone who is relatively new to the industry, realize that you and your staff will have to contribute any skills that your new Webmaster lacks.

PLAN YOUR SITE CAREFULLY

The most important thing to keep in mind during the planning stage is that all Web sites are works in progress. Getting your site up and running is only the beginning. Your Web site's content may change daily, monthly, or annually, depending on your goals and your audience. There is no surefire method for creating the right navigation and the right content. What works for one audience today may not work for another, or even the same audience one year from today. Remember that a Web site's elements can always be changed when they no longer serve your company's needs.

Armed with your business model and Internet strategy, your Web team should carefully review your company's various marketing methods. What has worked well, and what hasn't worked at all? Are there specific colors and fonts? Does a logo, or other images, collectively brand your company? Is there a company slogan or a specific marketing campaign that you plan to incorporate into your Web site's elements? If so, it's time to put all of this info on the table.

Spend plenty of time thinking about your target audience. How and why will your customers and potential customers use your Web site? Will they browse, shop, entertain themselves, or learn new information about your company, product, or industry? What do they want to know about your company? What will entice them to buy your product and to feel assured that your company can do what your Web site says it can? Are you offering product information, your client list, the company history, management background info, client testimonials, contact information for your company's various locations, press-related information? Does your target audience include investors or potential strategic alliance partners? If so, what information is most vital to them? Is it your annual statement, current stock price (if your company has publicly traded stock), or news of management changes, mergers, or acquisitions?

Before development can begin, information should be prioritized so that it is easier to create appropriate levels of navigation. Flat sites are those that make all information available on the home page or one level below the home page. Deep sites create multiple sublevels of information and require a little bit more exploring than flat sites. Some sites are very deep; requiring a site visitor to click five or more times before finding the needed information. (Most large corporations' Web sites are very deep.) Web site traffic (statistical) analysis will help you to stay abreast of the information that is most relevant to your site's visitors. More on that shortly.

If possible, create a focus group of 5 to 10 people who can provide feedback on your Web site's content, navigation, and overall usability. Obviously, it is preferable to choose people who fit your target audience and who will provide you with honest, objective information. Flexibility is important in site development, but you must not react to each and every piece of feedback. Keep track of feedback received from your focus group, as well as from other site visitors who make suggestions. When you review your site's look-and-feel every 6 to 12 months, consider this feedback and determine which suggestions are appropriate for your site's next renovation. Complaints and suggestions involving error messages and transaction processing should be handled immediately.

News stories have often reported the average site visitor's fear of security on the Web. You and your Web team should make sure that site visitors feel comfortable on your site, especially if the site is e-commerce-enabled or if you require registration. This might include adding a privacy policy or joining a privacy seal program.

The perfect site is one that is attractive, suits the company's overall image, displays meaningful (and, where appropriate, entertaining) information in an easy-to-navigate layout, and achieves your company goals. The site should load quickly and should let the site visitor know whom to contact for more information about a product or service, and how that person can be contacted. (I still see lots of Web sites that don't provide company telephone numbers, and some sites require a full-scale search to find a contact e-mail address.) Unless it's a publication, portal, or entertainment Web site, a business site should have a minimal amount of advertisements and affiliate buttons; they tend to clutter a Web site and can be quite distracting for some surfers. It's also a good idea to keep navigation buttons and contact information in the same place, on all pages of the site. Keep sentences short, and limit the amount of scrolling needed to get to information.

Carefully select ways to give your clients and site visitors added value. In addition to providing information about your company's products and services, a current frequently asked questions (FAQ) file, as well as relevant articles or tips written by company managers and employees, might be useful. Interactive features can be value-adds for site visitors, depending on time and financial resources. Webcasts, scheduled chats, live customer interaction solutions, and surveys could also be beneficial. Stay in touch with your clients, and ask them what they like and don't like about your Web site.

And last, but certainly not least, kill the clutter. There is a tendency for small businesses to attempt to turn their Web sites into portals. Later, the site owners abandon the sites because they overestimated advertising revenue and underestimated the amount of work required to maintain a portal site. Your clients can get free, branded e-mail addresses, entertainment news, and discussion boards just about anywhere on the Web. There's no need to clutter your business's important product and service information with these types of supposed value-adds. All elements of your company's Web site should serve to enhance your marketing goals, not distract from them. Focus on **your** company's target audience, not on the average Web surfer. Ask your clients what they want, and consider the consequences of new site features in terms of relevance, time, and financial investment.

ASSIGN STAFF DUTIES

Make sure that everyone on your staff knows what his or her Web-related responsibilities are, and the scheduled timelines or deadlines for their action items. Clearly establish who is responsible for developing site content, handling the site's marketing, and serving as the primary contact for the Webmaster or the Web design firm you have retained. Your staff also needs to be prepared to handle advertising sales, if necessary, and customer service-related e-mails. Employees should also be encouraged to check the site regularly, view competitors' sites, and make content suggestions.

If one of your employees is responsible for maintaining the site, make sure that he or she is properly trained. It is not enough to have a general knowledge of HTML. Web site design is becoming more and more complex; it requires continuing education to handle server-related issues and elaborate programming features.

COMPILE THE SITE'S CONTENT

Site content includes the company logo, history, contact info, product photos, staff biographies and photos, and other graphics. All content, except images, should be saved in text format. All logos and images should be saved in GIF or JPEG format. In most cases, your Web designer will assist you with this because most of the content will depend on the site's concept.

Your Web site goals (and your budget) will determine whether your site will be updated by the minute or once a year. The frequency of site updates should be estimated prior to the Web development process. Although content is king on the Web, there is no need for every business to become a portal. If you have properly assessed your time and the financial resources for your company's Web development, you should know how much time and money to dedicate to Web site updates. If your company is establishing an electronic brochure site, review the site at least once a quarter, and analyze site statistics monthly. Use site content and new features to increase clients' benefits, like posting product development announcements and giving notification of upcoming sales and events.

You and your Web team should have a system for performing updates. Once the frequency of site updates has been determined, set a specific day, date, or time for content delivery. Also, determine who will collect the information and how it should be transferred to the Webmaster.

SELECT A HOSTING SERVICE

Web hosting refers to the storage and serving of a company's Web files to site visitors. A Web site, as you may know, is simply a series of files that include text, images, and, sometimes, audio and video. When site visitors enter your Web site address into their browsers, they are connected to your Web host's server. The server responds by projecting the appropriate Web files onto the site visitors' screens. Larger companies often host their own Web files; most individuals and smaller companies use the services of an ISP (aka "Web host").

Most often, your Webmaster will select a hosting service, based on your predetermined needs. When you are selecting Web site hosting, look for:

- *Costs.* Web hosting fees can run from $10 to $200 per month, depending on a company's storage needs and features that are added to the site, including e-commerce and back-end software interaction (e.g., database, accounting). The average monthly hosting cost is $25 for small Web sites (under 100MB of storage space). Some hosts charge a one-time set-up fee, ranging from $25 to $150. Additional features may incur extra fees.
- *Up-time.* Your company's Web site needs to be accessible 24 hours a day, 7 days a week. The more up-time your Web site host provides, the better. (Up-time refers to the availability of your Web site's files.) You need to select a Web host that offers nearly 100 percent up-time. Web hosts should also back up their server files on a daily basis, just in case something happens to the server.
- *Disk storage.* This determines how much space is allotted for your Web site's files. Average disk storage available for smaller Web sites falls in the 25–100MB range. Large sites may require several hundreds of megabytes—or even several gigabytes—of storage space.
- *Data transfer.* This feature, measured in megabytes or gigabytes, determines how much bandwidth is available for traffic coming to your site. Needless to say, the more data transfer you have, the better.
- *Technical support.* Some companies offer technical support via e-mail only. Other companies offer 24/7 telephone and e-mail technical support. If your staff is not very Web- or server-proficient, you might want to select the services of an ISP that provides telephone support, in addition to e-mail support.
- *Security.* To give your customers peace of mind, it is important to know how secure your Web communications and customer data are. Ask how your host protects their servers from hack attacks, and what features, in your hosting package, will help you to maintain data integrity and confidentiality. The larger your company's site and the more features it has (e.g., e-commerce,

back-end software integration), the more enhanced security features should be included in your hosting package.

- *E-mail features.* Branded POP3 e-mail accounts allow you and your staff to send and receive e-mail using your company's domain ("name@yourcompany.com"). The vast majority of ISPs allow a limited number of POP3 e-mail addresses with business and personal hosting packages. Also, be sure to find out whether your host also offers e-mail forwarding and e-mail aliases (Figure 5.4).

- *Site activity and usage reports.* The vast majority of ISPs provide their customers with easy access to their Web site's statistics through a password-protected administrative page or a Web-based control panel. The data may come in the form of a combination of tables, graphs, and charts, or it may come in the form of raw log files, which require the use of a Web server log file analysis program, like WebTrends (www.webtrends.com) or Webalizer (www.webalizer.com). By reviewing your Web site's activity, you will know how much traffic your site is getting, how site visitors are finding your site, which pages are most popular, and how long site visitors stay on your site.

- *E-commerce.* Not every host offers e-commerce capabilities due to the necessary security elements required to process electronic transactions. Since e-commerce hosting prices are usually different than general hosting prices, you should always ask about additional e-commerce-related costs. Also, it's important to know how many products are allowed. Some

Figure 5.4   E-Mail Alias (Definition and example)

An e-mail alias does not provide a second e-mail account; it simply provides an alternate method of reaching the person's original e-mail Inbox. Each e-mail alias simply forwards e-mail on to any e-mail address that you specify.

E-mail aliases are often used to create handy replacements for long or difficult-to-remember e-mail addresses. They can also be used to create generic e-mail addresses such as info@yourcompany.com.

For example, if David Smith receives e-mail at david.smith @hiscompany.com and he wishes to have all company sales-related messages directed to his Inbox, he can create the e-mail alias sales @hiscompany.com and set it to forward to his e-mail account.

E-mail aliases are established by your ISP or via your ISP's Web-based control panel.

hosts impose limits on the number of sale items, or they may offer pricing levels based on the number of sale items. And some hosts require that you secure your own online merchant account and e-commerce gateway. We'll review the complete process for incorporating e-commerce in the next section.

Additional hosting features include:

- A Web-based control panel that allows you to easily view statistics, add new e-mail aliases, or forward e-mail messages to other addresses.
- Secure Socket Layer (SSL) encrypted ordering.
- Search engine submission.
- Web design software.
- Shopping cart software.
- Microsoft FrontPage server extensions.

Be sure to ask about special deals that include free domain name registration, free software, or discounts for prepaid services. Look for the ability to add à la carte services—additional POP3 mailboxes, more disk storage space, database, chat, or streaming video features. Some hosts are capable of serving such features; others are not. Ask, up front, for confirmation of these service offerings and their respective prices. If you have a large company or a site that receives an enormous amount of traffic, you might consider colocating your server (hosting and maintaining your own server on-site).

A site called The List (www.thelist.com) is a great place to find an ISP or Web host in your area. Additional resources for finding and comparing Web hosts include:

Freedom List	www.freedomlist.com
Host Index	www.hostindex.com
Host Search	www.hostsearch.com
Host Investigator	www.hostinvestigator.com
Top Hosts	www.tophosts.com
WebHosters.com	www.webhosters.com

If, at some point, you decide to change Web hosts, you or your Webmaster must contact your domain registrar so that your domain points to your new host's server. Also, your Webmaster will need to upload the files to the new server.

INCORPORATING E-COMMERCE

To process sales from your company's Web site, your company has three options:

1. Collect customer contact, billing, and transaction info off-line, via telephone or fax, for manual credit card processing.
2. Collect customer contact, billing, and transaction info via a secure Web server for manual, off-line credit card processing.
3. Collect customer contact, billing, and transaction info via your Web site for online, real-time credit card processing.

To accept credit cards for online purchases, your company needs to establish an Internet merchant account with a bank or a payment processing company that provides this service (Figure 5.5). Some payment processing companies are: PayPal (www.paypal.com), CheckSpace (www.checkspace.com), ProPay (www.propay.com), Charge.com (www. charge.com) and E-Commerce Exchange (www.ecx.com). Your merchant account provider (MAP) may also offer alternative payment processing for debit cards and electronic fund transfer (EFT) payments.

When you are selecting a merchant account provider, it is important to choose the right provider and an account arrangement that suits your business model and budget. Look for good service, competitive rates, and flexible limits. The size of your business and your business's creditworthiness, products, and anticipated sales will affect the type of account that you get and the fees that you will pay. Merchant fees can

Figure 5.5   Merchant Accounts

Not all merchant accounts are created equal. There are at least three different types of these accounts:

1. *Retail account:*   Used by merchants who swipe a customer's credit card through a point-of-sale (POS) terminal, request the customer's signature, and issue a credit card receipt on-site.

2. *MOTO (mail order/telephone order):*   Used typically for catalog ordering or for other merchant transactions for which a customer's card is not physically available. Merchants record specific customer information and process orders in batch form.

3. *Internet merchant account:*   Used by merchants for online transaction processing. Customer information is submitted on the company's Web site. Internet merchant accounts are similar to MOTO accounts, but transactions may be processed in batch form or in real-time.

---

take a sizable bite out of your profit margin, so pay close attention when comparing accounts and service providers. A variety of fees are involved with merchant accounts. They include set-up fees, security deposits, equipment leasing or purchasing, transaction fees (fixed charges applied to each transaction), discount rates (a percentage charged to you for each online sales transaction), chargeback rates (a percentage of total monthly sales, stemming from returned or rejected purchases), and chargeback fees (applied for every chargeback incurred).

After your company has achieved merchant status, you or your Webmaster will need to select a payment gateway. A payment gateway—a requirement for real-time, online transaction processing—is a secure link between your Web site and the credit card processor (Figure 5.6). A secure gateway ensures that, during transfer, your customers' contact

Figure 5.6   Steps Performed in a Real-Time
Online Credit Card Transaction

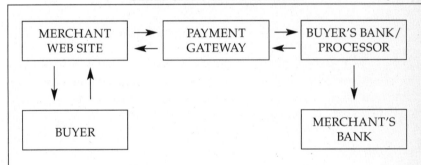

1. Buyer (site visitor) views Web site and selects goods/services to purchase.
2. Buyer submits credit card information on the Merchant's Web site.
3. Merchant sends credit card and sales information through the payment gateway, requesting authorization by the Buyer's card-issuing bank.
4. The card-issuing bank authorizes the transaction if the Buyer has enough available credit in their account. The card-issuing bank sends an authorization code (for approval or denial) back to the Merchant.
5. The card-issuing bank transfers the amount of the sales transaction, minus a fee, to the Merchant's bank.
6. Buyer receives, on screen and/or via e-mail, a transaction confirmation and receipt.

and financial information will not be intercepted or altered by hackers. The most widely known payment gateways are CyberCash (www .cybercash.com; purchased by Verisign in 2001), Authorize.Net, Cyber-Source (www.cybersource.com), and iBill (www.ibill.com). It is important to have a payment gateway that is compatible with your shopping cart program and your merchant account bank.

A shopping cart may or may not come with your Web site hosting account. Shopping cart programs—e.g., FreeMerchant (www.freemerchant.com), Miva (www.miva.com), and Mercantec's SoftCart (www.mercantec.com)—allow your company's Web site designer to create display and ordering pages for your products.

Micro-businesses on small budgets should consider options like Yahoo! Stores (store.yahoo.com), Microsoft bCentral (www .bcentral.com), BigStep (www.bigstep.com), or UMS eStore (www .umsestore.com). Some of these are integrated solutions that provide a Web storefront, hosting, secure transactions, and a shopping cart, all in one. Depending on the e-commerce solution, you may still have to acquire your own online merchant account and payment gateway.

Providing secure transactions can be a bit tricky. Most business owners assume that once they have a functioning Web site, a hosting package, and a shopping cart, they're all set to go for online sales. That's not the case. You must confirm—with your Webmaster, merchant account provider, and Web host—that your e-commerce transactions are secure. A secure server encrypts any data exchanged in order processing. The industry standard for secure servers is SSL (Secure

---

WEBSEARCH

E-COMMERCE RESOURCES

eCom Resource Center
www.ecomresourcecenter.com

eCommerce Guide
ecommerce.internet.com

MerchantWorkZ
www.merchantworkz.com

NetBusiness
content.techweb.com/netbiz

ZDNet: Business & Tech—E-Commerce
www.zdnet.com/enterprise/e-business

Socket Layer), but some of the major banks are developing an alternative standard called SET (Secure Electronic Transaction).

Last, but certainly not least, you will need to discuss state-to-state and international sales taxes with your corporate accountant. In virtual space, entrepreneurs tend to forget about the real world's borders and their own legal and tax responsibilities. Global opportunities also come with global liabilities, so be sure to protect your company from penalty assessments after the fact.

ANALYZE YOUR WEB SITE STATISTICS AND AUDIENCE

There are two primary trains of thought regarding Web site statistics. Some entrepreneurs think that the more Web site traffic they have, the more advertising dollars they can generate. Others think, "The more traffic my site has, the greater the chance that more people will buy my stuff." Actually, both groups are correct, but entrepreneurs' thinking cannot end at this point. There's a lot more to Web statistics than driving traffic with the *hope* of getting more ad dollars and the *potential* that a few people might buy a product. It's one thing to drive *traffic* to your site, whether you get 500 hits per month or 5 million page views per year. Converting traffic into *customers* is a whole other ball of wax. You can do this through regular analysis of your site's statistics.

Many of us realize the availability of Web site statistics, but few understand how these numbers translate into opportunity. With the two trains of thought above, entrepreneurs are, for the most part, leaving things up to chance and focusing on getting more "eyeballs" on their Web sites, rather than focusing on building a relationship with site visitors to keep those "eyeballs" coming back to buy the site's product(s). The Internet and World Wide Web are "new" media and are yet to have firmly established marketing and advertising standards. Nonetheless, strategy should be an integral part of any business-related activities online. As you gradually develop your company's marketing strategy and renovate your Internet presence, quite a few Web site statistics are available to help you structure your company's marketing and advertising efforts properly and effectively.

Web site statistics extend far beyond those little hit counters posted on Web site home pages (Figure 5.7). Technology exists that can tell you which pages on your site are viewed most often; how long visitors stay on your site; where site visitors are referred from; which page is usually the "exit" page for your site; and the day and hour when your site received the most traffic. These statistics are usually compiled by your Web host, but a number of site tracking software programs are

Figure 5.7   Web Site Statistics

Here are some of the top Web measurement statistics:

Hits (monthly, daily, hourly)
Page views (monthly, daily, hourly)
Unique visitors (monthly, daily, hourly)
User sessions (monthly, daily, hourly)
Ad views

Referring sites
   Top referring pages
   Top referring domains

Total number of visitors per hour
Total number of visitors per day

Total number of visitors per site page
Total number of visitors per referring site

Browser usage (type, version number, hits per browser type, percentage of total usage)

Screen resolution (type, hits per screen resolution, percentage of total hits)

Operating system (type, hits per operating system, percentage of total operating system)

Total number of errors (type, percentage of total errors)

Keywords used in search engine requests
   Top search engine keywords
   Top referring search engines

Top site entry pages
Top site exit pages

Most accessed pages
Least accessed pages

Most requested files, images, and downloads

Bandwidth (monthly, daily, hourly)

available. Before you rush off to purchase one, contact your Web host and find out how you can access your site's statistics. In most cases, you won't have to purchase a software program to achieve that access. You may find that your site's statistics are readily available in table, graphic, or raw log form. Many Web hosts will track your stats and

---

WEBSEARCH

WEB ANALYSIS TOOLS

EasyStat	Web Stat
www.easystat.net	www.web-stat.com
NedStat	Webalizer
www.nedstat.com	www.webalizer.com
HitBox Professional	WebTrends
www.hitboxprofessional.com	www.webtrends.com
Stats4You	
www.stats4you.com	

---

present them to you via a password-protected Web-based control panel; or, they'll provide you with a free (or discounted) downloadable Web analysis software package.

Before clarifying the definition of hits and other Web measurement tools, it is important to explain the difference between the terms "home page," "Web page," and "Web site." Home page refers to the main page of a Web site. It is also referred to as the "index" page of a Web site; hence, "index.htm" or "index.html" is sometimes found at the end of the site address. Home page is often used to describe an entire Web site, but this is incorrect. Web page refers to a single page within a Web site. A home page is also a Web page; it just happens to have its own special reference. A Web site is the compilation of all pages, images, and files for a single domain. A Web site can have one page or thousands of pages.

The most widely acknowledged Web statistical measure is the "hit." Unfortunately, this is also the most inaccurate way of measuring Web site traffic. Most people mistakenly assume that a hit refers to a single Web page that is viewed, or a person who visits a Web site. Contrary to popular belief, page views are much better measures of site traffic than hits. A "hit" actually refers to each of the elements on a single Web page—images, buttons, banners, and text. If a Web page has 12 images, one banner ad, text, and five button ads, its site statistics will reflect 19 hits when a visitor views this page. (*Note:* All of the content on a page registers as one hit, depending on how it is coded by the Web designer.) A "page view" refers to a single Web page that has been viewed by a site visitor. So, a single page on a Web site could register one page view and 19 hits. As you can see, page views are a lot more accurate. Given the differing Web design styles, tracking hits can become quite cumbersome.

Once you gain access to your site's statistics, you will be able to answer the following questions:

1. Are we meeting our quarterly, semi-annual, or annual goals for site traffic?
2. Are we meeting our quarterly, semi-annual, or annual goals for online revenue?
3. How are our site visitors finding out about our company's Web site?
4. Which information is most important to them?
5. Which information is least important to them?
6. What are the days or hours during which we get the most traffic? And why?
7. Which search engines have been most useful in our online marketing campaign?
8. How many unique visitors does our site attract each month?
9. How long do visitors stay on our Web site?
10. Which advertisements are viewed most often?

Make it a habit to review your Web site traffic on a monthly basis, and adjust your marketing efforts on at least a semi-annual basis. See whether traffic spikes after you distribute an electronic announcement or shortly after a direct mail postcard campaign. Also, look at ways that you can make changes to your content, to increase traffic on certain pages. Find out whether the majority of your traffic is coming from a specific search engine or a colleague's resource page. These statistics will help you to understand the effectiveness of your company's marketing and advertising efforts, and to adjust them accordingly.

To take things to the next step, e-commerce site owners need to determine their site's "customer conversion rate." This number reveals the ratio of online purchases to Web site visitors. (Divide the average number of monthly online purchases by the average number of monthly site visitors.) Obviously, the higher the conversion rate, the greater your potential for online profitability and the less expensive it should be for you to get new customers. Once you know your customer conversion rate, you'll have a better idea of how much traffic is needed to achieve your site's revenue goals. You can adjust your annual site traffic goals accordingly, and then analyze the success rate of each of

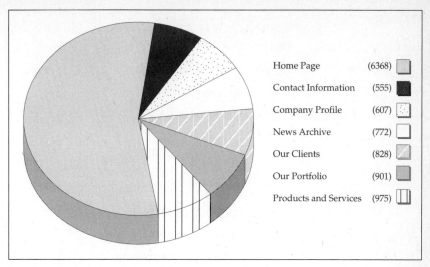

Sample statistical chart for monthly site visitors (by %), per page. Used with permission © Stats4You.com

your company's marketing efforts. (We'll look more closely at building a virtual brand and driving site traffic in Chapter 6.)

It is often much easier to increase one's customer conversion rate than to spend thousands of dollars trying to drive more traffic. Driving more traffic does not guarantee more sales, and it increases your company's customer acquisition costs. The notion of increasing your customer conversion rate is a close cousin to the principle that it costs more to get a new customer than it does to keep a current customer. Increasing your customer conversion rate is about working with what you've got. Many times, small adjustments like changing your site's navigation, updating content, adding a privacy policy, or even minimizing the number of affiliate programs on your home page—can make a huge difference in increasing the length of visitors' sessions and the possibility that they'll make a purchase. More significant changes, like streamlining the e-commerce transaction process, can produce significant increases in traffic and sales.

If your site does not have e-commerce, you should compare your monthly page views versus the number of e-mail inquiries received about your services. Also, take a look at the number of incoming phone calls requesting additional information based on a previous review of your site. Naturally, you should always ask how new contacts heard about your business. And, as much as possible, get feedback about your Web site from your current clients.

IMPROVING YOUR COMPANY'S
INTERNET ROI: RECAP

1. Choose your Web-based business model.

2. Develop your Internet strategy:

    (a) Clarify your target market(s).

    (b) Check out competitors' sites.

    (c) Prepare your staff for Web-related tasks.

    (d) Review your budget.

    (e) Create specific goals for your Internet presence.

    (f) Develop an integrated marketing plan.

3. Build a successful Web site:

    (a) Register one or more Web site addresses.

    (b) Secure your Web design team.

    (c) Plan your site carefully.

    (d) Assign staff duties.

    (e) Compile site content.

    (f) Select a hosting service.

    (g) Incorporate e-commerce.

    (h) Analyze site traffic and audience.

6

BUILDING A VIRTUAL BRAND

The level of widespread success for your company online depends on your ability to create a positive virtual brand. And what is a brand, exactly? A brand is an association of value with your company and its goods and services. It is a promise of quality. Your company's brand, above and beyond its pricing structure, can make or break your business.

When you think of companies like Nike, Nordstrom, Jaguar, or Ritz-Carlton, you immediately think of quality. There are obviously shoe manufacturers, department stores, auto makers, and hotels offering less expensive goods and services, but these names exude excellence and, to a great extent, the names alone justify the higher price that many customers are willing to pay for the goods and services of these companies. Companies like Target and Walmart don't encourage visions of grandeur and luxury, but they are successful brands nonetheless. Their brands are based on good product selection and great prices because their target audiences include working-class people who want variety and savings.

Contrary to popular belief, branding is not just about having a logo, a huge advertising budget, or a catchy slogan. A brand is an intangible aspect of who you are and what you offer. Your company's brand is what your customers collectively think about you, your business overall, and the products and services that your company offers. A virtual brand is the impression that customers, or potential customers, have when they see any part of your company's Internet presence—namely, your advertising; your Web site's colors, layout, and content; and your product or service information. Your company's virtual brand incorporates how you treat your online customers via e-mail and how you deliver (fulfill) your product or service. It also includes the customer service that is (or is not) provided when someone contacts you for more information. Whether your business is large or small, and whether or not you actively work toward building a brand for your company, it has one. And that brand can be positive or negative.

WHY VIRTUAL BRANDING MATTERS

A variety of books have been dedicated to the subject of brand marketing, and rightfully so. Building a positive, memorable brand requires a lot of time and exposure. It is a valuable asset that can give your company its competitive advantage. Your virtual brand is especially important because potential online customers have fewer means of contact with you and your staff. In this chapter, the intent is not to make you a branding expert, but to get you to understand the basic concept of virtual (online) branding, and each piece of the Internet marketing puzzle.

Branding isn't a new concept. The importance of branding has resurfaced due to technological developments and the evolution of Internet marketing. With so many global choices at a consumer's disposal, businesses must work harder to develop even a short-term relationship with Internet users. Also, with such aggressive competition in pricing and product features, it is becoming increasingly difficult to set one business apart from the next.

Examples of successful online brands include Yahoo!, NetNoir, America Online, BlackPlanet.com, and Amazon.com. Many African American-owned businesses don't have the budgets of the aforementioned companies, but it is possible—and important—for us to successfully create positive virtual brands for our companies, products, and services. Building brand familiarity and loyalty on the Web is a challenging but necessary priority for businesses of all sizes. Effective brand management can increase sales, help to retain customers, enhance a positive perception of goods and services, and shorten the business sales cycle.

Your company's overall brand incorporates your logo, colors, slogan, collateral pieces, traditional and online advertising, Web site, customer service, and product delivery. It affects your corporate culture, marketing and public relations efforts, and, most importantly, the perception that clients and potential clients have about your products and services. Your brand plays a great role in influencing how people feel about you. To create a truly successful virtual brand, it is vital for you to understand your target audience and all facets of your company's Internet presence.

COMPONENTS OF AN INTERNET PRESENCE

Marketing one's business online is a huge task, but this is often seen only as a matter of developing a Web site and optimizing search engine listings. Successfully marketing your business on the Internet encompasses a wide variety of elements—from using e-mail efficiently to providing excellent online customer service; from online media buying and selling to strategic Web site development. In essence, you need to create a complete Internet presence.

Most people think that an Internet presence and a Web site are the exact same thing. Actually, a Web site is an integral part of a company's Internet presence, but a lot more is involved. Before delving into the intricacies of an Internet presence, let's clarify the importance of your company's Web site as it relates to overall online marketing. A Web site is a marketing tool. Let me repeat that statement: *A Web site is a marketing tool.* It is not an instant panacea that will double or triple your company's sales overnight. By now, you should have heard—at least a few hundred times—that "build it and they will come" doesn't work on the Web. To effectively increase online sales, your company needs a solid business model and a clearly defined Internet strategy, both of which were discussed in the previous chapter.

An Internet presence includes, but is not limited to, the following elements:

1. E-mail marketing
   a. Regular e-mail contact with colleagues and clientele
   b. Direct e-mail distribution
   c. Electronic mailing list distribution
   d. Tag line
2. Online interviews and expert opinions
3. Employee representation in chat rooms, newsgroups, and e-mail lists
4. Online advertising
5. Online public relations

6. Web site
7. Listings in search engines and directories
8. Incoming links
9. Affiliate marketing
10. Other marketing options

Let's take a closer look at each of these elements and how you can utilize them to create a positive brand for your company.

E-Mail Marketing

E-mail truly is the "killer[1] Internet application" and will continue to be for a long time. E-mail allows you to stay in touch with clients and potential clients as often as you like. The networking and branding that you can do at little cost are astounding. It is, simply put, the easiest way to promote your business online, educate potential clients, and drive traffic to your site.

It is interesting to see how many people miss out on the opportunity to save money and generate new business via e-mail. A great way to capitalize on e-mail access and virtual networking is to forward *interesting and relevant* information to clients and colleagues when you find or receive it. They'll certainly remember you for it. I have personally maintained an international network for many years, just by using e-mail. I maintain contact with people not by sending out my own self-serving news but by sending information that is specifically important to them and their industry. This reinforces my reputation as a resource. I use my tag line to remind them of my company's services and contact information, as well as upcoming speaking engagements.

The biggest challenge with e-mail is the ease with which one can become overwhelmed with sending and receiving it. What with the millions of electronic mailing lists, spam, jokes, virus warnings, urban legends, and general information distributed, it is very easy for the average professional to receive hundreds of e-mail messages each day. A good rule is to set aside a specific time of each business day to check e-mail. It is understandably easy to become overwhelmed by a swelling e-mail Inbox, but it is imperative that entrepreneurs treat e-mail messages with the same respect they give to voice messages. It is pointless to include your company's e-mail address on your business card or Web site and never check your e-mail. To avoid missing out on business opportunities and important messages, scroll through the subject headers and respond immediately to client messages, and to product and service requests from potential clients. All other messages can be handled at another time. (You'll find more e-mail and online communication tips in Appendix A of this book.)

Another big challenge is relying too much on e-mail for marketing purposes. E-mail should support your overall marketing efforts. It should not be your sole online marketing method. Atim Annette Oton, executive vice president of *Blacklines* magazine (www.blacklines.net), notes, "Sometimes we rely on technology too much, especially for event announcements. One of the problems for us has been that people do not read their e-mail. Sometimes a phone call is much better and more direct." The quarterly publication, which targets black designers in architecture, interior design, construction, and the arts, also uses an electronic mailing list to distribute information and to save money.

Direct e-mail campaigns refer to the use of text or HTML advertisements, news, and announcements sent to a large group of people. Sometimes the distribution list includes clients, colleagues, and other people you know; sometimes the list includes potential clients and other unknown persons. Thousands of Web-based businesses use direct e-mail to distribute product, company, and industry information to their global target audiences.

Just as you can purchase mailing addresses for potential customers from mailing list brokers off-line, you can purchase e-mail addresses for potential customers in virtual space. The difference is that you must make sure that electronic list members have "opted in" or authorized the distribution of their e-mail addresses for the purpose of receiving specific information. Whether or not you know the individuals, it is a good idea to ask them if they're interested in receiving information from you. And, make it easy for them to unsubscribe from your distribution list.

Spam[2] ("junk e-mail"), as you may know, is a huge problem on the Web. Nearly all of us have received, at one time or another, mass-distributed business "opportunities," pornographic links, weight-loss product information, and alleged calls to action for some poor boy dying of cancer in some faraway country. Many of us have even been spammed by our colleagues and associates. Because of the ease with which someone can send e-mail to mass numbers of people, a lot of entrepreneurs have begun to abuse this privilege; resulting in our much overloaded e-mail Inboxes.

After many presentations and speaking engagements, I find that I am automatically subscribed to one or more e-mail lists on a variety of topics. The information on many of these lists often duplicates messages and resources that I already receive, so I immediately request to be unsubscribed, or I unsubscribe myself, if unsubscription instructions are available. Believe it or not, I have actually been scolded by list owners, both in person and via e-mail, for requesting to be unsubscribed from their lists! Worst-case scenario: If the person refuses to unsubscribe me, or adds my name to the electronic mailing list again (after I have unsubscribed), I set my e-mail filters to immediately refuse or trash any information coming from that person or list. (You just have to draw the line somewhere.) The point of the story: Ask before you send regular announcements or subscribe your colleagues to your electronic newsletter or discussion list. Sometimes your information may not be of interest.

If you purchase a list of e-mail addresses, make sure that it is from a reputable brokerage company and that the list members have opted to receive product information. Clearly identify who you are and what you are selling or announcing. Be respectful of those who request to be removed from your distribution list. And remember, just because you think that your information is not spam or that it is of the utmost importance to everyone, not everyone else will agree. Adding text that says "This is not SPAM" does not mean that your message isn't. Some ISPs actually put a limit on the number of simultaneously distributed e-mail messages and send notes out to violators of their mass e-mail distribution rules. Quite a few online marketers have lost their Internet access because of such transgressions. For more information about spam and avoiding the distribution of unsolicited commercial e-mail, contact the Coalition Against Unsolicited Commercial Email (www.cauce.org).

A successful direct e-mail or permission e-mail campaign lends itself to viral marketing, which is basically a fancy way of saying "word of

---

WEBSEARCH

Here is a list of reputable direct e-mail list brokers:

Direct Media, Inc.
www.directmedia.com

IDG Communications
www.idglist.com

Permission Direct
www.permissiondirect.com

PostMaster Direct
www.postmasterdirect.com

To find other brokers, in major search engines and directories use keywords on "direct e-mail" or "opt in list."

mouth" marketing. In virtual space, viral marketing involves the delivery of a message (which is, typically, an ad for your product, service, event, or a call to action) to a targeted audience who, in turn, forward your message to other people who may be interested. These new potential customers, triggered by your message, forward it to others, and so on. The key is content. Messages should be carefully constructed so that they provide "edutainment" (entertaining educational information) and are not obviously self-serving. To make a long story short, viral e-mail marketing campaigns turn your potential customers into an extended sales and marketing force for your company.

Thanks to free services like ListBot,[3] Topica (www.topica.com), and Yahoo! Groups (groups.yahoo.com), there is an *electronic mailing list* for every subject known to man. Electronic mailing lists are basically an easy way to regularly distribute news and information to a large number of people via e-mail. A list owner creates the list and invites friends, colleagues, fellow organization members, and/or coworkers to subscribe. Messages for the group are sent to the list's primary e-mail address (e.g., listname@yahoogroups.com), where it is subsequently distributed to all subscribers. Services like Roving's Constant Contact (www.constantcontact.com), SparkLIST (www.sparklist.com), and Microsoft's bCentral ListBuilder (lb.bcentral.com) offer electronic mailing list management services for a nominal fee. These products allow list owners to create HTML newsletters and promotions, and provide extensive reports for tracking list activity and results.

Sometimes, electronic mailing lists are used only for announcement purposes, to keep clients and potential clients abreast of products and services, pricing information, corporate events, and site content changes. For example, some companies use them to send out press releases, make special-event announcements, or drive traffic to the corporate Web site by including links in the e-mail message content. Often, electronic mailing lists are used as special-interest discussion groups based on race, gender, industry, entertainment, religion, parenting, or any number of other topics. Electronic discussion lists can be especially overwhelming to subscribers because many of them generate a lot of traffic (i.e., dozens of e-mail messages daily). Many lists have a "digest" version that allows list subscribers to receive up to 25 messages bundled in one message (versus receiving dozens of separate messages over the course of a day). Typically, when you subscribe to such lists, you receive instructions for requesting a digest version of the list, unsubscribing, posting messages to the list (if this is an option), and temporarily stopping the receipt of messages during your vacation or an extended period of time off-line (NOMAIL).

Initially, it was a great idea to distribute an online newsletter to clients and colleagues. The problem is that now everyone is distributing some sort of electronic list. And, to piggyback off of the previous topic, many list owners are automatically adding subscribers' names without asking first. Should you decide to create and distribute an electronic mailing list for discussion purposes or to announce your company's news, include content that is helpful and relevant to the list's subscribers. Don't automatically assume that clients and colleagues want to join your list. Ask whether a person is interested in receiving your information before automatically adding him or her to your distribution list. Also, ask subscribers for their opinions about the content. Make subscription and unsubscription options easy. Don't give people grief for unsubscribing! And lastly, monthly distribution is a lot easier on the Inbox than weekly announcements.

Another option is to find other electronic mailing lists with large subscriber bases (including your target audience, of course) and contribute news, tips, and other important information to those lists. There's no reason to reinvent the wheel, especially when other companies or consultants have already tapped into your target audience. I personally manage several electronic mailing lists, and to successfully do so requires dedication and a serious time commitment.

Tag lines, or "signature files" as they are also called, are lines of text automatically added to the top or bottom of outgoing e-mail messages. They are simple to create, and they can contain whatever information you want. Most often, they include business contact information (address, phone, fax, e-mail address, and Web site address). Some people get creative and add their favorite quote, a catchy slogan, or even an image created from text characters. Sometimes, tag lines include event information, a brief list of company services, or current sales info.

To add a tag line to your outgoing e-mail messages, open your e-mail client (e.g., Netscape Messenger, Eudora, Microsoft Outlook, AOL), choose Preferences, select "Signature file," input the tag line content, and you're set to go. Depending on your e-mail client, the instructions may be slightly different. If all else fails and you can't find "Signature file" on your drop-down menu, use the "Help" function. You can also create your tag line in word processing software, save the document as a text file, then select that filename (in your e-mail client) as your signature file. Lastly, you may have the option of adding a "vCard" (basically, an electronic business card) to your outgoing e-mail messages. Use the "Help" function and search on vCard to see whether this option is available. Some e-mail clients allow you to add graphics to your tag line. Be sure to keep images and animation to a minimum so as not to increase the e-mail message's size too much.

The great part is that tag lines are totally FREE and you can change them as often as you like. One warning though: Keep them simple. I have seen tag lines up to 20 lines long! This is especially horrendous in digest versions of electronic mailing lists because, to get to the next message, you have to scroll so far to get past each person's tag line. Nobody needs or wants that much information about your company on every outgoing e-mail message! Six to eight lines should be more than sufficient.

Interviews and Expert Opinions

One of the keys to low-budget traditional marketing is branding yourself as an expert in your industry. This is usually done by booking interviews and speaking engagements in radio, TV, and print media, as well as contributing to print publications. In virtual space, you can do the same thing. You can utilize your own or your employees' writing skills by adding articles to your company's Web site and to Web sites

Figure 6.1   Sample Tag Lines

*********************Turning Point Communications*********************

The small business and community development resource

***************http://www.turningpointmagazine.com*****************

_/ _/ _/ _/ _/ _/ _/ _/ _/ _/ _/ _/ _/ _/ _/ _/ _/ _/ _/
_/   Marketing Opportunities in Business & Entertainment _/
_/   www.mobe.com   _/
_/   _/
_/   "Visit our site for next year's event schedule."   _/
_/   info@mobe.com   _/
_/ _/ _/ _/ _/ _/ _/ _/ _/ _/ _/ _/ _/ _/ _/ _/ _/ _/ _/

i-strategy.com
P 310.858.5522
F 877.602.9775
E info@i-strategy.com
W www.i-strategy.com

"Don't just go to the Web. Compete. And succeed."

SERVICES: Multimedia development | Internet marketing | Consulting

---

that target your primary client base. You can also host chat sessions on your site or on other company or community Web sites. The chat session could focus on your product, industry, or company, or on the career or business success of one of your company's executives. For example, a CPA might offer regular tax tips or answer a "tax question of the week" on a Web site featuring financial content; or a graphic designer could offer logo or ad reviews in a chat session or in a discussion list featuring marketing information.

Lena L. West, president of xynoMedia Development, a technology solutions company in Yonkers, New York, recognized a need for knowledgeable women of color in her area of expertise and used her writing and speaking skills to obtain visibility for her company. By doing her homework and being courageous enough to ask for what she wanted, West became a contributing editor for SmallBizTechnology.com.[4] West says, "I started by writing articles for whoever would take them." That led to additional, paid writing opportunities. She did the same thing to secure speaking opportunities. "I started small, got some notoriety, and that led to all sorts of other opportunities, including other speaking engagements, book deals, Board/Chairperson/Steering Committee positions, conference founding, etc." So, in addition to marketing her company's services to secure new clients, she created new and different revenue streams, proving that a little bit of initiative can go a long way on the Web.

To follow West's example, you will need to perform Web market research to find sites that have chat-based interviews, Webcasts, and writing opportunities. Look for Web sites that target your primary client base (based on the profile previously discussed) and offer to contribute articles, tips, or a regular column. Be sure that your company's services and products somehow complement the targeted Web site's products, services, or content.

Employee Representation

The way that you and your employees communicate in virtual space reflects on your company. This is why it is important to perform regular keyword searches using your company, product, and executive managers' names. If someone does not like your company, your products, or one of your company representatives, he or she might express those sentiments in a newsgroup, on a Web site, or in an article. Former employees and customers have been known to dedicate electronic mailing lists and Web sites to venting their grievances about companies (e.g., kmartsucks.com). This is another reason why it's a good idea to stay in touch with your employees' needs. Along with opportunities for expanded marketing, the Internet also provides a global sounding board for unhappy employees and displeased customers.

It's impossible and somewhat intrusive to track every move that your employees make on the Internet, but keep in mind that e-mail aliasing (the use of your company's domain—"employee@yourcompany .com") reinforces your brand—positively or negatively—depending on what your employees do online and how they communicate with other people. Your employees' online participation and expert opinions indirectly keep your company's name in the public eye and can lend credibility to your brand. From a proactive standpoint, encourage your employees to participate in electronic mailing lists, newsgroups, and chat rooms for recruiting, networking, and research on behalf of the company. Be sure to reward them for any opportunities resulting from their efforts.

Remind employees to use a soft touch when participating in electronic mailing lists, newsgroups, and chat rooms. Obnoxious, in-your-face sales tactics can provoke flames. Special attention should be paid to the list threads (conversations) before jumping in with product and service announcements. The best results will come from a long-term investment in the list, rather than from a disruption of the normal flow of conversation to try to get immediate sales.

Online Advertising

Prior to recent technological advances, we were already bombarded with over 3,000 advertisements each day on billboards and television screens, in newspapers and other print media, and on the radio. Thanks to the fact that the Internet is the fastest growing medium in history, ads are truly everywhere—on our phones; in banners and buttons on our computer screens; in pop-up and pop-under boxes as we surf the Web; on our handheld screens; and in attachments to incoming e-mail messages. Web ads come in text and image form, and terms like "interstitial," "advertorial," and "rich media" have been added to our vocabulary. Media buyers have the extraordinary task of choosing from a wide variety of advertising options that are attached to every available communication form. Advertising does not come cheap, so it can be quite difficult for a media buyer to know where to spend his or her ad dollars in virtual space. Media sellers now have the task of wading through the online ad sales puddle to find acceptable rates based on their site's often confusing Web statistics.

Web banner ads have taken quite a beating in the past few years, due to dismal returns on investment and an overall consumer desensitization to banner ad content. Other online advertising options—button ads, link and banner exchanges, content sponsorships, interstitials, advertorials, and classified ads in electronic newsletters—have created equal amounts of confusion because of a lack of industry standards. In 1996, The Interactive Advertising Bureau[5] (www.iab.net) stepped in to create some method to the madness, but the new terminology—CPMs, clickthroughs, pay-per-click, pay-per-sale—has complicated matters even more.

Internet advertising's early years were mostly about expensive experimentation. Most companies' marketing plans have some element of experimentation; the problem begins when the experiments outnumber the proven methods. Initially, media buyers weren't the only experimenters; online media sellers had just as difficult a time gathering information about their site visitors and creating somewhat meaningful ad rates. Things are a bit better nowadays, and we can reasonably request more detailed information about Web site audience measurement from online media sellers.

Regular reports show that the top 10 Internet advertisers are typically companies that have massive ad budgets (e.g., America Online, Microsoft, AT&T) and can therefore afford to focus primarily on long-term branding versus immediate sales. It would seem that small to mid-size firms couldn't possibly make enough of an impact online to affect sales in the short term. With an overall ad budget of a few hundred to possibly a few thousand dollars, your company's primary focus will lean toward immediately generating sales. Whatever the size of your advertising budget, a targeted approach will be most effective. In short, spend your ad dollars where you're most likely to get the highest rate of return. The clearer you are about your company's audience profile, the greater the likelihood that you'll spend your ad dollars in the right places. We'll review the finer points of online media buying and selling shortly.

Online Public Relations

If you haven't considered online public relations, think about the fact that a number of highly trafficked content portals and new media outlets have a wider distribution base than many print publications. However, getting press online can be just as tedious, if not more so, as it is off-line. It should definitely be considered for companies that have newsworthy announcements (e.g., mergers, acquisitions, venture capital funding, exceeding reported revenue figures, strategic alliances). If your company can afford to retain a public relations agency, make sure that your PR representative is familiar with online public relations. If

---

WEBSEARCH

**ONLINE PUBLIC RELATIONS AND
NEWS WIRE RESOURCES**

Business Wire   www.businesswire.com

CorporateNEWS—The   www.corporatenews.com
Internet PR Solution.

- For a small fee, a DigitalWork professional writer will craft a professional press release. The company also offers press release distribution to over 22,000 media outlets.

    DigitalWork   www.digitalwork.com/publicrel/

- Online news and press release distribution and submission services.

    eReleases   www.ereleases.com

- Offers articles, tips, and resources for online advertising and public relations.

    Internet PRGuide   www.internetprguide.com

- Press release distribution and online media monitoring service.

    Press Release Network   www.pressreleasenetwork.com

- A promotion tutorial and a collection of articles and resources for online marketing.

    Promotion World   www.promotionworld.com

- Free online press release distribution services.

    PRWeb.com   www.prweb.com

---

you have a smaller company you can still pursue press opportunities on and off the Web. Here are some tips:

1. Have something truly newsworthy to tell. (The fact that your company just renovated its Web site is not newsworthy.)
2. Make sure that your press release answers the "Who," "What," "When," "Why," and "Where" questions. Try to keep the release to one page in length, with double-line spacing. Your media representative's contact information should be prominently displayed.

3. Do your homework to make sure that you're sending your press releases to the right persons.

4. Make your Web site media-friendly by offering media contact information, minimizing graphics, and including your company's most recent press releases on your Web site.

5. Do not call or e-mail reporters to find out whether they received your mailed, faxed, or e-mailed message.

6. Use a spelling and grammar check for all messages and press releases.

7. For distribution via e-mail, send all press release content in the body of the e-mail message, not as an attachment.

8. Use the "BCC" (blind carbon copy) e-mail address function when sending a press release to several reporters.

You can either utilize an online press release distribution service or perform research to develop your own customized list of online media outlets. Naturally, you'll want to include major content portals as well as Web sites for traditional media.

Web Site

Your company's Web site is the central point of your entire Internet presence. Without it, you're shooting yourself in the foot. If you're going to make the investment, plan carefully (as discussed in the previous chapter). Your company's Web site is, most often, someone's first impression of your company's products and services. Take a critical look at Web sites when you're surfing. Make a note of what you like and don't like about other sites. Then take another look at your own site.

Compare your site to your company's collateral pieces—stationery, print ads, and brochures. Does your Web site display the appropriate colors, logo, images, slogan, and font? If not, it should. Image is everything, and if you intend to effectively brand your company in virtual space, your image should be uniform.

Whether your Web site's purpose is to sell products or to serve as an electronic brochure that displays your company's service information, your Web site should be functional. There must be a clear purpose for your site. Clarify what you do, who you are, and how site visitors can contact you for additional information. Nothing is more frustrating than visiting a Web site and not being able to locate contact information. That's like having a storefront with no salespeople. Make it easy for your site visitors to buy from you and to contact you. Remember: They are potential customers.

Your company's Web site should be easy to navigate, whether your site map is flat or deep. Maps don't have to look the same way. They just have to be functional, informative, interactive, and attractive.

Stop and think like a customer for just a moment. How much clicking are you willing to do to get the information you want? Even if the site has a search function, the content should be succinct and strategically connected for easy navigation. The point is to simplify the process of getting service and product information. I think not. Keep it simple and minimize the scrolling.

Load time is important. Remember your target audience's profile. Not everyone is using DSL and cable modems. How quickly does your site load at 56k bps or 33k bps, especially at peak Internet access hours? Images should be compressed. Video and audio should be kept to a minimum, unless yours is an entertainment site. There are plenty of ways to give a site some flavor without overwhelming it with Flash, applets, streaming video, audio, and pop-up boxes.

Resource and link choices are important to content development. Remember that all business Web sites are not meant to be portals. Choose resources and links that will be most valuable to your primary target audience. Your link choices should also complement your products and/or services. If you sell beauty products, it makes sense to add links to salons that sell your product. If you choose to include links to Web sites with unrelated content, like entertainment or news sites, categorize them so that site visitors can easily locate the information that is most relevant to them. It is also important to check your outgoing links regularly, to make sure that they are not "broken." (Broken links are links that no longer work because the referenced Web site is no longer available, or the link has been coded improperly and returns an error message when a site visitor clicks on it.)

Be careful about link placement. Do you really want to add outgoing links on the home page of your site? That's like inviting someone into your business and immediately sending them across town to another store that carries a different product. This is another reason why banner ads have lost their luster. You might make a few bucks on banner advertising, but if your site visitors click on the advertiser's banner on your home page, you've lost a potential client.

To reiterate an earlier point, kill the clutter. Remember the purpose of your company's Web site. Odds are, it is not about providing free ad space for every telecommunications, software, and affiliate program on the Web. Unless there is a huge difference in your Web site's display from one browser to the next, or unless you have a special relationship with a browser manufacturer (which is highly unlikely, in most cases), no one needs to see the preferred browser buttons ("This site is best viewed with . . ."). Also, traffic counters are no longer regarded as great ideas for Web site elements. Plenty of sites still display counters, despite their dismal readouts. My personal favorites are the sites that display "Last update: September 1998" messages. I always wonder whether these sites have simply been abandoned or if people just don't take a critical look at their sites. Site statistics can be reviewed on the back end, and there are plenty of options for letting potential customers know when you've updated your Web site's content.

You can use a variety of new media elements to drive traffic to your site and to add value for your clients (and potential clients). Consider hosting chat sessions on your site (or someone else's) to promote your product or service. Businesses might use audio or video on their sites for minicommercials or client testimonials. Webcasts (live or recorded broadcasts of workshops, interviews, presentations, or news) are another great way to take your site to the next level.

If your site design is unusual or if your site's content is exceptional, you, your Webmaster, or one of your clients can nominate your company's Web site for a number of Web site design awards. There are literally thousands of "site of the day," "best of the Web," and other Web design awards. Depending on the type of award, winning or even being nominated may add credibility to your brand and generate visibility on the Web and in traditional media.

If you've got the budget, you can use one-to-one marketing features to personalize your Web site and create visitor and customer loyalty. You may have noticed a number of sites that greet you by name ("Welcome, David"), offered product suggestions based on previous purchases, or provided you with preferred or customized content ("personal pages"). Naturally, it costs a bit more to incorporate some of these features, but personalization is the ultimate way to market and is a primary goal for all media outlets. Take good care not to overstep the privacy boundaries of your target audience as you seek to provide a personalized Web experience for your site visitors.

Interactive Web site features can also be used to brand your company and expand your customer base. E-cards (electronic greeting cards) are great tools for sites featuring art, motivational products, entertainment figures, or informative quotes. Affirmations, Inc. (www.affirmgoals.com), a Chicago-based company that sells motivational products targeting people of color, incorporated e-cards into its Web site to draw attention to its products. Along with personalized messages, site visitors can send images of motivational posters, themes, and quotes to their friends via e-mail. Like BlueMountain (www.bluemountain.com) and Virtual Flowers (www.virtualflowers.com), the recipient is provided with a pick-up number and a link back to the Web site so that he or she can read the incoming message.

Sites featuring up-to-the-minute news, articles, product reviews, and educational information can use tell-a-friend e-mail referrals to drive traffic and to circulate great content. Such sites add an "E-mail this page to a friend" link that allows you to input a colleague's e-mail address and a personalized message. If your Web site is graphics-heavy, consider adding printer-friendly, text-only versions of important articles. Site visitors can then print and distribute your materials off-line, increasing your company's exposure and potential client base.

Opinion polls and quick surveys are yet another way to involve site visitors. For events, white papers, articles, and interviews, consider adding a "Tell us what you think" form on your site. This option is especially great for high-traffic Web sites because it is likely to get a measurable amount of feedback. A survey or poll on a relevant news issue, with dynamically generated results, offers an attention-grabbing element to your site's content. You can also use online surveys and forms to request testimonials and product reviews from customers and site visitors. These testimonials and reviews may be used as future site content, to add credibility.

Listings in Search Engines and Directories

The race for better search engine listings is never-ending. Unlike Yellow Pages placements that remain static for at least a year, your company's listing in a popular search engine or directory can change every day. Is it important to get your company listed in popular search engines and directories? Certainly. Is it insane to spend the majority of your marketing efforts attempting to stay at the top of search engines and directories? Absolutely.

Let me start by defining the difference between search engines and directories. A search engine, like Lycos (www.lycos.com) or Alta Vista (www.altavista.com), compiles Web site addresses into a massive database, which is searched based on keywords that you type. Yahoo!, contrary to popular belief, is not a search engine; it's a directory. The primary difference is categorization. Yahoo! and other directories compile Web site addresses and list them in a number of predefined categories, allowing you to search by keyword or category. Based on Yahoo!'s brand and average daily page views, a lot of people prefer directories over general search engines. This has provoked a lot of search engines to add categorized listings to their sites. (For a list of some of the more popular search engines and directories, see Appendix B.)

Some search engines allow you to "buy" keywords so that your company's Web site address or banner advertisement comes out on top or near the top (for a predetermined period of time), based on the specified keyword searches. RealNames Corporation (www.realnames.com) provides a global addressing service that allows you to purchase keywords to be used in lieu of your Web site address. In other words, if your company name is "RARE Enterprises" and you register your company name as a RealName keyword (assuming that it's available), site visitors could type "RARE Enterprises" into their browsers instead of your Web site address, and they'd be redirected to your Web page. These keywords work with Microsoft's Internet Explorer browser as well as the MSN, LookSmart, EuroSeek, DogPile, and MetaCrawler search engines. To strengthen your brand, you might consider RealName registration for your company's slogans, special product names, or any trademarks that your company owns.

Initial search engine placement occurs when your company's Web site gets added to search engines and directories via manual requests, electronic submission, or search engine and directory "spiders." Manual requests require that you, your Webmaster, or a staff member visits each search engine or directory and submits your company's Web site address, site description, and/or keywords. Be very selective about who makes your submissions. It can be difficult to make changes without the appropriate log-in and password info for each of the major search engines. You can also buy software that makes the submission requests for you. Over the past few years, hundreds of companies have surfaced that will charge you to manually or electronically submit your site to search engines and directories. It is yet to be proven which method is best. Either way, results are usually not immediate. As a matter of fact, so many site owners are requesting search engine and directory listings that your site listing may not show up for several months.

Last but not least, if you do not manually or electronically submit your site, it may get picked up by "spiders" or "webcrawlers"—software programs sent by search engines and directories in search of Web site addresses to be added to their databases. In this case, the "spiders" will use your Web page titles, META tags, and content to classify your site.

Search engine optimization is an ongoing task. Some site owners have resorted to daily manual submissions in order to increase their site's placement. This plan can actually backfire because many search engines will exclude listings for companies that request excessive submissions. Prior to spending lots of time and money trying to keep your site at the top of the major search engines, assess how your clients typically find your business. Check your Web site statistics on a regular basis to identify the most popular referring links. If the numbers are substantial, consider search engine optimization as an important investment.

The easiest way to ensure that your site is properly listed in search engines and directories is to make sure that your Webmaster uses appropriate Web page titles, META tags, and Alt image tags in your Web site code. Web page titles are the words in the uppermost border of your Web browser (Figure 6.2). A lot of people don't regard this area as important, but you'll often notice that search engine listings use these words to reference a page, based on the keyword search. If you don't utilize the words properly, your site may not be indexed correctly, and any reference to your Web site pages may show "Home page" rather than the name of your company or a more appropriate page identifier.

META tags (units of HTML code that are not required but are useful in search engine placement) are used in the header of each Web page's source code to highlight important items—for example, descriptive content or keywords that may be used to search for your company, products, or services. META tags should be used on all pages of your company's site for proper indexing. Be sure to give your Webmaster the keywords that Internet surfers are likely to use when they are looking for you, your company, or your products or services. Update your META tags when new products, services, and content are added.

Alt image tags are descriptive names used for graphics and photos on a Web page. If a Web page image doesn't load, you may see a filename

Figure 6.2   Web Page Title

or descriptive phrase. This is an Alt image tag. The tag is important because many search engines use this information, in addition to page titles and META tags, for proper indexing. Also, it is helpful to site visitors who may have missed out on the image (if it doesn't load properly). At the very least, these visitors will have a general idea of what they were supposed to see.

Among the additional, oft-overlooked listing options are: cooperative linking, link exchanges, Yellow Pages, and specialty online directories. Cooperative linking involves exchanging Web site links with fellow colleagues. Link exchanges, like LinkLeads.com, are Web sites that allow you to list your site for free and to search for other companies that provide complementary services (allowing an exchange of Web site links). Online search engines and directories have caused many entrepreneurs to completely forget about traditional Yellow Pages directories and their respective Web sites. However, they still exist and they're still used by tens of thousands of consumers and business owners. Be sure that your company's Yellow Pages listings are current in print and on the Web. Most online Yellow Pages allow you to update your listing on the Web. Competitive and general market research will uncover specialty online directory sites (including Afrocentric search engines, Yellow Pages, and link lists) that provide a variety of subject-specific links, one or more of which may be well suited to your company. I have noticed, on many occasions, that site owners focus more on getting listed in popular search engines than on getting visibility via industry resource pages and sites frequented more often by their target audiences. For instance, an architect would be better served by submitting his firm's Web site address to home improvement directory sites, architectural industry resource lists, and general design-oriented search engines.

The opportunities listed above may often prove more successful than general search engine listings because competing links are fewer and are targeted to a specific audience, rather than to the general surfing Internet community. Check your listings regularly to make sure that your references and contact information are current, and that incoming links are not broken.

Incoming Links

Who's linking to your Web site? It's a good idea to find out because a link can add—or take away—credibility for your company. Also, it helps to know where your site visitors may be coming from. As you are now aware, popular search engines and directories are not the only ways for your clients and potential clients to find out about your company. A general search on the Web and an analysis of your Web site statistics will help to uncover referring Web sites.

WEBSEARCH

Perform regular Web searches on your company's name, special product names, trademarks, and the names of your company's managers, especially if these individuals are publicly visible. The purpose is to find out who is referencing your company, and in what way. This can also assist your corporate marketing strategy and help to maintain a proactive stance for your company (for the purposes of spin control).

You might be amazed to find out what turns up!

You may notice, when you check incoming links, that another site is directing people to the wrong address or to a page that no longer exists on your Web site. If this occurs, be sure to set the referring site owner straight. Send a nice letter thanking him or her for the incoming link, and request an update of your Web site address and available information. If you find that your company is listed on a site that may somehow lessen your site's or your company's credibility, respectfully request to have the link and any references to your company removed. (In late 2000, there was an alleged exchange between Apple Computers and the Church of Satan. Apple Computers discovered that the Church of Satan was displaying "MADE WITH MACINTOSH" badges and hyperlinked Apple logos on its Web site. Apple's attorney requested the removal of the badges, logos, and links due to "alleged trademark dilution.")

Affiliate Marketing

Web-based affiliate marketing programs have been around since the mid-1990s, but they gained prominence around 1999, when Amazon.com's program gained prominence. The basic premise of Web-based affiliate marketing is using a network of merchants to drive traffic and increase the possibility of sales.

Affiliate marketing programs are basically banner, button, or link-driven advertising opportunities that pay a commission to referring companies for impressions, click-throughs, or sales. It is difficult to find a portal that doesn't reference at least a few affiliate marketing programs. Everyone, from ISPs to online communities, has incorporated affiliate programs into their Internet marketing strategies, in hopes of generating traffic and sales. Barnes & Noble has an affiliate marketing program; American Express, Xerox, OfficeMax, 1-800-Flowers, and several hundred other companies have affiliate or "associate" programs that pay anywhere from a few cents per click-through to several percentage points per referred sale. Due to the popularity of these programs, several revenue-sharing networks such as Commission Junction (www.cj.com), LinkShare (www.linkshare.com), and Be Free, Inc. (www.befree.com) have formed to serve as centralized processing, tracking, reporting, and payment systems for merchants and affiliated participants.

Great care should be taken when developing an affiliate marketing program as well as when selecting appropriate affiliate program participants. The desire to make a few bucks through affiliate marketing programs has led to a proliferation of cluttered sites that feature any number of affiliate buttons and banners throughout. A site owner may enhance his or her company brand and drive additional traffic, but the biggest challenge will be competing with the myriad programs in existence.

According to many online experts, affiliate marketing programs are fundamental components in online success. The problem is that, nowadays, affiliate marketing programs are so commonplace that they've lost their luster. On one hand are claims that these so-called revenue-sharing programs are generating major traffic and hundreds of billions of dollars in e-commerce sales. On the other hand, thousands of merchants claim never to have seen one thin dime from the variety of affiliate programs in which they participate.

Let's look at both sides of the affiliate marketing coin.

On the *affiliate* side, these programs seem to be the Holy Grail of retail-based e-commerce, but there are plenty of pitfalls. Program administration can be a nightmare. How do you properly track the clicks, especially for site visitors who don't make a purchase in an affiliate program that pays per click-through (versus pay-per-sale)? Do you use a third party solution or handle the program's administration in-house? How do you handle your affiliate program's overwhelming success? Do you have a scalable program or process in place to handle dozens (or hundreds) of merchants? Can you effectively provide support for all of your affiliated merchants? What happens if your program is overwhelmingly unsuccessful? How do you tweak it so that it works for you? And, at what point do you make the decision to dismantle the program?

Some affiliate programs are like multilevel marketing opportunities; they offer several tiers. In other words, merchants are rewarded for bringing new merchants to the fold, and they may receive a commission on sales brought in by the newfound merchants. Can your program handle this?

You also have to consider the best way to build a network of site owners who are committed to working with you. Even if your company has a recognizable brand, marketing your program can be a huge task because it's next to impossible to stick out in the affiliate crowd nowadays. How do you structure a program to incentivize your affiliates to stay with you for the long term? How do you help them promote your products on their sites? If your company does not have a well-known brand, how do you get affiliates to buy in? How do you keep affiliates informed? All of these questions should be answered via a preliminary feasibility study. You have to research your competition and your options to see whether an affiliate marketing program fits your company's business model and Internet strategy.

On the *merchant* side, by participating in many affiliate marketing programs, you've chosen to send incoming site traffic—and potential clients—away from your site. (Be sure to find out whether the affiliate program actually sends site visitors away or allows them to stay on your site to make their purchases.) Calculate what you expect to make in affiliate program commission and compare that amount to what you could make if the site visitor stayed on your site and actually made a purchase. Is it worth it? And what is too much "revenue sharing"? In their effort to make a few bucks, Web site owners have allowed affiliate programs to overtake their Web site space. Each quarter, review your affiliate revenue and decide whether you should terminate some of your affiliate relationships.

Also, consider the fact that you're now trying to drive traffic not only for your product, but also for the variety of affiliate programs to which you belong. In a perfect world, your company's target audience is also a primary target audience for your affiliates' products and services. If that is not the case, then what? How much more money and time can you dedicate to driving traffic for someone else, let alone for your own site? And, is it worth the additional work to clutter your own site's content and gain a few extra pennies here and there?

Merchants should pay close attention to the fine print in their affiliate contracts. Some affiliates and revenue-sharing networks have exclusivity clauses that prevent participation in other affiliate programs. Also, pay attention to payment arrangements. Some affiliates pay monthly; others pay commissions quarterly or semi-annually.

Lastly, and of utmost importance, find out what your regular site visitors want. As always, your target audience's needs should be at the

Figure 6.3   Important Steps in Developing a
Successful Affiliate Marketing Program

1. Anticipate the best- and worst-case scenarios; establish specific goals and exit criteria.

2. Create a formal program with a contract.

3. Make it easy to join your program with an online application and easy-to-find company contact information.

4. Add a Frequently Asked Questions (FAQ) list to your site.

5. Make sure that your merchant banners and buttons reinforce your brand.

6. Provide support for your merchants by dedicating one or more staff members to administer your affiliate program.

7. Keep your merchants informed with e-mail announcements and regular statistical reports.

8. Maintain your merchants' privacy.

9. Provide a competitive commission structure.

10. Promote your program on your Web site, in search engines, via e-mail, in your traditional marketing materials, and in affiliate program directories such as:

Affiliate Announce	www.affiliate-announce.com
Associate Programs, Inc.	www.associateprograms.com
Associate-It	www.associate-it.com
CashPile.com	www.cashpile.com
i-Revenue.net	www.i-revenue.net
Refer-It	www.refer-it.com
Referral Madness	www.referralmadness.com

11. Educate your merchants so that they contribute more to the affiliate network.

12. Keep your program current by adding new opportunities and products.

13. Actively recruit new merchants.

14. Establish a plan to detect merchants' fraud techniques.

forefront of your online marketing and revenue-generation decisions. Will your participation in the popular ClubMom (www.clubmom.com) affiliate program offer value to your clients? Are your customers likely to click on a link to subscribe to their favorite magazines from your Web site? Are your site visitors more likely to go directly to 1-800-Flowers, or will they come to your site and click through?

Other Marketing Options

Creativity is the name of the game on the Web. Just because something hasn't been done before doesn't mean that it isn't possible. Many of the following options are merely twists on traditional media marketing opportunities. Others are new ideas based on technological capabilities. Remember to check with your corporate attorney before broaching ideas or opportunities that might require a trademark or service mark.

- *Frequent surfer points program.* Even the smallest airlines have frequent flyer mileage programs nowadays. To piggyback on this idea, a number of sites have initiated frequent Web surfer points programs. Companies like MyPoints.com, as mentioned in the previous chapter, allow you to advertise in their incentive programs and drive traffic to your site by sending "push"-oriented e-mail messages to program participants. However, site owners always have the option of creating their own programs. Such a program allows you to collect site visitor information to personalize your marketing message, increase your potential client database, and add value to your content and products.

- *Promotional giveaways and free stuff.* Like their counterparts in traditional space, people in virtual space love free stuff. By giving away free promotional items, you can collect potential customer information and strengthen your company brand. Free stuff doesn't always have to be a physical product or branded item. Some sites give away service or consulting hours, or they provide access to something useful on their Web sites. For example, a travel agency might include an online currency converter on its Web site. Or, a meeting planner site might provide a formula for calculating room-size requirements for an upcoming event.

    Promotional giveaways are not as hot as they used to be, especially if you're giving away pens, mugs, or mouse pads. These items are used so frequently that most entrepreneurs have dozens of them. Also, online consumers are making every effort to protect their personal information, due to online privacy issues and a desire to minimize spam and regular junk mail. A little creativity on your part can certainly get beyond these concerns. Depending on your efforts to alleviate site visitors' fears about providing their personal info, there is still plenty of potential for a successful promotional giveaway campaign. When budgeting for online promotional giveaways, keep in mind the associated shipping costs.

- *Sponsored content.* In the past few years, increasing numbers of Fortune 1000 companies, especially banks and technology businesses like Hewlett Packard, Wells Fargo, Bank of America, Sprint, AT&T, and IBM, have sponsored content and communities on Web sites targeting people of color. By sponsoring a community or content on another Web site, you can indirectly promote your company, product, or service, and strengthen your virtual brand. The targeted area should obviously attract your primary target audience. Sponsorship makes your company and product name synonymous with a certain quality, so the site, community, or content that you choose to sponsor should complement your company's products and services.

- *Web-based games and contests.* Contests are a great way to incorporate interactive features into your Web site while informing customers about your product, service, or industry. You could promote product news and information via a trivia-based game, contest, sweepstakes, raffle, or scavenger hunt. If your Web site draws a lot of traffic, a strategic alliance partner might consider providing a luxury prize, such as airfare, money, computer equipment, or an automobile.

- *Product reviews on other sites.* The best way to add credibility to your company is to get your products reviewed on other Web sites. Because the reviews are likely to come from objective parties, site visitors will be more inclined to trust the feedback and purchase your products.

- *Webrings.* A webring is a subject-specific group of Web sites that are linked together, usually by randomly generated banner ads on the linked member Web sites. The supposed benefit of belonging to a webring is much like cooperative linking. Site visitors will visit other member sites to find more information about the subject or focus of the ring. Webrings were initially quite popular around the Web, but many have fallen out of favor because of the speed with which the member Web sites become obsolete.

  Worldwide, there are thousands of webrings focusing on every subject known to humans—rainforests, babies, celebrities, recycling black dollars, antique collecting, various television programs, and fashion. To find, join, or create a web-ring that fits your company's product, service, or industry, go to www.webring.org (now owned by Yahoo!).

- *Coupons.* E-mail or printable coupons are a great way to get your company's name and product in front of a large audience. This works especially well if you have a brick-and-mortar presence. Coupons can be issued to loyal customers, electronic mailing list subscribers, or any site visitor who is interested in purchasing your product within a specified period of time. Needless to say, if you have a popular or very useful product and if the coupon offers a substantial discount, visitors will tell their friends.

- *Free stock giveaways.* When TravelZoo.com was launched in the mid-1990s, the company executives took an alternative route to garner visibility and drive regular traffic to their site. Rather than buying lots of ad space online and in traditional media, TravelZoo.com offered three shares of stock to anyone who visited its Web site within the first few weeks of its site launch. I personally received the e-mail message about the stock giveaway at least 10 times! (And yes, I'm a shareholder.) The premise behind the free stock giveaway is that shareholders will be more likely to visit the site often, tell friends, and do business with the company as often as possible, in order to drive up the stock price. As I write this book, TravelZoo.com appears to be alive and well, despite the meltdown of dot-coms. Not a bad idea for giving away free stuff and encouraging customer loyalty.

- *CD-ROM business cards.* The concept behind CD-ROM business cards is that you can send your Web site to a customer, rather than sending the customer to your Web site. CD-ROM business cards are basically CD-ROMs that are the size of a business card and include your company's brochure, Web site (with hypertext links), demos, product descriptions, audio, video, and interactive features. They are usually purchased in bulk quantities—like business cards and promotional items—and distributed via mail or at trade shows.

- *Online mall.* Although they have been much maligned, quite a few online malls are still floating around. If you hope to become an online mall e-tailer, it is best to check out the current mall tenants and ask lots of questions about the incoming traffic and mall marketing.

Before selecting any of these (and other) marketing options for your company, consider the brand that you're trying to establish or reinforce for your company. *Where* you advertise is just as important as your marketing message. Rather than saying, "Oooh, it's FREE!," think about your target audience and the environment in which your brand will be referenced. If you are targeting affluent customers, link exchanges may not be the best bet, free or not. It is important to get your message to the largest audience possible. But, strategically speaking, your efforts should focus on the media that will put you in front of the largest audience base that *fits your targeted profile,* not just any and every Internet user.

Each of the referenced marketing elements has several books dedicated to its proper development, use, and analysis. The point of the previous list is to get you to understand all of the elements that might play a role in developing and enhancing your virtual brand. As noted, your company's Web site is the central focus of your Internet presence, but there is so much more that goes into being truly successful online. Just as an entrepreneur should be concerned with the cleanliness of his or her store, the attitude of his or her employees, the store's inventory, and the appearance of company advertising and print collateral pieces, so should entrepreneurs concern themselves with their entire Internet presence. Everything that you and your employees do—or don't do—on the Internet affects your business. Unanswered e-mail, a Web site that doesn't load quickly or contains outdated content, distributing spam, and displaying broken Web site links are counterproductive to your company's objectives.

Keep in mind that an Internet presence should be "a work in progress." Do not feel that you must incorporate every new technology and marketing method into your Internet presence. Some of these methods are suitable for particular businesses, and some are not. Once you've assessed your resources—time, energy, and money—you will have a better idea of which methods will work best toward achieving your specified goals.

The list is obviously not exhaustive. Entrepreneurs can employ many other creative ideas, such as using direct mail Web cards (www.web-cards.com, www.modernpostcards.com, and www.americasprinter.com) to announce new site developments, and building relationships with other site owners via link or content exchanges.

The average entrepreneur will use a combination of the previously reviewed marketing options. When you are developing your Internet strategy and choosing options to reinforce your company's brand, you must take great care. The most common mistakes that I've witnessed, relating to virtual brand development and Internet marketing, are:

1. Underestimating the power of the Internet and grassroots marketing.

2. Overestimating the power of the Internet and grassroots marketing.

3. Web site development with limited or no active marketing.

4. Spamming.

5. Lack of targeted marketing—trying to be all things to all people.

6. Emphasizing search engine listings only.

7. No regular analysis of marketing efforts.

Effective online marketing and branding involve strategy, creativity, realistic expectations, and a long-term investment. Before you create or revise your company's Internet strategy, try thinking like your customers. Make a quarterly review of your company's marketing and advertising performance results. There's no point in establishing success parameters if you don't check to see if you've reached them.

ONLINE MEDIA BUYING AND SELLING

The mechanics of online media buying are not completely unlike those of traditional media buying. Both share the "impression" measurement. Online media buying adds a new twist in that online space is constantly changing (often up to the nanosecond), and it incorporates flexibility and personalization on levels rarely imagined. Whereas a print advertisement in a magazine remains static, offering "impressions" to anyone and everyone who views the publication for years to come, Web site banner ads can be dynamically generated to suit each new site visitor, at any given time of day. Print ads are typically restricted to quarter-page, half-page, and full-page sizes; a Web site owner has the wherewithal to put any portion of his or her site up for grabs, based on placement, time of day, or the profile of the current site visitor. Talk about complicating things! Most entrepreneurs have enough difficulty understanding the basics of traditional media buying; now we have a whole new lexicon to deal with.

The cool thing about online media buying and selling is that we can track the connection between ad viewing and product purchases a lot easier than we can when we're using traditional media. This obviously drifts into the complicated waters of online privacy issues. But even the most basic and less intrusive Web statistics can deliver helpful information to properly structure online ad models. Tracking and understanding online performance measures may be "cool," but it is anything but easy. Apart from learning the new lingo, a site

Table 6.1 Marketing Methods—Costs, Advantages, and Disadvantages

Method	Cost	Advantages	Disadvantages	Notes
Signature/tag line	Time invested to create and update (minimal)	Reinforces company information on all outgoing e-mail	None	Should be no more than six to eight lines. Time-sensitive information should be updated regularly
Banner ad	Depends on ad host; may be a flat fee for a specified length of time; may range from a few cents to tens of dollars per click-through	Good ad method for branding Free banner advertising through LinkExchange	Cost for banner creation (graphic design) and placement; also time invested to locate host sites	Preferred form of advertising for numerous successful sites
Search engine/directory submission	FREE to $250 per listing depending on method used to submit; time invested for manual submissions	Allow Web surfers to successfully search for Web site	Listings must be checked and optimized regularly to maintain position	Submissions can be made manually or electronically (via a software program)
Press releases and articles	Varies. At minimum, time invested for creation and submission to appropriate online and off-line publications. Hiring PR firm may cost several hundreds to several thousands of dollars	Potential to create widespread interest in Web site	None	Must be properly timed to generate interest
Print advertising	Hundreds to thousands of dollars per publication (depending on run time)	Potential to create, increase, or renew interest (locally, regionally, or internationally)	Expensive	Listed as second-highest method for Internet surfers to locate Web sites (*USA Today*)

Include Web site URL on all printed materials (stationery, ads, etc.)	Hundreds to thousands of dollars for reprinting	Reinforces Web presence	Aside from initial cost to reprint, no other disadvantages	Web site URL and a general e-mail address should be listed on marketing materials
Electronic mailing list	Time investment for development and administration; if outsourced, cost based on number of subscribers or number of messages distributed	Opportunity to reinforce Web site; also, an opportunity to interact with interested individuals; can be used to "push" participants back to your Web site	May be difficult to gain subscribers due to proliferation of electronic mailing lists	List must be "opt-in" (recipients must give their expressed permission to be included on the list; otherwise, this effort could prove more damaging than helpful)
TV/Radio	Hundreds to thousands of dollars per ad, per station	Reinforces Web presence and company brand	Costly (for time and production of commercials)	Cost not as much a factor if TV/radio advertising is already part of company marketing efforts
Online forums/chat rooms/listservs	Time investment for staff	May drive traffic to Web site	Requires a substantial time investment for multiple staff members; must be carefully used because direct and obvious marketing efforts are highly frowned upon	Time is also required to locate appropriate forums, chat rooms, and listservs for advertising and participation
Links (incoming and outgoing)	Time invested to locate new sites for outgoing links and to check incoming links	Strategically selected outgoing links can add value to a Web site; incoming links expose a site to more people	Some time investment to locate new sites for both incoming and outgoing links	Links should be useful, strategically placed, and checked regularly

owner must understand how ads are technologically served, be able to analyze Web site statistics, and meaningfully communicate those statistics to potential buyers. Another challenge involves online ad performance measurement—specifically, the way these data can become polluted from all of the servers and people involved in the information collection process.

Online advertising can take the following standard formats:

- *Banners:* Rectangular ads, typically placed along the top, bottom, or sides of a Web page.

468 x 60 Full banner

234 x 60 Half banner

88 x 31 micro bar

- *Buttons:* Usually square ads, placed in the left or right margin of a Web page, or interspersed within the text.

120 x 60 Button

120 x 90 Button

125 x 125 Button

- *Skyscrapers:* Vertical rectangularly shaped ads that extend along the length of the left or right margin of a Web page.

120 x 240
Vertical banner

120 x 600
Skyscraper

160 x 600
Wide skyscraper

- *Pop-up/Pop-under ads:* Square or rectangularly shaped ads that appear in a separate browser window when a Web page loads. Pop-up (aka "pop over") ads appear on top of a primary browser window; pop-under ads appear behind a primary browser window. They often go unnoticed until you log off and close your primary browser window.

250 x 250 Square pop-up

300 x 250 Medium rectangle

180 x 150 Rectangle

336 x 280 Large rectangle

- *Interstitials:* Interactive ads that appear in a separate browser window while a Web page loads. Interstitials may or may not automatically close after a few seconds. Pop-up and pop-under ads are forms of interstitials.
- *Advertorials:* An advertisement designed to resemble editorial content.
- *Classified:* A text-based ad that appears in an electronic mailing list or on a Web page.

Please note that most of these ad forms may include animation and usually link to a page on the advertiser's Web site.

Online media are typically sold based on:

1. The number of ad impressions.
2. The number of click-throughs.
3. The number of transactions generated from an ad click-through.
4. A specified environment (e.g., specific keyword search).

Figure 6.4   Sample Web Advertising Rate Card*

	Placement	Ad Rate	Ad Development	Specifications**
Full banner	Placed prominently on the top of approved content pages	$45 CPM[†‡]	$100 standard $175 animated	468 × 60 10kb JPEG[‡] or GIF[‡]
Half banner	Run of site[‡]	$30 CPM	$50 standard $85 animated	234 × 60 JPEG or GIF
Button #1	Run of site	$20 CPM	$75 standard $130 animated	120 × 90 JPEG or GIF
Button #2	Run of site	$15 CPM	$75 standard $130 animated	120 × 60 JPEG or GIF
Square button	Run of site	$25 CPM	$75 standard $130 animated	125 × 125 JPEG or GIF
Micro button	Run of site	$10 CPM	$25 standard $40 animated	88 × 31 JPEG or GIF
Skyscraper	Run of site	$50 CPM	$100 standard $175 animated	120 × 600 JPEG or GIF
Large rectangle	Placed on primary site exit pages	$50 CPM	$100 standard $175 animated	336 × 280 JPEG or GIF
Vertical rectangle	Run of site	$30 CPM	$100 standard $175 animated	240 × 400 JPEG or GIF
Square pop-up	Loads along with home page	$60 CPM	$100 standard $175 animated	250 × 250 JPEG or GIF

*Per Interactive Advertising Bureau standards (www.iab.net).
**Measured in pixels.
†Minimum buy-10,000 impressions.
‡See the Glossary (Part V).

Given the lack of regulated industry standards, Web site owners employ a number of advertising sales options, including:

- Offering rotating banner ads at lower prices than static banners. (Rotating banner ads change each time the Web page is loaded. Static banner ads remain the same.)
- Offering banner and button ad development.
- Requiring a minimum or maximum time commitment (three months or six months) for ad buys.
- Offering lower fees for lengthier advertising commitments and ads on multiple pages.
- Imposing a memory maximum (10 kb, 12 kb, etc.) in addition to other specifications.

In terms of pricing structure, I have seen an amazing range: from 0.02 CPM for small business sites to upward of $100 CPM for portal sites. Because of the obvious confusion, many online media sellers set flat-rate pricing on their ad inventory. You might find a site owner who offers banner ads at $500 per quarter, or button ads at $75 per month. Rather than using Web site statistics and trying to value their media inventory based on suggested or average costs per thousand, these site owners just guesstimate and see how quickly they can sell all of their available ad space. Mine is not to judge whether these site owners are right or wrong; my task is only to let readers know what they are in for when they attempt to purchase or sell online media.

Like traditional media purchases and sales, online media buying or selling is based on target audiences. Media buyers purchase space based on options, including geographic location, browser type, content, gender, race, age, income, education, operating system, time of day, e-mail address domain, or Web site content. If you've done your homework, you already have a target audience profile, so your online media purchases should be a bit easier to make than those of a new site owner who has no idea what his or her typical customer profile looks like. If you know your audience profile, select your media buys based on that profile. If not, your best bet is to purchase media across a few different sites, with slightly different audiences. Either way, you must take the time to analyze the results and be patient. You may have heard that a potential customer needs to see your marketing message at least seven times before he or she actually makes a purchase. The situation is similar in virtual space. Reinforcing your marketing message and branding your company take time. Depending on your campaign's results, you need to decide between tweaking your message or shifting your media buys to another outlet. Testing is critical for finding the outlets that help you meet your traffic and sales goals. It is best to broaden your overall audience by keeping your campaign fresh and attracting new "eyeballs" to your site.

Most online media are severely overpriced and much of their product goes unsold. The easiest way to buy ad space, especially on smaller sites, is to approach the site owners or ad representatives directly. Many sites offering ad space nowadays have a rate card available online. Others require a completed form that details your needs, and a phoned or e-mail follow-up. Smart entrepreneurs will employ online ad auctions to get space on popular sites at low cost. Even the smallest businesses can get low-priced online ad buys at popular Web sites and portals by using online ad auctions and advertising networks. Online ad auctions bring buyers and sellers together so buyers can bid on available ad space (usually offered at discounted rates). Before buying auctioned ad space, make sure the sites you have selected will actually deliver the audience you want to reach.

If ad management gets far too complicated but still appears to be worth the investment, consider retaining the services of a media buyer or an online ad network like Engage (www.engage.com) or Match-Logic (www.matchlogic.com). When your budget reaches this level, you'll be able to dynamically serve your Web site ads, based on the specific profile of the current site visitor. Whatever choice you make in purchasing online advertising, be sure to request a report so that you can review your campaign's results and make sure that you got what you paid for.

When buying ads, pay special attention to guarantees, and ask questions about ad contract requirements, agency commission fees (usually 15 percent), ad placement, the close date (deadline for submitting ads), and the opportunity to use ALT image copy. Be sure to give the appropriate Web site address, and confirm receipt of any ad copy or images sent to the Web site owner or ad sales rep. And, of utmost importance, before signing anything or handing over any cash, find out who the site's other advertisers are. Since we're talking about branding, what's the use of paying for ad space if your ad is right next to your biggest competitor's, or if your ad is smack in the middle of three or four affiliate program buttons? It's important, in any advertising medium, to keep great company. Don't be intimidated if the other advertisers are Fortune 1000 companies. As long as you have taken great care of your brand, created great ad copy, reviewed your budget, and properly targeted your market, go for it.

From the media sellers' perspective, who your advertisers are says a lot about your business. You must also look at your brand. If

---

WEBSEARCH

**ONLINE ADVERTISING RESOURCES
AND NETWORKS**

24/7
www.247.com

Ad Central
www.adcentral.com

Ad Outlet
www.adoutlet.com

Ad Resource
www.adresource.com

AdsGuide
www.adsguide.com

DoubleClick
www.doubleclick.com

Ezine Ad Auction
www.ezineadauction.com

fastclick
www.fastclick.com

i-Clicks
www.i-clicks.net

OuterPlanet
www.outerplanet.com

PennyWeb
www.pennyweb.com

Standard Internet
www.standardinternet.com

ValueClick
www.valueclick.com

---

your Web site content targets families, you would obviously take great care not to sell advertising to alcohol or tobacco companies. That's an obvious choice; the point is to do your homework. Not all advertisers are who they say they are. Perform your due diligence. Check to see who owns the domain that banner ads will link to. Make sure that your contract appropriately states the types of advertisers that you do not want. And, needless to say, your corporate attorney should approve any advertising contracts before you accept them.

I can imagine that quite a few readers, viewing the confusing state of online media buying and selling, will ask, "How much should I spend on online advertising?" and "Which online advertising will be most effective for my business?" These are good questions but not questions for me. My mantra, throughout this text, has been: Focus on your target audience. How are your customers finding you? What does your budget look like? Based on your responses, your marketing and advertising might be distributed like this:

Print	20 percent
TV	0
Radio	5
Outdoor	15
Direct mail	45
Online	15
Total Ad Budget	100 percent

You might want to break the formula down further and reference specific newspapers, radio stations, online outlets, or direct mail pieces as primary sources of new business. Keep tabs on your customers. Find out where they see your marketing messages. Pay attention to how site visitors respond to your ad copy. This is a necessary chore that most entrepreneurs don't make time for, but it can make or break your business in the long run. The best advice that I can give you is to look for media buys that balance targeting, prestige, audience, quality, and pricing in a way that works for your company.

The keys to effective online buying are:

1. Have a clear message.
2. Selectively choose your online media outlets.
3. Ask lots of questions.
4. Be consistent in your marketing message, image, and site content.
5. Regularly review the effectiveness of your ad campaign, and learn from your mistakes.

Figure 6.5   Marketing Schedule

Daily
 Check e-mail; respond to clients' and potential clients' requests.

Monthly
 Review Web site statistics.
 Review online ad campaign results.
 Pursue new online media outlets.

Quarterly
 Review affiliate program activity.

Bi-annually or Annually
 Review Web site layout, navigation, and content.

The keys to effective online media selling are:

1. Have a clear understanding of your site's average visitor profile.
2. Have a clear understanding of your site's ad rates.
3. Be selective about your advertisers.
4. Provide your advertisers with site statistics and traffic reports for their ad buys.
5. Stay abreast of innovative online ad technology.

RACIAL ANONYMITY ON THE VIRTUAL PLANE

A major selling point of the Internet is that it gives business owners and professionals an opportunity to bypass the usual stereotypes and preconceived notions that some consumers have about African Americans. Many of us are familiar with having to jump through extra hoops and having to work ten times harder than our competitors because of racial prejudice. On the Internet, you have a chance to cross lines and sell to customers whom you may not have had the opportunity to sell to before.

When you choose to incorporate an Internet presence into your corporate marketing strategy, keep this in mind. When developing your presence, consider your primary target markets. Don't just market to the African American consumer if other groups may find convenience, quality, or a great price in your product or service. Having a true knowledge of your target audience is critical to effective marketing and sales. All too often, African American business owners target their goods and services strictly to the African American community when they could very easily expand their market to include other nationalities or markets outside the United States.

I'm not suggesting that you market to all of the hundreds of millions of Internet users, but I have noticed a prevalence among Afrocentric site owners to target their site content and design strictly to African American consumers by consistently decorating their sites with kinte and mud cloth patterns, as well as African motifs and watermarks, even if the product is not necessarily Afrocentric. This touches a very serious issue within the community. Do you "pass" or do you showcase your cultural pride?

I am not suggesting that African American business owners deny their cultural pride and identity. My message should be very clear: You are in business to make a profit, and *all* of your primary potential customers should be considered when your site is developed. That's it; plain and simple. Your business's representation, online and in traditional media, should be a market-driven choice. On the flip side, if an African American entrepreneur's Web site does not display an Afrocentric symbol or motto, its absence does not mean that he or she lacks cultural pride. The entrepreneur is merely taking advantage of the opportunities available in the online environment.

Needless to say, this is a sensitive and very important issue. Because African Americans do not have a separate language or a primary way of identifying one another (aside from our physical features), it is often quite difficult for us to identify African American-owned businesses in virtual space. If you are interested in "recycling black dollars" online, how can you be sure that you're buying from a black-owned business? I have surfed thousands of sites, and I have run across several posts in listservs and newsgroups where the discussion focused on a site with an Afrocentric theme but the site had been developed or was owned by a Caucasian person or a person of a different cultural background (e.g., the now defunct "blackfamilies.com").

Until an *Afronet* magazine article, written by Cinque B. Sengbe, ran a few years ago, most African Americans would have been completely unaware that many of the popular Web sites targeting African Americans were not owned or operated by African Americans. Inspired by the article, the owners and managers of Search Black (an Afrocentric search engine) and the Association of African American Web Developers (AAAWD) initiated the BOCC program, which stands for Black Owned, Controlled, and Conceived. The mission of the program is to allow site visitors to identify African American-owned Web sites and businesses. Program participants simply have to display the BOCC button on their Web sites and register their site in the Search Black directory.

This takes me back to the civil uprising in Los Angeles many years ago. Many Asian and Jewish store owners purchased or made Afrocentric signs and posted them in their store windows. The signs claimed that the stores were "Black owned," to keep them from being trashed. On the Web, this takes a slightly different form. Companies that may or may not be African American-owned will include "black," "*noir*," "jet," "ebony," or even "Africa" in the company name or domain name, to entice African American consumers. And how are we to know the difference? Without the ability to "screen" registrants, what's to stop any business owner from using an Afrocentric theme or image to insinuate minority ownership?

Honestly, without direct knowledge of the business owner or a reference from a trusted source, you just don't know whether a company is African American-owned. Even if the site is listed in an African American directory or virtual shopping mall, there are no guarantees. In the case of many of these directories and link lists (and the Networking Directory in Part III of this book), sites are listed that may be "of interest" to African Americans.

To find out more about a business's ownership, ask for references that are local to the business. Also, ask for references within your virtual circles. Maybe someone in one of your electronic mailing lists, newsgroups, or chat rooms has had a direct experience or contact with the business owner or Web site author. And, don't forget to use your traditional community resources—churches, black business associations, black chambers of commerce, Urban League—for referrals. In this respect, the Web cannot be the end-all for us. We should continue to support brick-and-mortar businesses in our local communities to recycle our black dollars.

7

MANAGING AN E-BUSINESS

The online economy is far from finished. Computers and Internet access have become ubiquitous in business and, despite the volatility of the industry and its respective stocks, technology continues to drive the economy and create a more leveled playing field for minority entrepreneurs.

Technology includes much more than the Internet. Computer hardware and software, cellular phones, pagers, networks, PDAs, and the like all play an important role in business development. The reason that the Internet has taken center stage above and beyond other emerging technologies is because of the myriad opportunities it affords entrepreneurs. Having the ability to locate new suppliers and access new markets, get quicker access to government and corporate contract opportunities, perform business-related research, streamline data transfer, and offer clients additional communication methods are all simplified by Internet-based technologies.

The smart entrepreneur recognizes that information technology is a tool for addressing needs, rather than an end in and of itself. It is a path, not a destination. Using information technology (IT), we can learn to increase and manage knowledge so that the "Digital Divide" does not become an ever-increasing "Knowledge Divide."

Successful entrepreneurship involves vision, creativity, and long-term planning. In the new economy, entrepreneurs must use information and technology to take relationships to a new level. Not only do they have to strategically integrate technology developments into their businesses, they must now focus on swiftly and effectively managing high volumes of information and globally connected employees, clients, and vendors.

E-business has little to do with being a dot-com and everything to do with utilizing information and technology to be more competitive, to enhance customer relationships and form strategic alliances, to improve communication, and to streamline business processes for efficiency. All businesses should strive to become e-businesses, whether they're architectural firms, manufacturers, advertising agencies, farms, or home-based Web businesses. By identifying their businesses on this larger scale, African American business owners and managers can propel their companies beyond previous limitations such as lack of access to capital, inadequate communication methods, unskilled labor, and lack of information about contract opportunities.

DEFINING E-BUSINESS

For many entrepreneurs, e-business has been strictly associated with having a Web site, when the reality is that:

e-Business = Knowledge Management

Successfully managing an e-business involves all of the tasks addressed in previous chapters—strategically integrating new technology developments, staying connected while on the road, hiring capable IT employees and vendors, developing a Web site, and building a virtual brand. A Web site is at the heart of e-business management. Additional elements include:

- Electronic Customer Relationship Management (eCRM).
- Minimizing Internet user security concerns.
- Evaluating and minimizing electronic risks.
- Managing virtual employees and telecommuters.
- Forging strategic alliances.

Electronic Customer Relationship Management (eCRM)

eCRM describes a combination of practices used by a company to collect and analyze customer data (including contact information and shopping habits). eCRM also refers to software applications that are used to streamline sales and marketing processes. The use of such practices and applications allows a company to better serve its customers and to build stronger relationships with them.

Succeeding in e-business involves being committed to customer retention. Most of us realize that it costs more to get a new client than it costs to maintain a current client relationship. In virtual space, it is even easier to lose clients than it is in the traditional business arena. The ongoing Internet euphoria of the past 10 years has begun to wane for those entrepreneurs who realized—the hard way—that the limitless online opportunities available to them are also available to all of their international competitors, thus requiring a greater effort to maintain customer loyalty.

The Internet demands a much greater respect from entrepreneurs who initially planned to gain so much by investing so little. Managing an e-business involves smart marketing, providing superior customer service, and regular performance analysis. It requires having a clear understanding of your customer's needs; protecting their interests; and investing your time, energy, and money in solidifying those relationships. A successful e-business manager realizes that growing the company's Web site beyond the electronic brochure stage demands a shift in mind-set and strategy. Rather than feeling satisfied with merely having a Web site, he or she focuses on creating additional value for clients through a full-scale Internet presence. The company's eCRM growth strategy might include adding electronic order tracking, live help for sales or customer service via chat or return phone call (e.g., LivePerson—www.liveperson.com), automatically making purchase suggestions via e-mail based on previous orders, and maintaining a server-based profile and wish list for regular Web site visitors.

The key to mastering eCRM is personalization. In addition to creating an engaging and safe environment, an entrepreneur must constantly analyze the customer and his or her transactions to further develop the company's marketing and Internet strategies. While it's important to fully understand a company's target audience, technology now allows even the smallest business to pinpoint the preferences of an individual customer. A successful e-business manager realizes that not all site visitors view the company's Web site for the same reasons. Previously, sophisticated CRM technology tools were typically reserved for larger companies with big budgets. Thanks to Web audience measurement systems and the proliferation of application service providers (ASPs) targeting small business, smaller companies now have access to information and programs that help convert Web site traffic into revenue and simplify marketing decisions.

MINIMIZING INTERNET USER SECURITY CONCERNS

In Chapter 2, we addressed ways to protect business and client information that is stored at your business or maintained on your company's computers. Information that is transferred over the Internet has an entirely different set of problems. Customers' greatest apprehension to doing business online is the fear of having their contact and financial information stolen or misused.

Due to the proliferation of spam, hacking, and Internet fraud, Web site visitors are demanding to know how their information is being protected and used. To help e-business managers build online consumer trust and to protect consumer privacy, a number of privacy seal programs, like TRUSTe (www.truste.com), have been created. TRUSTe is a nonprofit organization offering a licensing program that allows approved businesses to carry the TRUSTe seal—or "trustmark"—on their Web sites, adding credibility to the sites and sending a message to visitors that the company has taken measures to protect visitor and client data. To carry the seal, a Web site owner must complete a license agreement and self-assessment form, create and post a privacy policy on their Web site, adhere to TRUSTe's Program Principles, and pay an annual fee. In addition to providing its seal, TRUSTe also assists licensees with consumer privacy complaints. Other privacy seal programs include PriceWaterhouseCoopers' BetterWeb Program (www.pwcbetterweb .com) and the Better Business Bureau's Online Privacy Program (www.bbbonline.org/businesses/privacy/index.html).

If your Web site uses cookies[1] or collects Web site visitor information (e.g., name, contact, or financial information) via registration or contact forms, it is important to add a clearly written privacy policy that explains why this information is being collected and how it will be used. For more information about privacy policies and protecting customer data, check any of the above-referenced privacy seal program sites, or contact the Electronic Privacy Information Center (www.epic.org), or the Online Privacy Alliance (www.privacyalliance.com).

For e-commerce, it is especially important to secure your site for the receipt and exchange of customer financial information. Customers need to feel confident that their information will not be altered or intercepted by hackers before they move beyond merely browsing to actually purchase your products. It's one thing to post a privacy policy on your site telling visitors how you'll be using their information; it is an entirely different task to protect that information from prying eyes. You or your Webmaster should confirm that your Web server employs Secure Sockets Layer (SSL) technology to secure Web communication. SSL technology encrypts any information exchanged between your customers and your company's Web server. SSL Server IDs, also known as digital certificates, can be obtained from VeriSign (www.verisign.com), a leading provider of corporate Web site infrastructure services. (Prices start at $349 for the first year; renewals are $249.) VeriSign also provides an additional level of security that requires authentication before customers can access previously input information, minimizing impostor access to your client data. Sites using VeriSign's Server IDs are noted by the VeriSign security seal.

Providing potential customers with options for interaction and transaction completion is integral to operating a successful e-business. Without direct and personal contact with potential customers, the way that you present your services and products, as well as how you respond to customer questions, speaks in a much greater volume than in traditional space. I cannot emphasize enough the importance of creating a professional and useful experience for your company's Web site visitors. Potential customers should feel that they and their information are safe. They should know how to reach you and they should clearly understand what products and services your company offers. Customers should have no trouble navigating through your site to find the information that they need. Site visitors should not be penalized for making their purchases online (versus in-store) and they should receive the purchased products without incident. Return policies should be clearly displayed.

Evaluating and Minimizing Electronic Risks

With the accelerated rate of change in the global marketplace and the increasing reliance of business on technology, e-business exposes entrepreneurs to a whole new set of operational risks. Minimizing these risks will undoubtedly play a major role in the success of a company's Internet strategy.

Consider the following questions:

- If I use a digital signature on a contract, is it valid? Are there states or countries that don't yet recognize digital signatures? How can I confirm that someone's digital signature is authentic?
- Can our site link to any other Web site without penalty?
- What happens if an employee or a hacker steals company or client data and distributes it to the public?
- Am I able to legally add my favorite music to the company Web site without authorization from the artist or distributor?

- Do we have to charge sales tax to out-of-state or international customers who buy products from our Web site? If so, what is the rate?
- Can I legally register a domain name that resembles my competitor's company name?
- Am I allowed to use content from other Web sites on mine? If so, how much information am I allowed to use before it's considered copyright infringement?
- What recourse do I have if a former employee creates a Web site or discussion list just to badmouth our company?
- If our Web server constantly fails and our company loses stockholders and market share, can we sue the ISP?
- Is the company legally responsible for employing the latest ergonomics solutions?

These are questions that may or may not have crossed your mind but they are a growing part of the unique set of legal and tax-related challenges brought on by e-business. Issues like digital signature authentication, trademark and copyright infringement, cybersquatting, defamation, linking rights, Internet fraud, online gambling, electronic publishing, computer crime, and state-to-state and international taxation are finding their ways into litigation on a daily basis. E-business risks extend beyond technology systems to include human resources, intellectual property rights, and real-time loss assessment.

To minimize electronic risks, e-business managers must:

- Prepare for the unexpected (e.g., fraud, server down-time, natural disasters, theft). (See Chapter 2.)
- Build capacity. What if your e-business takes off? Are you ready to handle an influx of e-commerce transactions or massive amounts of traffic on your Web site? Your company's next stage of e-business development should be in mind as (or even before) the previous stage is implemented. Your support staff should be prepared for the best- and worst-case scenarios.
- Make sure that your business attorney is familiar with new media and Internet legislation, and address contractual and operational issues with him or her in advance.
- Check with your CFO and CPA before aggressively engaging in international e-commerce. Both representatives should stay abreast of Internet tax laws to keep your company out of hot water. Always consider tax effects before decisions are made.

- Instruct your computer consultant, network administrator, or Webmaster to implement security features in all company technology components and periodically test them.

- Protect Web site, Intranet, and Extranet content with a copyright statement. It is all too easy to cut and paste information found on Web sites. Some designers have taken measures to minimize this by incorporating text into the images, thereby eliminating the ease with which someone can take it. Have your business attorney develop the appropriate copyright and trademark verbiage to protect your information.

- To protect sensitive e-mail message content, send outgoing messages in an encrypted format. (Check your e-mail client for instructions.) Also, some e-mail users include the following content in all outgoing messages:

> The information transmitted is intended only for the person or entity to which it is addressed and may contain confidential and/or privileged material. If you are not the intended recipient of this message, please do not read, copy, use, or disclose this communication and notify the sender immediately. It should be noted that any review, retransmission, dissemination or other use of, or taking action in reliance upon, this information by persons or entities other than the intended recipient is prohibited.

- Contracts with freelance Web designers should assign ownership of all site elements—text, images, and overall design—to your company upon completion or termination of the project.

- Minimize reliance on a single person or a small team for handling IT issues by maintaining a current list of back-up technical support consultants or firms.

- Have your bookkeeper pay close attention to telephone bill charges. An increasing number of companies are defrauding businesses by "cramming" (placing unauthorized charges on telephone bills) fees for Internet, telecommunications, and new media-related services.

Last, but certainly not least, is the issue of doing business without boundaries. Most entrepreneurs realize that it can be expensive to expand your market throughout your home state, let alone targeting potential customers in other countries. The fact that the Internet automatically opens up global possibilities does not imply any guarantees

---

WEBSEARCH

INTERNET LAW RESOURCES

GigaLaw.com	www.gigalaw.com
Internet Law and Policy Forum	www.ilpf.org
The Internet Law Journal	www.tilj.com
Nolo Self-Help Law Center	www.nolo.com

---

that your efforts will be successful. A good number of sites that receive international traffic often do so by chance because international trade is about more than displaying your products on the Web or getting listed in a search engine. E-business managers must realize that there are quite a few issues that can arise when providing services and products to global customers such as language differences, currency conversion, increased shipping costs, and international taxation. E-businesses have to be proactive about these opportunities and keep in mind that their corporate attorney and accountant need to be involved in the development of the company's Internet strategy, especially if international product and service requests are expected.

Managing Virtual Employees and Telecommuters

Corporate culture, a common set of beliefs shared by a company's employees or project team members, is sometimes purposefully established; most often it occurs by happenstance. Either way, it can make or break a business. A fragile corporate culture can dissolve even the strongest business with the best product. Difficult employees, ineffective managers, a lack of company or project ground rules, or a weak mission statement can each contribute to an unproductive work environment. A solid corporate culture can decrease employee turnover or solidify a company during a merger or acquisition.

In a traditional business environment, the company founder or president is most often responsible for instilling and reinforcing the values and principles that make up a business's culture. Coworkers collaborate and develop camaraderie while working in the same department or at the same location. In e-business, such camaraderie may not develop through constant face-to-face interaction.

An e-business manager faces the challenge of creating and/or reinforcing a corporate culture with employees, consultants, and vendors who may never meet face-to-face. Project participants may reside on opposite ends of the globe yet work "together" on a daily basis. Luckily, technology plays a vital role in making up for the lack of in-person communication. With telephones, pagers, digital cameras, and video-, Web-, and teleconferencing, instant messaging, and e-mail, a multimillion dollar business with no two employees in the same city can operate as efficiently as a Fortune 1000 corporation.

Virtual employees are commonplace nowadays and can improve efficiency and save money for businesses. To effectively manage virtual employees and telecommuters, e-business owners and managers must:

- Clarify what your company stands for (commitment to excellence, superior customer service, quality). These values should be reinforced through leadership, the company's slogan, and its overall brand.
- Practice extremely selective hiring. Hire based on skills *and* attitude. Start each employee on a small project and regularly review their timeliness, quality of work, communication skills, and overall contributions to the project and company.
- Take into account that work ethics differ from industry to industry, country to country, and person to person. Establish very clear work and communication expectations at the forefront.
- Promote tolerance. Emotions and intent are not always conveyed well via e-mail or other electronic means. Before reprimanding an employee, follow up by phone and ask him or her to clarify their electronic statements.
- If geographically possible, schedule at least one face-to-face meeting for employees to meet each other and connect on a more human level. If this isn't possible and video- or Web conferencing isn't an option, exchange photos electronically so team members can attach faces to names and voices.
- Hold regular staff/team meetings via chat, instant messaging, or other electronic means that allow you to "log" the discussion content.
- Clarify each staff/team member's role in the company/project.
- Action items should have clear deadlines and interim milestones.
- To create seamless communication, only one person should be assigned as the client contact and all others, whether contract workers or employees, should be clear as to whether and when they can approach the client.
- Compliment employees on a job well done and offer your support. Remember to tell them what they're doing right. It makes

it much easier to approach them when something has gone wrong. Also, virtual employees still require motivation and often may feel isolated, especially if there are actual on-site employees.

- Minimize technology addiction by keeping meetings to a minimum. Also, clarify when employees should make themselves available to answer questions and to discuss issues that arise.
- At virtual meetings, request input from each participant to keep them from tuning out.
- Make sure that company and project information is freely available via an intranet or by other electronic means.

These tasks should be undertaken by any business or project manager, whether they're dealing with on-site or virtual employees. In an e-business, clarity of purpose is much more significant because you don't have the benefit of geography that allows you to directly supervise employee performance. Managing virtual employees requires patience and improved communication skills, especially for those managers who have previously worked only in a "touch" environment.

Forging Strategic Alliances

No one is an island. And that certainly is the case in virtual space. Strategic alliances have been forming in record numbers for the purposes of increasing online sales and enhancing corporate brands. A strategic alliance can be a simple collaboration on a single project or a long-term union between two or more companies to add value to each participating company's products or services.

Many so-called strategic alliances are honor-based agreements between companies. Typically, Company A provides one service and Company B provides another to fulfill a contract. Or, Company A agrees to market Company B's products in exchange for discounted or bartered services.

A strategic alliance is defined as a formal joint effort between two or more firms to market a product or service for a profit. "The combined effort should exploit a perceived market advantage," says Stephanie Ardrey, principal of Ardrey Associates International. "It is important for strategic alliances to provide clearly defined benefits to all parties involved. And, it is vital that the strategic alliance has specific goals and an exit strategy."

Unlike a full-scale merger, a strategic alliance brings the strengths of two or more firms together for a predetermined period of time and for a clearly specified purpose. Each company benefits by broadening its market base, concentrating on its strengths, and sharing the over-all—and possibly, reduced—risk. Affiliate marketing programs are a form of strategic alliance.

SuccessNet and AztecaNet, two Los Angeles-based minority-owned Internet Service Providers, formed a strategic alliance that saves them several thousands of dollars in operating costs each month. The founders of the two companies realized that each company had access to dial-up lines needed by the other so they combined their available lines, decided to share an office, and are now able to target an international audience.

Another minority-owned ISP, Atlanta-based Nubonyx.com, has formed strategic alliances with several technology businesses to offer additional services and portal features to its growing customer base. The company has saved the cost of having to pay a contractor or hire an employee to develop custom applications and features. Subsequently, the year-old company has grown by leaps and bounds.

Due to increased corporate contract bundling, more and more minority-owned businesses will need to form strategic alliances to be competitive. Analyze your target market and consider those services or products that may add value for your customers. Pursue alliance partners before opportunities arise so that you're not left at the last minute scrambling to find someone to help you win or fulfill a contract. Also, have your attorney develop or review strategic alliance agreements so that your risks are minimized.

The "e" in e-business does not stand for "easy." The challenges are as limitless as the opportunities. The key factors involved in e-business are creating a usable site with relevant content; providing security (for both your clients and your business); providing excellent customer service and timely product fulfillment; selecting an effective team of employees; and forging legally binding, mutually beneficial alliances to deliver added value. Entrepreneurs who are more adept at these tasks are more likely to succeed in their online efforts.

THE ROLE OF AFRICAN AMERICAN ENTREPRENEURS

The question for African American business owners and managers is certainly not "*Should* I incorporate new technology into my business?" but "*How* do I productively incorporate new technology and position my business for success?" Unless we employ strategic planning, technological limitations can and will impede business development and economic survival. This is not just about getting a Web site; it's about doing what's best for your business's productivity overall.

African American entrepreneurs must find a way to effectively target the "Black Digerati"—those of us who have grown up with technology firmly integrated in our lives—without alienating the generations who are catching up (or resisting).

We are well positioned to benefit from the digital revolution, but we must not allow the Knowledge Divide to widen. We must continue to develop traditional and virtual communities, based on industry, geography, or special interest that serve as conduits of information. African American entrepreneurs should participate in communities such as MOBE (Marketing Opportunities in Business and Entertainment), founded by Kofi and Yvette Moyo, and produced by their company, Resource Associates International (Chicago, IL). MOBE has expanded from an annual symposium series to include the MOBE Institute, a virtual learning and business building center. This organization was one of the first to recognize African American technology innovators with their annual MOBE IT award. They also hosted a White House Briefing in 2001 that brought minority entrepreneurs from around the country to discuss access to capital and marketing opportunities with the Bush administration. Their Web site features marketing news, a message board, and a schedule of events. This global network of African American movers and shakers is an inspiring example of how we can utilize technology to achieve the American dream.

Other inspiring communities that have emerged to bridge the Digital and Knowledge Divides include:

- The Market Store (Philadelphia, PA; www.mobe.com/next/tms.html)

  Bruce Rush started the TMS Online Entertainment Marketing News e-zine in October 1998 to promote his business. The twice monthly distributed e-zine now reaches 6,500 subscribers and features useful ethnic, entertainment, and online marketing news. TMS is chockful of Internet marketing information; a calendar of national technology, marketing, and general business conferences, workshops, and seminars; academic, artistic, and creative opportunities, and multicultural marketing facts. Not only has he generated considerable business inquiries, he has consummated several deals and has generated ad income.

- The Multicultural Advantage (Philadelphia, PA; www.tmaline.net)

  The Multicultural Advantage, founded and operated by Tracey Minor, is best known for its portal Web site and two online e-zines, "Power Moves for People of Color" and "The Multicultural Advantage Staffing Report." The e-zines provide resources, tools, and information that are designed to help minority professionals and business owners succeed. The Web site also serves to assist those who are seeking to hire, service, or market to minority professionals and business owners.

- dimelist (New York, NY; www.redibis.com)

McIntyre's dimelist is "a free-flowing environment for technological career networking." She launched the list at the height of her Internet career, when she realized that she had "few if any professionals of color with whom to network. Members circulate current technology news, discuss industry and community issues, and network. "What I'm most proud of is what happens 'off the list.' Generally, lots of business relationships are blossoming among the members and that's what I wanted to happen."

African Americans do not have the luxury of dealing with technology issues later, especially when this is one of the first times in history that we have a chance to get involved in the early stages of the online economy. We must maintain awareness, not only of new and emerging technologies, but available business management information, programs, and resources offered by local technology centers and professional organizations, government agencies, and corporations to assist underserved communities. An actively expressed interest in this vital area—including verbal acknowledgment and participation—will continue the development of such programs, at a time when some politicians and corporate representatives believe that the Digital Divide is closed or, at the very least, narrow enough to be "old news."

According to Mitch Duncan, group program manager at Microsoft, "African American entrepreneurs should leverage technology that enables them to adapt quickly and flexibly to fast-changing business conditions and customer needs. The effectiveness of e-commerce use by the African American community will lay the foundation and create new possibilities and opportunities for these businesses to market and deliver their goods and services to this target market, in a competitive environment."

Globalizing African American business is more than a notion and African American professional organizations have to take a stand as well. They must go beyond merely seeking sponsorship from major technology corporations to implementing hands-on demonstrations and workshops for member business. Zana Billue, president of Zana Cakes, Inc. in Cleveland, Ohio, says that "African American organizations spend most of their efforts highlighting advertisements from major companies who sponsor their annual events, more so than assisting African American businesses with becoming more competitive."

Organizations should also provide more information about getting access to capital through minority-focused venture capital firms, like idealflow (www.idealflow.org), Springboard (www.springboard2000.org), and BLG Ventures (www.blgventures.com).

RAISING THE LEVEL OF CORPORATE CONSCIOUSNESS

To take matters to another level, we must speak up. Few technology companies will go out of their way to find us—for employment, business-to-business opportunities, or as consumers—so we need to let them know that we exist. If our voices are loud enough, intelligent executives and program directors with a desire for equal access (and expanded market share!) will do a better job of marketing their products and programs to us.

IBM has made a conscious effort to target their marketing to the African American entrepreneurial community. By working with the National Black Business Council, the U.S. Hispanic Chamber of Commerce, and the National Association of Women Business Owners, IBM is able to effectively send their messages to African American, Hispanic, and women business owners. Above and beyond offering their logo for branding purposes as so many other companies do, IBM sponsors workshops, provides speakers, offers discounts on their products and services, and places advertising in specific publications in these markets.

ON THE HORIZON: A DIGITAL LIFESTYLE

The harsh reality is that if you don't have a computer and Internet access, your education, communication, career, and business opportunities will be limited. Technology development isn't expected to slow down any time soon. Within a few years, home networks will be commonplace. PC prices are expected to drop even farther. More and more technology products will have advanced speech recognition abilities and we'll be using "smart" appliances, which will reset themselves after power outages, turn themselves off when not in use, and adjust themselves for energy efficiency. We'll be using "self-repairing software" in our businesses and our "smart houses" will come equipped with automated on-and-off scheduled lights and appliances, video doorbells with facial recognition software, and servers that control major household power sources. Interactive television will allow us to "click" on TV ads for more information, instantly.

Whether you're ready or not, things are happening and changes are being made. It's up to you to get with the program or get left behind. New technology can and will enhance any business that uses it properly.

Consider this book to be a technology bootstrapping guide. It is my hope that you have not only received information but also a cause for action. The government and Corporate America cannot close the Digital Divide (or the Knowledge Divide) without our help. These entities are scrambling for survival themselves and when, if ever, they are able to and choose to come to our aid, it will be far too late.

The challenge has been defined for you. Solutions and opportunities have been presented. So, what are you going to do?

NETWORKING DIRECTORY—WEB SITES OF INTEREST TO AFRICAN AMERICAN ENTREPRENEURS

Several hundred Web sites are included in the following list. The sites listed are categorized based on the primary site elements and target market. Some of the sites listed are not owned or operated by African American content providers, but the information may be of importance to African American entrepreneurs.

Keep in mind that sites go up and come down as fast as you can blink your eyes. If you go to a Web site address listed in the directory and an error message is returned, double check what you typed. If there is a forward link, click on it and be sure to update your bookmarks. If there is no forward link and you've typed in the correct address, try using a search engine to locate the organization or information.

DIRECTORY CATEGORIES

Banking & Finance

Afro-Caribbean
www.afrocaribbean.com

Ariel Capital Management, Inc.
www.arielmutualfunds.com

Ascend Venture Group, LLC
www.ascendventures.com

Finance & the African American Family
www.blackwealth.com

BlackStocks
www.blackstocks.com

Blaylock & Partners
www.blaylocklp.com

BLG Ventures
www.blgventures.com

Carthage Venture Partners
www.carthage.net

Carver Federal Savings Bank
www.carverbank.com

Coalition of Black Investors (COBI)
www.cobinvest.com

Coalition of Black Investors, 2001.

Community Financial Investment Groups Association
www.investblack.com

Creative Investment Research
www.creativeinvest.com

eChapman
www.echapman.com

eFundsAssist
www.efundsassist.com

Jamaica Stock Exchange
www.jamstockex.com

National Federation of Community Development Credit Union
www.natfed.org

Operation Hope
www.operationhope.org

Rainbow/PUSH Wall Street Project
www.financialproject.com

Seaway National Bank of Chicago
www.seawaynb.com

Syndicated Communications, Inc.
www.syncomfunds.com

Urban Bankers Coalition, Inc.
www.ubcny.org

Business Services

1124 Design
www.1124design.com

ACT*1 Personnel
www.act1personnel.com

ACT*1 Technical Services
www.act1tech.com

Admin Resources Plus
www.adminresourcesplus.com

African American Speakers Bureau
www.aasb.net

Alert Staffing
www.alertstaffing.com

The Amoore Group, Inc.
www.amooregroup.org

Ark Capital Management
www.arkvc.com

The Baker Group
www.tbakergroup.net

Black Butterfly Press
www.maxinethompson.com

Black Speakers Online
www.african-american-speakers-online
.com

C. Ottley Strategies, Ltd.
www.cottley.com

CEO Express
www.ceoexpress.com

Chaslo Promotional Items
www.chaslo.com

Chisholm—Mingo Group
www.chisholm-mingo.com

Code One Communications
www.code1.com

Diversity Speakers
www.diversityspeakers.com

Duncan Resource Group, Inc.
www.duncanresource.com

EZCertify.com
www.ezcertify.com

EZ Biz Leads
www.ezbizleads.com

George Fraser's Fraserville.com
www.fraserville.com

The Huffmon Group
www.huffmongroup.com

i4 Consulting Group
www.i4cg.com

iClique
www.iclique.com

i-Dealflow
www.idealflow.org

Inner Caucus Entertainment
www.innercaucus.com

International Franchise Association
www.franchise.org

Justice & Sustainability Associates, LLC
www.justicesustainability.com

Kimberly Stansell, Entrepreneurial Author & Trainer
www.kimberlystansell.com

LaGrant Communications
www.lagrantcommunications.com

Masai Design
www.masaidesign.com

MBELDEF
www.mbeldef.org

MBS Educational Services & Training
www.mbs-enterprises.com

The Medley Group
www.medleyrecruits.com

Minority Business Global Network
www.mbnglobal.com

Minorities In Business
www.minoritiesinbusiness.com

Minority Executive Search
www.minorityexecsearch.com

The MWBE Development Center, Inc.
www.mwbe.com

Northern Illinois Minority Contractors Assn.
www.tricomweb.com/nimca

Oakland Consulting Group
www.ocg-inc.com

Possibilities
www.possibilitiesbbs.com

Renaissance Entrepreneurship Program
www.rencenter.org

Robertson Treatment
www.robertsontreatment.com

SeminarSource.com
www.seminarsource.com

SingleShop.com
www.singleshop.com

**Speakers etc. Bureau &
Coaching Firm**
www.speakersetc.com

SRB Productions
www.srbproductions.com

Sullivan International
www.sullivaninternational.com

Swilley Graphics & Design
www.swilleygraphics.com

Target Market News
www.targetmarketnews.com

TEC Law Group
www.teclawgroup.com

Tobin & Associates PR
www.tobinpr.com

Triple J Word Processing
www.triple-j.net

Tyler-James
www.tyler-james.com

VSS CyberOffice
www.vsscyberoffice.com

Washington Linkage Group
www.washingtonlinkagegroup.com

Western Direct, Inc.
www.western-direct.com

World Business Exchange Network
www.wbe.net

The Write Image
www.thewriteimage.net

Career & Education

BlackCollege.com
www.blackcollege.com

Black Collegian Online
www.blackcollegian.com

**Black Fraternity & Sorority
Paraphernalia & Info**
www.stepshow.com/events
/calendar.shtml

Black Greek Network
www.blackgreeknetwork.com

Black Issues in Higher Education
www.blackissues.com

Black Quest
www.blackquest.com

Break Through Online
www.breakthrough.org

**Career Center for Workforce
Diversity—EOP Publications**
www.eop.com

Children's Scholarship Fund
www.scholarshipfund.org

**fastWeb: Financial Aid Search
Through the Web**
www.fastweb.com

**Diversity/Careers in Engineering &
Information Technology**
www.diversitycareers.com

Diversity Employment
www.diversityemployment.com

Diversity Expo
www.diversityexpo.com

DiversityInc.com Career Center
www.diversityinc.com

DiversityInc.com (Reproduction of any kind is strictly prohibited.)

Diversity Job Bank
www.imdiversity.com

Education Highway
www.eduhwy.com

Financial Aid Information Page, The
www.finaid.org

Gates Millennium Foundation
www.gmsp.org

GreekShow.com
www.greekshow.com

HBCU Alumni Center
www.hbcu.com

HBCU Central
www.hbcu-central.com

Hire Diversity
www.hirediversity.com

Homecoming: The Networking Magazine for Black Graduates
www.homecoming.com

InfiniteGreek.com
www.infinitegreek.com

Mind Productions: Social Concerns of Black People
www.mindpro.com

Minorities Job Bank
www.iminorities.com

Minority Executive Search
www.minorityexecsearch.com

NAACP Diversity & Job Fair
www.naacpjobfair.com

National Association for Equal Opportunity in Higher Education
www.nafeo.org

National Employment Minority Network
www.nemnet.com

The Ron Brown Scholarship Program
www.ronbrown.org

Teach for America
www.teachforamerica.org

The Telecom Opportunity Institute
www.ttoi.org

United Negro College Fund
www.uncf.org

Workplace Diversity
www.workplacediversity.com

Community & Social Organizations

100 Black Men of America
www.100blackmen.org

America's Promise
www.americaspromise.org

Ask Heartbeat
www.askheartbeat.com

Benton Foundation
www.benton.org

Black Men In America
www.blackmeninamerica.com

Black Success Foundation
www.blacksuccessfoundation.org

Buppie Network
www.buppienetwork.com

Chocolate Singles
www.chocolatesingles.com

Congress of National Black Churches
www.cnbc.org

Crenshaw Christian Center/Ever Increasing Faith Television
www.faithdome.org

First Friday of Seattle
www.firstfridayofseattle.com

Gentlemen of Distinction
www.gentlemenofdistinction.com

Greater Sacramento Urban League
www.sul1.org

Greater Washington Urban League
www.thursdaynetwork.org

"I Have A Dream" Foundation, The
www.ihad.org

Initiative for a Competitive Inner City
www.icic.org

Inroads, Inc.
www.inroadsinc.org

Iota Phi Theta
www.iotaphitheta.org

MAD-DADS
www.maddadsnational.com

Magic Johnson Foundation, Inc.
www.magicjohnson.org

Morino Institute, The
www.morino.org

NAACP Legal Defense Fund
www.ldfla.org

NAACP Online
www.naacp.org

Nation of Islam
www.noi.org

National Organization of Concerned Black Men, Inc.
www.libertynet.org/~cbmno

National Coalition on Black Voter Participation, Inc.
www.bigvote.org

National Council of Negro Women, Inc.
www.ncnw.com

National Summit on Africa
www.africasummit.org

Onyx Coalition, Inc.
www.onyxcoalition.com

The Refugee Project
www.refugeeproject.com

Rockford Branch of the NAACP— Rockford, IL
www.tricomweb.com/naacp

The Ron Rice Foundation
www.theronricefoundation.org

The Runners' Club
www.runnersclub.org

Southern Poverty Law Center
www.splcenter.org

Street Soldiers/Omega Boys Club
www.street-soldiers.org

Tookie's Corner
www.tookie.com

West Angeles Church of God in Christ
www.westa.org

With Ownership Wealth
www.wowcbcf.org

Conferences, Conventions, Expos & Trade Shows

African American Male Empowerment Summit
www.aamesummit.com

African American Women on Tour
www.aawot.com

© 2001 by Pepie Designs for African American Women on Tour.

Building Wealth Conference
www.cmgbuildingwealth.com

DesigNation—Organization of Black Designers
www.designation.net

Los Angeles Black Business Expo
www.blackbusinessexpo.com

Indiana Black Expo
www.indianablackexpo.com

International Black Buyers & Manufacturers Expo & Conference
www.ibbmec.com

International Black Summit
www.mbnet.com/ibs/index.htm

Marketing Opportunities in Black Entertainment
www.mobe.com

Consumer Products & Resources

Affirmations, Inc.
www.affirmgoals.com

African American Biographical Database
aabd.chadwyck.com

African American Cyber Marketplace
www.aacmp.com

African American Health
www.africanamericanhealth.com

African American Images
www.africanamericanimages.com

African American Shopping Mall
www.aasm.com

African Pride
www.african-pride.com

AfroWorld
www.afroworld.com

Ahneva Ahneva
www.ahnevaahneva.com

All Black Books
www.allblackbooks.com

Black Classic Press
www.blackclassic.com

Black DVD Online
www.blackdvdonline.com

Black Expressions
www.blackexpressions.com

Black Facts
www.blackfacts.com

Black Fraternity & Sorority Paraphernalia & Info
www.stepshow.com

Black Health Network
www.blackhealthnetwork.com

Black Hollywood Education & Resource Center
www.bherc.org

Black Issues Book Review
www.bibookreview.com

Black Literature
www.blackliterature.com

Black Movie.com
www.blackmovie.com

Black Music Archive
www.blackmusicarchive.co.uk

Blacklist for Black Consumers
www.javanet.com/~yvonne

Blackonomics
www.blackonomics.com

BottomDollar.com: The Shopping Search Engine
www.bottomdollar.com

Chef Ashbell's Foodstop
www.foodstop.com

Christine's Genealogy Web site
www.ccharity.com

CultureLink: Premier Retailer of Cultural Merchandise
www.culturelink.com

Cush City
www.cushcity.com

Darnell's Black Radio Guide
www.radioblack.com

Electronic Urban Report (EurWeb: The Urban Cyberstation)
www.eurweb.com

Encyclopedia Britannica Guide to Black History
www.blackhistory.eb.com

EOE International
www.eoeinternational.com

Ethnic Grocer
www.ethnicgrocer.com

Frederick Douglass Designs
www.fddesigns.com

Go Fatima
www.gofatima.com

GreekShow.com
www.greekshow.com

Harlemm Network
www.harlemm.com

Healthy Sisters
www.healthysisters.com

Jewel Diamond Taylor
www.jeweldiamondtaylor.com

Juneteenth Worldwide Celebration
www.juneteenth.com

Kwanzaa
www.globalindex.com/kwanzaa

Martin Luther King Jr. Day
www.mlkday.com

MG Publishing Co.
www.mgpublishing.com

Moments in Black History
www.momentsinblackhistory.com

Mosaic Books
www.mosaicbooks.com

MotherLand Foods
www.motherlandfoods.com

Music Specialist, The
www.asha.com

My Man Printing, LLC
www.mymanwear.com

Negro Baseball Leagues
www.blackbaseball.com

Negro League Baseball
www.negroleaguebaseball.com

Pay 2 View 2000
www.pay2view2000.com

ProLine Corp.
www.prolinecorp.com

Public Eye Certified Shopping Sites, The
www.thepubliceye.com

Soul House
www.soulhouse.com

Splendid Rain Enterprise
www.splendidrainenterprise.com

Tavis Smiley Foundation
www.tavistalks.com

Tony Brown Productions, Inc.
www.tonybrown.com

Urban Goods
www.urbangoods.com

**Willie Jolley—Speaker /
Singer / Author**
www.williejolley.com

Wilson Brown Gallery
www.wbgallery.com

Government

**Biographical Directory of the
U.S. Congress**
www.Bioguide.congress.gov

**Black Population U.S.—U.S. Census
Bureau**
www.census.gov/population/www
/socdemo/race/black.html

**Bureau of Alcohol, Tobacco &
Firearms**
www.atf.treas.gov

Bureau of Labor Statistics
www.Stats.bls.gov

Bureau of Transportation Statistics
www.bts.gov

Census Bureau
www.census.gov

Center for Disease Control
www.cdc.gov

Central Intelligence Agency
www.odci.gov

Congress.Org
www.congress.org

Congressional e-mail addresses
www.congress.org/elecmail.html

Congressional Quarterly, Inc.
www.cq.com

**Consumer Products Safety
Commission**
www.cpsc.gov

Environmental Protection Agency
www.epa.gov

Federal Bureau of Investigation
www.fbi.gov

**Federal Communications
Commission**
www.fcc.gov

**Federal Deposit Insurance
Corporation (FDIC)**
www.fdic.gov

**Federal Emergency Management
Assistance (FEMA)**
www.fema.gov

Federal Gateway
www.Fedgate.org

Federal Trade Commission
www.ftc.gov

**Fedix—Your Source of Federal
Research and Education**
www.rams-fie.com

**FedNet—Broadcast Coverage of the
U.S. Government**
www.fednet.net

FedWorld Information Network
www.fedworld.gov

FirstGov.com
www.firstgov.com

Food and Drug Administration
www.fda.gov

General Services Administration
www.gsa.gov

Great American Website
www.uncle-sam.com

Internal Revenue Service
www.irs.ustreas.gov

International Trade Administration
www.ita.doc.gov

Library of Congress
www.loc.gov

Minority Business Development Agency
www.mbda.gov

Minority Telecommunications Development Program
www.ntia.doc.gov/opadhome
/mtdpweb/outline.htm

NASA
www.nasa.gov

National Science Foundation
www.nsf.gov

National Telecommunications and Information Administration
www.ntia.doc.gov

Occupational Safety and Health Administration
www.osha.gov

Office of Minority Enterprise Development (SBA)
www.sba.gov/MED

Patent & Trademark Office
www.uspto.gov

Public Citizens' Congress Watch
www.citizen.org/congress

Roll Call Online: The Newspaper of Capitol Hill
www.rollcall.com

SBA Office of Minority Enterprise Development 8(a) Business Development
www.sba.gov/MED

Small Business Administration
www.sba.gov

Social Security Administration
www.ssa.gov

Trade & Development Agency
www.tda.gov

U.S. Department of Agriculture
www.usda.gov

U.S. Department of Commerce
www.doc.gov

U.S. Department of Defense
www.defenselink.mil

U.S. Department of Education
www.ed.gov

U.S. Department of Energy
www.doe.gov

U.S. Department of Health and Human Services
www.os.dhhs.gov

U.S. Department of Housing and Urban Development
www.hud.gov

U.S. Department of Interior
www.doi.gov

U.S. Department of Justice
www.usdoj.gov

U.S. Department of Labor
www.dol.gov

U.S. Department of State
www.state.gov

U.S. Department of Transportation
www.dot.gov

U.S. Department of Treasury
www.ustreas.gov

U.S. Department of Veterans Affairs
www.va.gov

U.S. Embassies
www.usembassy.state.gov

U.S. Postal Service
www.usps.gov

White House
www.whitehouse.gov

Industry & Professional Organizations

African American Association of Innkeepers International
www.africanamericaninns.com

African American Business Alliance
www.a-aba.com

African American Teachers' Lounge
www.members.tripod.com
/~teacherslounge/index.html

African American Women in Business Conference
www.aawibc.com

African American Women In Technology
www.aawit.org

American Association of Blacks In Energy
www.aabe-mich.org

American Health & Beauty Aids Institute (AHBAI)
www.proudlady.org

Association of African American Web Designers
www.aaawd.org

Association of Black Cardiologists
www.abcardio.org

Association of Black Psychologists
www.abpsi.org

Black Broadcasters Alliance
www.thebba.org

Black Business Association, Los Angeles
www.bbala.org

Black Business Association, Broward County
www.bbaol.org/Broward

Black Business Association, Memphis
www.bbamemphis.org

Black Chambers of Commerce
www.blackchambers.com

Black Coaches Association
www.bcasports.org

Black Data Processing Associates Online
www.bdpa.org

Black Entertainment Sports Lawyers Association
www.besla.org

Black Entertainment & Telecommunications Association
www.betaonline.org

Black Pilots of America
www.blackpilots-america.org

The Black Sports Agents Association
www.blacksportsagents.com

Black Urban Professionals (Buppies) Online
www.buppie.com

Black Women in Publishing
www.bwip.org

Black Writers Alliance
www.blackwriters.org

Blacks In Government
www.bignet.org

Boston Association of Black Journalists
www.babj.org

Chicago Black MBAs
www.ccnbmbaa.org

Collegiate Entrepreneurial Organization
www.c-e-o.org

Conference of Minority Transportation Officials
www.comto.com

Dayton Association of Black Journalists
www.activedayton.com
/commmunity/gropus/DABJ/

Executive Leadership Council & Foundation
www.elcinfo.com

First Friday, Atlanta, GA
www.1stfridays.com

First Friday, NJ/NY Metro
www.hometown.aol.com/ffriday
/index.html

**Greater Los Angeles African
American Chamber of Commerce**
www.glaaacc.org

**International Society of African
Scientists**
www.dca.net/isas

The Leaders Forum
www.leadersforum.org

Minority E-Commerce Association
www.themeca.org

**Minority Information Technology
Professionals**
www.mitp.org

**National Action Council for
Minorities in Engineering, Inc.**
www.nacme.org

**National Alliance of Black School
Educators**
www.nabse.org

**National Association for Equal
Opportunity in Higher Education**
www.nafeo.org

**National Association of African
Americans in Human Resources**
www.naaahr.org

**National Association of Black
Accountants—NY Chapter**
www.nabany.org

**National Association of Black
Customs Enforcement Officers**
www.nabceo.org

**National Association of Black
Female Executives in Music and
Entertainment**
www.womenet.org

**National Association of Black
Journalists**
www.nabj.org

**National Association of Black Law
Enforcement Executives**
www.noblenatl.org

**National Association of Black
Management Consultants**
www.nabmc.org

**National Association of Black
Telecommunications Professionals**
www.nabtp.org

**National Association of Blacks in
Criminal Justice**
www.nabcj.org

**National Association of Market
Developers**
www.namdntl.org

**National Association of Minorities
in Communications**
www.namic.com

National Bar Association
www.nationalbar.org

National Black Business Council
www.nbbc.org

**National Black Business Trade
Association**
www.myfreeoffice.com/nbbta
/nbbta3.html

**National Black Chamber of
Commerce**
www.nationalbcc.org

**National Black MBA
Association, Inc.**
www.bmba.com

**National Black MBA Association,
Inc.—Atlanta**
www.atlbmba.org

**National Black MBA Association,
Inc.—Dallas**
www.nbmbaa-dallas.org

**National Black MBA Association,
Inc.—NY**
www.nyblackmba.org

National Black Media Coalition
www.nbmc.org

National Black Nurses Association
www.nbna.org

National Black Police Association
www.blackpolice.org

National Black Programmers Coalition
www.nbpcinc.org

National Black State Troopers Coalition
www.nbstc.com

National Coalition of Black Meeting Planners
www.ncbmp.org

National Council of Black Engineers & Scientists
www.ncbes.org

National Minority Supplier Development Council of Florida
www.nmsdcfl.com

National Newspaper Publishers Association
www.nnpa.org

National Organization of Minority Architects
www.noma.net

National Society of Black Engineers (NSBE)
www.nsbe.org

National Technical Association
www.huenet.com/nta

The New Leaders, Los Angeles
www.newleaders.org

The New Leaders, Columbus
www.newleaderscolumbus.org

NIH Black Scientists Association
www.nih.gov/science/blacksci

Northern California Black Engineers
www.ncalifblackengineers.org

Northern Illinois Minority Contractors Assn.
www.tricomweb.com/nimca

Orange County Black Chamber
www.ocblackchamber.com

Organization of Black Airline Pilots (OBAP)
www.obap.org

Organization of Black Designers
www.core77.com/OBD

PRAME: Public Relations, Advertising, Marketing & Excellence New Media Professionals
www.prame.org

South Africa USA Chamber of Commerce
www.southafricausachamber.com

South Bay Black Nurses Association
www.blacknurses.org

International/Global Connections

Africa 2000
www.africa2000.com

Africa-America Institute
www.aaionline.org

Africa Online
www.africaonline.com

African Connections
www.melanet.com/connections

African Information Services Center
www.africaservices.com

African National Congress
www.anc.org.za

Africanet
www.africanet.com

AfricaNews
www.africanews.com

AllAfrica.com
www.allafrica.com

Africa.com
www.africa.com

Bahamanet
www.bahamanet.com

Black Britain
www.blackbritain.co.uk

Black Presence in Britain
www.blackpresence.co.uk

BlackNet UK
www.blacknet.co.uk

Café de la Soul—Your Source to Black Paris
www.cafedelasoul.com

Copyright 1998/1999/2000/2001.

Caribbean Newspapers
www.caribbeannews.com

CyberPlex Africa
www.cyberplexafrica.com

iAfrica
www.iafrica.com

Kabissa
www.kabissa.org

KenyaWeb
www.kenyaweb.com

Nigeria on the Net
www.nigeria.com

Nigeria Central
www.nigeriacentral.com

Nigeria Exchange
nigeriaexchange.com

Orientation South Africa
www.orientation.co.za

South African International Trade Exhibition
www.saitex.co.za

Southern Africa Places
www.places.co.za

US Africa Online
www.usafricaonline.com

The Voice: Britain's Best Black Newspaper
www.voice-online.co.uk

Woyaa
www.woyaa.com

Newspapers, Magazines & Web Zines

African Americans On Wheels
www.onwheelsinc.com

The Afro-American Newspaper Co. of Baltimore, Inc.
www.afroam.org

Afronet Online Magazine
www.afronet.com

Atlanta Tribune Online
www.atlantatribune.com

The Atlanta Voice Newspaper
www.theatlantavoice.com

Baltimore Times
www.btimes.com

Black Business Journal
www.bbjonline.com

Black Enterprise Online
www.blackenterprise.com

Black Headlines
www.blackheadlines.com

Blacklines of Architecture, Inc.
www.blacklines.net

Black News Online
www.blacknewsonline.com

Black Press USA
www.blackpressusa.com

Black Talent News Interactive
www.blacktalentnews.com

Catch-A-Fire: The Net's 1st Black Web Station
www.catchafire.com

Challenger News Network
www.challengernews.com

Charlotte Post
www.thecharlottepost.com

Chicago Standard
www.chicagostandard.com

CYH Magazine Online
www.cyhmagazine.com

CityFlight Newsmagazine
www.cityflight.com

Essence Online
www.essence.com

Exodus Newsmagazine
www.exodusnews.com

The Final Call Online Edition
www.finalcall.com

Homecoming: The Networking Magazine for Black Graduates
www.homecoming.com

In the Black Magazine
www.intheblackmagazine.com

Jacksonville Advocate
www.jacksonvilleadvocate.com

Michigan Citizen
www.michigancitizen.com

Minority Business Reports
www.mbreports.com

Mississippi Link
www.mississippilink.com

Monroe Free Press
www.monroefreepress.com

Network Journal—Black Professional & Small Business News
www.tnj.com

Northeast Florida Advocate
www.northeastfloridaadvocate.com

Philadelphia News Observer
www.pnonews.com

Prince George's Post
www.pgpost.com

San Francisco Bay View
www.sfbayview.com

Turning Point Magazine
www.turningpointmagazine.com

Urban'Rom DVD Magazine
www.urbanrom.tv

U.S. Black Engineering Magazine
www.blackengineer.com

The Vine Online
www.thevineonline.com

Politics & Activism

Black America's Political Action Committee
www.bampac.org

Black Democrats
www.blackdemocrats.org

Black Electorate
www.blackelectorate.com

Black Politics Daily
www.blackpoliticsdaily.com

Congressional Black Caucus Foundation
www.cbcfonline.org

E-The People
www.ethepeople.com

Joint Center for Political & Economic Studies
www.jointcenter.org

The Glass Ceiling
www.theglassceiling.com

National Council of Black Republications
www.members.nbci.com/BlackGOP

Political Dictionary
www.fast-times.com/political
/political.html

Pop and Politics
www.popandpolitics.com

Ronald H. Brown Foundation
www.rhbf.org

Urban Institute, The
www.urban.org

Portals & Directories

The African American
www.theafricanamerican.com

African American Business Directory
www.africanamericanbusinessdirect
ory.com

African American Internetwork, The
www.afamnet.com

African American Web Connection
www.aawc.com

Africana.com
www.africana.com

Afrocentric Resource Center
www.jazm.com

BET.com
www.bet.com

BigBlackBook
www.bigblackbook.com

Black Chicago Online
www.blackchicago.com

Black Market, The
www.theblackmarket.com

Black Online Exchange
www.bole.net

Black-Owned.com
www.black-owned.com

Black People
www.blackpeople.com

Black Planet
www.blackplanet.com

BlackSeek
www.blackseek.com

Black Source Network
www.blacksource.com

Black to Basics
www.blacktobasics.com

Black Voices
www.blackvoices.com

Black Web Network, The
www.blackweb.net

Black Web Portal
www.blackwebportal.com

Black World
www.blackworld.com

Black World Today, The
www.tbwt.com

Blackapolis
www.blackapolis.com

Body In Black
www.bodyinblack.com

DallasBlack.com
www.dallasblack.com

DiversePRO
www.diversepro.com

EbonyCare.com
www.ebonycare.com

Empowerment Network for African Americans
www.globalmecca.com

EverythingBlack.com
www.everythingblack.com

Indigo Blu
www.indigoblu.com

LittleAfrica! Village Marketplace (Portal)
www.littleafrica.com

MelaNet
www.melanet.com

Minority Business Network Global
www.mbnglobal.com

MyBlackWeb.com
www.myblackweb.com

NetNoir
www.netnoir.com

Northern California/Bay Area African American Resources on the Internet
www.tomato.com/~baydrum

Osiris One Network
www.osirisone.com

Reunion Online—Black New England
www.blacknewengland.com

SABLEnet
www.sablenet.com

San Diego BLAACK Pages
www.sdbp.com

Search Black
www.searchblack.com

Soul Search
www.soulsearch.net

Soul Society's Minority Links
www.soulsociety.com/minlinks.htm

Urban Live
www.urbanlinklive.com

VirtuallyBlack
www.virtuallyblack.com

What's the 411?
www.whatsthe411.com

Recreation

4 Seasons West Ski Club
host.scbbs.com/~4sw

A Separate Cinema
www.separatecinema.com

African American Golf Association
www.aaga.com

African American Literature Book Club
www.aalbc.com

African American Travel
www.bdsummit.com

African Americans on Wheels
www.automag.com

Afrogolf
www.afrogolf.com

Alvin Ailey American Dance Theater
www.alvinailey.org

Baltimore County African American Cultural Festival
www.aaculturalfestival.com

Bid Whist
www.bidwhist.com

Black Outdoorsman
www.blackoutdoorsman.com

Black Travel Online
www.blacktravelonline.com

Blues Festivals Directory
www.bluesfestivals.com

The Body Clinic
www.the-body-clinic.com

Books for African Americans
www.japhelps.com

Cancun All-Star Fiesta
www.allstarfiesta.com

Cinnamon Traveler On-line
www.cinnamontraveler.com

City-Alert.com
www.city-alert.com

The Community Chest
www.thecommunitychest.com

Creative Travel Planners
www.chocolatetravel.com

eSoul
www.esoul.com

Screen shot taken from esoul.com.

Funk Jazz Kafe
www.funkjazzkafe.com

Harlem Globetrotters
www.harlemglobetrotters.com

Jamerican Film & Music Festival
www.jamericanfilmfest.com

Jazz Emporium
www.jazzemporium.com

National Association of Black Scuba Divers
www.nabsdivers.org

National Brotherhood of Skiers
www.nbs.org

Onnidan's Black College Sports Online
www.onnidan.com

Original Southwest Louisiana Zydeco Festival, The
www.zydeco.org

Sinbad's Soulmusic Festival
www.soulmusicfestival.com

Soul of America
www.soulofamerica.com

Soul4U.com
www.soul4U.com

Urban Events
www.urbanevents.com

Urban Hang Suite
www.urbanhangsuite.com

Urban Music Festival
www.urbanmusicfestival.com

Urban Sports Network
www.urbansportsnetwork.com

What 2 Read—African American Literature
www.what2read.com

Supplier Diversity Programs & Info

b2b Diversity
www.b2bdiversity.com

Diversity e-Commerce
www.diversityecommerce.com

MinorityAmerica.com
www.minorityamerica.com

National Minority Supplier Development Council, Inc.
www.nmsdcus.org

NBC Sourcing
www.nbcsourcing.com
/supplierdiversity/

State of North Carolina, Office of Historically and Underutilized Business
www.doa.state.nc.us/hub/

SupplierGateway
www.suppliergateway.com

Try US Directory
www.tryusdir.com

WelcomeInfo.com
www.welcomeinfo.com

Technology

A Touch of Classics
www.atouchofclassics.com

Aerolith
www.aerolith.com

African Technology Forum
web.mit.edu/africantech/www

AlphaData Corporation
www.alphadata.com

Answer Austin
www.answeraustin.com

Ashanti Technology
www.ashantitech.com

Used with permission of Ashanti Technology Inc.

August Fifth
www.augustfifth.com

B2eMarkets
www.b2emarkets.com

bd Systems, Inc.
www.bdsys.com

Black Americans of Achievement
www.baoa.com

Black Enginer
www.blackengineer.com

Black Family Technology Awareness Week
www.blackfamilynet.net

Black Geeks Online
www.blackgeeks.com

Black Pioneers of the Internet Forum
www.delphi.com/blackpioneers

Blinks.Net
www.blinks.net

Break Away Technologies
www.breakaway.org

Café Future and Gallery
www.cafefutureandgallery.com

CC-OPS, Inc.
www.ccops.com

Center for Neighborhood Technology
www.cnt.org

ChaseCom
www.chasecom.net

Community Technology Centers Network (CTCNET)
www.ctcnet.org

The Conduit
www.theconduit.com

Cyber Group Network, Inc.
www.cybergroupnetwork.com

CyberCrime Corporation
www.cybercrimecorp.com

Dallas Area Technology Alliance
www.tekitup.com

Diversity/Careers in Engineering & Information Technology
www.diversitycareers.com

e22 Digital
www.itutu.com

The GilWil Group, Inc.
www.gilwilgroup.com

Gray Systems
www.graysys.com

Herbie Hancock's Rhythm of Life
www.rolo.org

Imperito
www.imperito.com

Inner City Software: Brains in the Hood
www.innercity.com

Intellitech
www.intellitech.net

Interpretech
www.interpretech.com

IXI Technologies
www.ixitech.com

JMMS Enterprises, Inc.
www.jmmsenterprises.com

Kinetic Media, Inc.
www.kineticm.com

M-Cubed Information Systems
www.m-cubedc.com

Marsh Communication Services, Inc.
www.marshcom.com

Mr. October 4 Kids
www.mroctober4kids.com

MTS Technologies, Inc.
www.mtstech.com

National Action Council for Minorities in Engineering, Inc.
www.nacme.org

National Black Programmers Coalition
www.nbpcinc.org

National Society of Black Engineers
www.nsbe.org

Network Commerce, Inc.
www.networkcommerce.com

Network Data Links
www.ndl.net

Nia Promotions
www.niapro.com

OurSpace Consulting
www.ourspace.com

Peasy Head, Inc.
www.peasyhead.org

Pepie Designs
www.pepiedesigns.com

Philip Emeagwali
www.emeagwali.com

Places of Color
www.placesofcolor.com

Playing 2 Win
www.playing2win.org

Sentel
www.sentel.com

Solutions Now
www.solnow.com

Soul of Technology
www.souloftechnology.net

Spy America Online
www.spyamericaonline.com

TechDiva.com
www.techdiva.com

Tech Museum of Innovation, The
www.thetech.org

Technology Access Foundation
www.techaccess.org

The Teqnology Group
www.teqnology.com

U.S. Black Engineering Magazine
www.blackengineer.com

Universal Solutions, Inc.
www.usi-online.com

USBOL
www.usbol.com

Venardis
www.venardis.com

xynoMedia
www.xynomedia.com

Technology—Consulting

Digital Rhythm Interactive
www.digitalflow.com

i-strategy.com, llc
www.i-strategy.com

Information Brokers, Inc.
www.infobro.com

Jamila White—Internet Strategist
www.jamilawhite.com

Kweku Computer Solutions
www.kweku.com

Oakland Consulting Group
www.ocg-inc.com

Technology—ISPs & Hosting

Black Cyberspace Online
www.blackcyberspace.com

Innetix Wireless
www.innetix.com

Khpra International
Communications
www.khpra.com

Nubonyx
www.nubonyx.com

PCS WorldNet, Inc.
www.pcsworld.net

SuccessNet
www.successnet.net

U.S. Black Online
www.usbol.com

Technology—Multimedia Design

Ashay
www.ashay.com

Bay Tomato Company, The
www.tomato.com

Destee Design & Publishing
www.destee.com

DME Interactive Holdinsg, Inc.
www.digitalmafia.com

EasyWeb, Inc.
www.easywebinc.com

Ember Media
www.embermedia.com

ImageCafé
www.imagecafe.com

Imaginuity, Inc.
www.imaginuity.com

Imhotech New Media Design
& Publishing
www.imhotech.com/imhotech

Inside Image Web Design
www.insideimage.com

JNAD Web Design
www.jnad.net

Knox Design
www.knoxdesign.com

Mcnetec Webpage Services
www.mcnetec.com

Michelle Traylor Data Services
www.mtdsnet.com

Midnight Online
www.midnight-online.com

Copyright Midnight Online, 1996–2001.

Mitchell Holden Group
www.mhgonline.com

ohsdesign, inc.
www.ohsdesign.com

RaberWeb
www.raberweb.com

TechnikOne
www.technikone.com

Todd A. Kelley Design Services
www.takmedia.com

TriCom
www.tricomweb.com

Ty Webbin
www.tywebbin.com

Technology—Software

African & African American Clip Art Series
www.erols.com/tdpedu/clip.htm

Gikuuri Software
www.glsoft.com

Inner City Software
www.innercity.com

Women

Black Living
www.blackliving.com

Black Women in Publishing
www.bwip.org

Black Women in Sisterhood for Action (BISA)
www.feminist.com/bisas1.htm

Black Women's Health
www.blackwomenshealth.com

Blackgirl International
www.blackgirl.org

Celebrating Life
www.celebratinglife.org

Center for Women's Business Research
www.womensbusinessresearch.org

Digital Women
www.digital-women.com

DOE Network
www.doenetwork.com

The Gathering—A Women Of Color Expo
www.the-gathering.com

HauteZine
www.hautezine.com

International Association for Women of Color Day
www.womenofcolorday.com

Moca Couture
www.mocacouture.com

National Association of Women Business Owners
www.nawbo.org

Nia online
www.niaonline.com

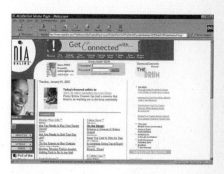

Onyx Woman
www.onyxwoman.com

Oprah
www.oprah.com

Real Divas
www.realdivas.com

Sistah Space
www.sistahspace.com

SistaSearch
www.sistasearch.com

Sisterfriend Soul Journeys
www.sisterfriendsouljourneys.com

Sisterfriends
www.sisterfriends.com

Sisters 4 Sisters
www.sisters4sisters.com

The Sisters Community
www.do4self.org

StyleWorks
www.styleworks.com

Women's Executive Network
www.thewen.com

Women's News Bureau
www.womensnewsbureau.com

Appendix A

ONLINE COMMUNICATION TOOLS

This appendix includes some Netiquette (Internet etiquette) tips to enhance your online communication skills and e-mail marketing efforts, and keep you from getting flamed via e-mail, chat rooms, Usenet Newsgroups, or electronic mailing lists. The most important thing to remember is that although the online world is a relatively new and different culture, it is still a network of human beings, not just a bunch of globally connected machines. The golden rule ("Do unto others . . .") applies here as well.

Even if you're a seasoned Netizen, review these tips. You just might learn something new.

1. *Check your e-mail regularly.* Nothing drives me crazier than people who check their e-mail once every two weeks—if that often. Don't make your e-mail address accessible unless you're going to check it regularly and respond. Checking your e-mail should be as important as checking your voice mail. Remember, this is a new and different culture. People typically expect responses to e-mail messages within 24 hours (if not immediately).

2. *Use descriptive subject headers in your e-mail messages.* I'm sure that many readers identify with me on this. I typically get 100 to 300 e-mail messages each day. So, when I get an empty e-mail subject heading or one that says "Letter" or "Very important," I'm less likely to open it on the first go-round. If you want a faster response to your message, be descriptive, but brief, in your e-mail subject header.

3. *Type in ALL CAPS only when you intend to shout.* Typing in all caps is not only hard on the eyes but, in e-mail messages, chat rooms, and posted public messages, it's considered the same as shouting. (This is usually the easiest way to spot a Newbie.) Initially, you may get a soft reminder to type in lower or sentence case. After that, expect to get flamed.

4. *Use smileys for emphasis.* Online communication is based on typewritten text, so it's more difficult to express any type of extreme emotion (negative or positive). To get your point across briefly and with attitude, you can use smileys (aka "emoticons," short for "emotion icons"). Other forms of expression include typing in all caps (shouting) and using acronyms (e.g., "btw" for "by the way"). See Figure A.1 for a list of commonly used smileys and acronyms.

5. *Keep tag lines short.* Tag lines (aka signature files), typically attached to the bottom of outgoing e-mail messages, should be no more than six to eight lines long. They usually contain information about the sender: his or her name, a business name, and contact information. Sometimes, tag lines include info on an upcoming event, a favorite quote, or a special business or personal announcement. See samples of tag lines in Chapter 4.

6. *Do not forward personal e-mail without the original author's consent.*

7. *Cut the headers* when forwarding jokes and other e-mail messages that have traveled over the Internet numerous times. It's quite annoying to get a five-line message that's at the bottom of 100 lines of headers.

8. *Do not include the entire content of a previous posting/message in your reply.* When you respond to an e-mail message or public posting, include only its relevant parts, especially when the original message is lengthy.

9. *Keep it simple, sweetie.* Unless you and a friend, colleague, or associate commonly send each other lengthy messages, keep yours short, sweet, and to the point. On the Net, brevity is key. Keep in mind those people who get dozens, if not hundreds, of e-mail messages daily. Especially when posting to an electronic mailing list or Newsgroup, do *not* post a dissertation, unless absolutely called for.

Figure A.1   Smileys and Internet Acronyms

Without face to face interaction, sometimes you just can't get that atti-tude to shine through! I've included here some of the most commonly used smileys and acronyms. New ones are created every day, so by no means is this list exhaustive. With a simple search in your favorite search engine, you will undoubtedly find a number of Web sites dedi-cated to maintaining databases of smileys and acronyms. The list below is more than enough to get you started.

SMILEYS

Smileys, or "emoticons" as they are sometimes called, are online facial expressions. Here's how they work:

Basic Smiley Construction

: ; | =	Eyes
- * (or blank)	Nose
>) o (<	Mouth
8 B = c { } E	Accessories

Smiley Examples

:-)	Happy
;-)	Winking
:-(	Frowning
:-I	Ambivalent or indifferent
:->	Devilish or sarcastic

(NOTE: If you still haven't figured out how smileys work, tilt your head to the left.)

More Smileys

>:-(	Angry
:'-(	Crying
;-)=)	Grinning
:-D	Laughing
:-X	Mute
:'-)	So happy, s/he is crying
:-"	Whistling
;->	Winking and devilish combined
:-@	Screaming
:-V	Shouting
:-/	Skeptical
:-O	Surprised/shocked
:-o	Surprised
:I	Hmmm...
—-<—{(@	A rose
:-P	Tongue-in-cheek comment
@:-)	Afro-smiley (Courtesy of MissDC, BlackGeeks)

(continued)

Figure A.1   (Continued)

ACRONYMS

In addition to the numerous acronyms referring to computer and Internet hardware and software (e.g., ASCII, DRAM, PCMCIA), now we've got online communication acronyms. These are a lot more fun, a whole lot easier to remember, and, at times, much more valuable.

Online communication acronyms can be developed from just about any phrase, company name, or witticism that you regularly use. (btw, they are typically used in lower case.)

TIP: When you create a new one, remember to spell it out the first few times you use it and when you begin to use it outside of your normal online circle of friends and associates.

2U2	To you, too
ASAP	As soon as possible
B/C	Because
BRB	Be right back
BTW	By the way
C4N	Ciao for now
CFD	Call for discussion
CU	See you
CUL(8R)	See you later
F2F	Face-to-face
FAQ	Frequently asked questions
FWIW	For what it's worth
FYI	For your information
IMHO	In my humble opinion
IOW	In other words
LOL	Laughing out loud
NC	No comment
OTOH	on the other hand
RO(T)FL	Rolling on the floor laughing
SO	Significant other (e.g., boyfriend, girlfriend, husband, wife)
THX	Thanks
TIA	Thanks in advance
TTFN	ta-ta for now
TTYL(8R)	Talk to you later
W/	With
W/O	Without

10. *Watch those attachments,* especially when posting to a list! Not everyone has a high-speed Internet connection, so attachments can still take a while to transfer. Be sure to let the recipient(s) know what the attachment is and which software to open it with.

11. *Do not spam!* Spamming refers to sending unsolicited commercial e-mail, typically in mass amounts. There are many ways to sell a product on the Net without spamming! If you insist on sending unsolicited commercial e-mail to potential customers who are not from an *opt-in mailing list,* expect to get flamed. You can also lose your e-mail account and/or get blacklisted on the Web.

12. *If you receive spam, notify your ISP.* Don't reply to spam; it will only confirm to the spammer that your e-mail address is live. Many times, your reply will just "bounce" back to you anyway. Pay close attention to any available unsubscribe/remove instructions in the body of the original spam message (just in case there's a different e-mail address for unsubscribe messages).

WEBSEARCH

OPTIONS FOR FIGHTING SPAM

Coalition Against Unsolicited Commercial E-mail
www.cauce.org

Junk E-mail Resource Page
www.junkemail.org

Official Internet Blacklist
www.blacklist.com

SpamCop
www.spamcop.com

Spam Recycle
www.spamrecycle.com

---

13. *Do not forward chain letters.* Expect to get them every so often. Even if a letter says something like "You'll die in 7 days if you don't forward this to 59 people," delete it. These are just as bad as, if not worse than, chain letters received in Snail mail because they travel a lot faster (and there are so many of them

floating around!). Chain letters typically have some wonderful story about life, love, or friendship, and their endings read like this:

> Do not keep this message.
> This must leave your hands within 96 hours.
> Send copies and watch what goes on in the next four days.
> You'll have a pleasant surprise.
> This is true, even if you're not superstitious.

or

> Send this message to at least five people and your life improves.
> 0–4 people: Your life improves slightly.
> 5–9 people: Your life improves according to your expectations!
> 9–14 people: You'll have at least five surprises in the next three weeks.
> 15 or more people: Your life improves drastically and your dreams start to take shape.

14. *Respect copyright and license agreements.* Do not reprint or forward any information without the author's consent. Also, do not sell or distribute previously licensed software.

15. *"Lurk" before you leap.* When you join an electronic mailing list, chat room, or Newsgroup, "lurk" first. This simply means checking out how the group's participants interact with each other. This will definitely keep flames to a minimum.

16. *Check the FAQ (Frequently Asked Questions file) first.* When you're new to a Web site, electronic mailing list, or Newsgroup, check the FAQ file before you start asking questions. Many electronic lists send a "Welcome" e-mail message to new subscribers with all of the pertinent info about the group. FAQs and Welcome messages usually answer questions like:

Who's the list/site/group administrator?

How do I unsubscribe from this mailing list?

How do I post messages?

Are sponsorship or advertising opportunities available?

Can I mention my products and services on this list?

17. *Don't post a public message when a direct e-mail will suffice.* If you are responding to a very specific but somewhat off-topic information request in a small group or on an electronic mailing list, send your response directly to the person requesting the info, not to the entire list.

18. *Don't flame!* Flaming refers to the use of insults and derogatory language directed toward another person. It is often the result of a disagreement between one or more persons in a chat room, on an electronic mailing list, or in a Newsgroup. People have been known to disagree online (considering the fact that the interacting parties could be from different cultures, backgrounds, or mind-sets), but pursuing an all-out flame war is a whole other matter. Simply agree to disagree and move on. Calling each other names or swearing is completely unnecessary.

19. *Be open-minded and don't preach.* As stated earlier, people who interact online are often from very different backgrounds and situations. Keep this in mind. Every person is entitled to his or her opinion. Read what a person has to say and be respectful of the viewpoint expressed. Also, leave your soapbox in the closet. It's okay to express your opinion, but don't become a "missionary of your lifestyle" who is trying to convert anyone and everyone who'll listen.

20. *If someone harasses you, report him or her to your ISP and to the appropriate list or system operator immediately.* If a person sends inappropriate e-mail messages to you, report them immediately, keep copies of the messages, and do whatever your ISP, the sender's ISP, or the electronic mailing list owner tells you to do. In some cases, the person's messages to you can be blocked. Flaming the person may only antagonize him or her and make the situation worse. Also, most e-mail software allows you to block or filter out messages from certain e-mail addresses, or based on subject header or message content.

21. *Never give out personal information (address, home phone, passwords, Social Security number, credit card numbers, etc.) in a posted message.* Most of us have heard stories about couples who've met and fallen in love on the Internet. That's wonderful, but remember that there are just as many crazies on the Web as there are walking up and down the street. Just because you are sitting in the privacy of your home or office while you're online doesn't mean that you're safe. Take the same precautions that you would in the real world. If you are purchasing a product from a Web site, read about the source's security and encryption policy before you input your credit card number. Never include personal information in publicly posted messages. A direct e-mail is somewhat safer, but nothing is foolproof—not even the U.S. mail! Use common sense when giving out information.

22. *Respect other people's privacy.* Protect your contacts by using "BCC:," which stands for "blind carbon copy." It never ceases to amaze me how people send out mass e-mail messages with all of their contacts' e-mail addresses openly available. Odds are pretty high that you wouldn't just hand over your print or electronic contact lists. Then why not protect their e-mail addresses? Just as spider programs exist to sniff out Web site addresses for search engine and directory listings, there are programs that were created to sniff out e-mail addresses for spamming. Also, there's nothing to stop the recipients from sending direct e-mail to each other, which is not always such a great thing, especially if you have high-profile colleagues or clients.

23. *Ask permission to link to another person's site.* Better to be safe than sorry. You would think that it would be a compliment to someone if you link to his or her site because of the potential for increased traffic. But, in April 1997, Ticketmaster sued Microsoft for "deep linking" to its site without authorization. The primary argument for the suit was that the traffic originating from Microsoft's site bypassed TicketMaster's home page advertising.

24. *When you download files, run a virus check on them before opening them.* Forgetfulness and laziness can cost you a lot of time and money. Viruses picked up during transmission over the Internet can destroy files on your hard drive, including vitally important system files. Also, regularly back up your hard drive files.

25. *When you hear about a new virus, investigate it further.* Confirm the validity of the virus before forwarding any related news to colleagues. (See more about viruses in Chapter 2.)

26. *Confirm that it's okay to forward e-mail jokes, prayers, and nonbusiness-related messages.* On average, I get at least 20 new e-mail jokes, prayers, and social announcements per day. Some of them are relevant to my life; most are not. What's worse is that a lot of these messages are repeats. Always ask whether a colleague is interested in receiving any general messages.

27. *Be careful when forwarding e-mail messages that sound like "urban legends."* Don't just take a lazy person's approach and forward the message to 20 of your friends and associates. Check it out first. No need to create hysteria where there is none. By the way, Bill Gates is not going to send you $1,000; Disney is not giving away a free vacation; there is no kidney theft ring in New Orleans; Neiman Marcus does not sell a $200 cookie recipe; and there is no little boy in England who is dying of cancer and

wants you to send cards to get him into the *Guinness Book of World Records*. Consult urbanlegends.miningco.com before forwarding any of these types of e-mail messages. Click on "Current Net Hoaxes." (See Appendix D for more information about validating urban legend-type e-mail messages.)

THE TEN COMMANDMENTS FOR COMPUTER ETHICS

1. Thou shalt not use a computer to harm other people.
2. Thou shalt not interfere with other people's computer work.
3. Thou shalt not snoop around in other people's files.
4. Thou shalt not use a computer to steal.
5. Thou shalt not use a computer to bear false witness.
6. Thou shalt not use or copy software for which you have not paid.
7. Thou shalt not use other people's computer resources without authorization.
8. Thou shalt not appropriate other people's intellectual output.
9. Thou shalt think about the social consequences of the program you write.
10. Thou shalt use a computer in ways that show consideration and respect.

© Computer Ethics Institute, 1991. Author: Dr. Ramon C. Barquin.

Appendix B

SURF TIPS AND SEARCH BASICS

SEARCH ENGINES VERSUS DIRECTORIES

Some of the Web sites listed in the following tables are classified as search engines; others are called directories. What's the difference? It boils down to categorization. Yahoo!, although commonly called a search engine, is technically a directory. So is Infoseek. Lycos and Alta Vista are search engines. Directories often make searching easier because you can search by category or by keyword.

Here are some of the Web's top search engines, directories, and Yellow Pages listings:

Search Engine/Directory	Web Site Address (http://)
About	www.miningco.com
All Business: Champions of Small business	www.allbusiness.com
Alta Vista	www.altavista.com
Ask Jeeves	www.askjeeves.com
CNet's Search.com	www.search.com
Direct Hit	www.directhit.com
Dogpile	www.dogpile.com

Search Engine/Directory	Web Site Address (http://)
Excite	www.excite.com
Go2	www.go2.com
Google	www.google.com
HotBot	www.hotbot.com
LincOn	www.lincon.com
Lycos	www.lycos.com
Mamma	www.mamma.com
Metacrawler	www.metacrawler.com
Northern Light	www.northernlight.com
Oingo	www.oingo.com
Open Directory Project	www.dmoz.org
Overture (formerly GoTo.com)	www.overture.com
SuperPages	www.superpages.com
Switchboard	www.switchboard.com
WebCrawler	www.webcrawler.com
WhatUSeek	www.whatuseek.com
Yahoo!	www.yahoo.com
Yellow Online	www.yellowonline.com

WORLDWIDE SEARCHING

For those of you who do business globally or are simply interested in international searches, here are a few international search tools:

Search Engine/Directory	Web Site Address (http://)
Ananzi South Africa	www.ananzi.co.za
Aonde (Brazil)	www.aonde.com
Caribbean-Search.com	www.caribbean-search.com
CubaWeb	www.cubaweb.cu
Egypt Search	www.egyptsearch.com
EuroPages: The European Business Directory	www.europages.com
goGreece	www.gogreece.com
Homer: The Canadian Search Directory	www.homer.ca
Lokace (France)	www.lokace.fr
MexMaster (Mexico)	www.mexmaster.com
Nomade (France)	www.nomade.fr

Search Engine/Directory	Web Site Address (http://)
Search Dragon (Asia)	www.searchdragon.com
Search Engine Colossus: International Directory of Search Engines	www.searchenginecolossus.com
Swiss Search (Switzerland)	www.search.ch
Web Watch (Belgium)	www.webwatch.be
Web Wombat (Australia)	www.webwombat.com.au
WEPA! (Puerto Rico)	www.wepa.com
Woyaa! (Africa)	www.woyaa.com

Yahoo! also features "Local Yahoo!s" for various international locations.

For a list of Afrocentric search engines and directories, see the Networking Directory.

WHICH SEARCH TOOL IS THE BEST?

It depends on your personal preference and what you're searching for. Each search engine and directory is created for different reasons. A lot of people prefer Yahoo! because of its categories; others prefer Alta Vista or Northern Light because of their immense databases. Here are a few pointers:

- If you're just browsing, start at Yahoo!
- If you're looking for maximum results, try Alta Vista or Lycos.
- Use Deja.com for Usenet Newsgroup searches.
- To search several engines and directories at once, use a metasearch engine like Metacrawler or Dogpile.
- No matter where you start, always be prepared to use other search tools.

Here are some basic Web search tips and tricks:

- **Enter as many subject-specific search terms or phrases as possible,** to limit your search.
- **Enter your search subject in singular terms.** Most search engines will return singular and plural versions of search terms.
- Always **check your spelling!**
- Try **multiple spellings** where appropriate (e.g., afrocentric, afro-centric).

- Use **lowercase spelling.** Results will include upper- and lower-case spellings on most search engines.
- Use **synonyms** (e.g., black owned businesses, African American owned businesses).
- Wherever possible, use **wildcards** like * and **?** to generalize a subject search (e.g., "art*" will return search results for art, arts, artists, artistic).
- If you are looking for a specific name or title, **use quotes.** (Example: Instead of Colin Powell, type in "Colin Powell.") This will change your search results significantly.
  - Or, use a **prepend operator** between the words (e.g., Colin+Powell). "+" requires that results must include all search terms; "-" prohibits a specific term.
- **Word order** affects search results as well. Try searching on "government procurement" and "procurement government." You may get totally different results.
- Use **Boolean logic** (AND, OR, NOT) to limit search results. For example, type in: **soul food NOT movie.** This search will give you Web sites and references to soul food recipes and restaurants, not sites featuring or mentioning the movie *Soul Food*.
- **Each search engine has its own Help page and search tips.** Be sure to check the Help page if you have trouble finding what you're looking for.
- If at first you don't succeed, **try another search engine!!**

ADDITIONAL TIPS

- When searching for a **major corporation's Web site,** try using the following format first: www.companyname.com. For example, if you're looking for the Web site for *USA Today,* try www.usatoday.com.
- To find an electronic **mailing list** on any subject, go to Yahoo!Groups (groups.yahoo.com), Topica (www.topica.com), or CataList (the official catalog of LISTSERV lists—www.listserv.net/catalist.html).
- Don't forget to **ask people for help.** If you cannot find specific information by using search tools, post a public message in a relevant special-interest group or in an electronic mailing list. Also, send e-mail to friends and colleagues who may be familiar with the subject matter; you never know who has the answer to your question.

- Search the **Library of Congress** Web site when looking for books and articles: www.loc.gov.
- If you're looking for articles from a specific major publication (e.g., *Wall Street Journal, Los Angeles Times, New York Times*) **go to the archive section on the publication's Web site.** (NOTE: Some publications charge to access the archive section on their Web site.) Another good place to find newspapers and articles is the **Newspapers On-line** Web site: www.nando.net
- **Be persistent and creative.** Prepare to supply the ingenuity needed to make search tools as effective as they were meant to be.

NOTE: There are numerous books and Web sites dedicated to Internet and Web searching. The purpose of this section is not to make you an expert online searcher but to provide you with a few pointers for quick online searches.

Millions of pages are on the World Wide Web; but, they have not all been documented. Search engine spiders are hard at work, every second of the day, seeking new Web pages to be included in their massive databases. This means that no online search should be considered exhaustive. If you don't find what you're looking for on the Web, it doesn't mean that the person, company, item, or information does not exist. It may simply not be indexed in search engines or it may not be on the Web yet. Try off-line reference sources (e.g., print publications, government agencies, colleagues).

Appendix C

GETTING THE RIGHT DATA

KNOWLEDGE VERSUS INFORMATION OVERLOAD

One of the biggest disadvantages of new technology is information overload. Given today's cell phones, pagers, fax machines, e-mail, and text messaging, we've become accessible to information bombardment 24 hours a day, 7 days a week.

It's not unusual to get 50 to 100 pieces of e-mail daily from electronic mailing lists, clients, colleagues, and spammers. (I'm the lucky recipient of 100 to 300 pieces daily!) If your e-mail address is on your business card and/or in your tag line, your fax machine might be burning less paper but you'll make up for it in e-mail.

Here are some tips for managing e-mail without losing your mind:

1. *Utilize the filtering mechanism in your e-mail software to sort e-mail and to exclude messages with certain headers and keywords.* E-mail filters allow you to block and sort e-mail by keyword, size, and sender (name and/or e-mail address). This can be especially helpful if you receive lots of jokes and spam.

2. *Check the sender's name and the e-mail subject header so that you can respond to the familiar and most urgent e-mails first.* If you get

a lot of e-mail, you don't have to respond on a first-in, first-out basis. Check the headers to determine which ones are more important. Naturally, messages that arrive with a high priority should be checked first.

3. *Buy yourself some time by using e-mail autoresponders.* Netizens expect quick e-mail responses—usually, within 24 hours. If you know that your current schedule won't allow you to respond to your overflowing e-mail immediately, create an e-mail autoresponder notifying the sender that his or her e-mail has been received and that you will respond within the next few days. Check with your MIS manager, in-house techie, or ISP if you don't know how to do this.

4. *Set aside a specific time of day to respond to your e-mail messages.* The exception to this rule is replying to urgent messages from clients and colleagues who require an immediate response. All other message responses should be relegated to early morning or late afternoon. Why? Because if you respond to your messages four or five times a day, responses to your responses will arrive as often. A lot of people respond to e-mail as it comes in. If your recipient does the same, you're actually creating more e-mail than you're eliminating.

VALIDATING INFORMATION

On a daily basis, we receive information from TV, radio, newspapers, magazines, memos, e-mail, facsimile machines, advertisements, people, and a bunch of other sources. Unfortunately, people tend to assume that most of these sources supply valid information simply because of their mass distribution appeal. Think of the many times people have argued with you about the validity of a piece of information, when the basis of their argument was: "But, I saw it on the news!" or "It was in the paper. It has to be true." No source is without its flaws, and this is especially important because of the speed with which information travels on the Internet. I've seen urban legend-type e-mail messages pass through my Inbox several times during the course of a week, no doubt having circulated the globe numerous times in the interim. Remember the story about Tommy Hilfiger making racist claims on "Oprah"? That story has been circulating the Web since 1997, and no matter how many times Oprah and Tommy Hilfiger have denied and disputed the story, it continues to circulate.

How do you know whether the information that you receive is true? By asking questions; that's how. Needless to say, no one has time to research every piece of information received, so you have to pick your battles carefully. The difference with the Internet versus other media is that *you* play a key role in the dissemination of the information. If you see something on the news, you might be likely to tell one or two friends, colleagues, or associates in person or via telephone. If you get something in your e-mail Inbox, odds are that you'll forward the message to 10 or 20 people immediately. Get the picture? If you thought bad news traveled quickly before, now it moves at lightning speed.

Here are a few things to remember:

- Don't believe everything you read.
- Chain letters don't always look like chain letters. Sometimes they look like simple "FYI" notes or calls to action.
- Passing along bad information is as bad as, if not worse than, not receiving valuable, valid information.

When you receive a questionable e-mail message that is a call to action about some so-called recent event, or if the message sounds like an urban legend, don't just pass it on without validating it. Ask yourself:

1. Who is sending this information?
2. Where did the sender get it? Is the original source listed?
3. What are you being instructed to do, if anything?
4. What purpose does this information serve?
5. Is it time-sensitive?

Typically, these messages claim that a person, group, or corporation committed a crime or injustice against someone else. The messages typically have dozens of lines of headers and intertwined notes claiming verification that the information is correct. Before passing it on, forward the message to a community leader or someone who can verify or disprove it.

I'm sure that many readers have received an e-mail announcing that African Americans will lose their right to vote in the next few years. This message was circulated on the Net dozens of times before somebody had the good sense to forward it to the NAACP. Finally, the information was publicly disproved, and a statement to that fact was posted on the NAACP Web site. A week after the NAACP disproved the information, I received the invalid information for an umpteenth time.

It takes just as little time to verify or disprove information as it does to forward the info to 20 of your friends. Don't be a part of the Internet's misinformation circles. Verify or disprove information before you pass it on!

Appendix D

SIDETRACKING INTERNET SCAMS

Technology creates viable business opportunities for everyone, including for the dubious characters of the world. Con artists are finding newer, better, and faster ways to scam people out of their money with fraudulent business opportunities and investments. Among the top ten "dot cons" according to the U.S. Federal Trade Commission, are fraudulent Internet auctions, multilevel marketing and pyramid opportunities, travel and vacation plans, "miracle" health cures, credit cards, investment opportunities, general business opportunities, free Web sites, and other free Internet services.

When you are presented with an investment or business opportunity, by telephone or by e-mail, always take the time to thoroughly check all the information you receive. Remember that if it sounds to good to be true, it usually is.

Ask the following questions:

1. Where did you get my name and telephone number/e-mail address?
2. Can you send me written materials to back up your claims?

3. What are the risks involved in this investment?
4. Would you be willing to explain your proposal to my attorney, accountant, or banker?
5. What government agency supervises your activity?
6. How long has your company been in business?
7. How much of my money will go for fees and commissions?
8. Where, exactly, will my money be held?
9. What type of written statements do you provide, and how often will I receive them?
10. Who are your firm's principals? Can you provide references for them?

The National Fraud Center and the U.S. Federal Trade Commission can assist you in determining whether an opportunity is legitimate. You should also contact them if you think that someone is trying to scam you.

National Fraud Center
www.nationalfraud.com
Four Horsham Business Center
300 Welsh Road, Suite 200
Horsham, PA 19044
Phone: (215) 657-0800
Fax: (215) 657-7071
Toll-free: (800) 999-5658

U.S. Federal Trade Commission (FTC)
www.ftc.gov (Click on "Consumer Protection")
Department of Consumer and Regulatory Affairs
614 H Street, N.W.
Washington, DC 20001
Phone: (202) 727-7120
Fax: (202) 727-8073/7842

GLOSSARY

Advertorial—An advertisement designed to resemble editorial content. Also refers to a paid newspaper or magazine article about an advertiser. Advertorials must have worthwhile information and be interesting to the reader. They should read like a news story.

Affiliate marketing—Affiliate marketing is any form of online marketing or advertising where the advertiser pays for results rather than paying just to reach a certain audience. Affiliate participants promote the advertiser's products or services on their Web site in exchange for commission on leads or sales that result from their Web site visitors' acting on these offers.

AIM—America Online (AOL) Instant Manager.

ALT image tag—An *HTML* code typically used to describe to site visitors what an image represents. If an image on a *Web* page doesn't load properly, the site visitor can read the ALT image tag to know what would have been displayed. This information is also used by *search engines*.

Angel investor—A financial backer, usually a friend or relative, who provides venture capital funds for start-ups. Angel investors are typically successful entrepreneurs who want to help other entrepreneurs get their business off the ground. Funding estimates vary, but usually range from $150,000 to $1.5 million. (The term "angel" comes from the practice, in the early 1900s, of wealthy businessmen investing in Broadway productions.) Today, "angels" typically offer expertise, experience, and contacts, in addition to money.

Applet—A program or "little application" designed to be executed from within another application. Applet typically refers to a small Internet-based program that is written in *Java* (a programming language for the Web), is usually embedded in an HTML page on a Web site, and can be executed from within a browser.

ASCII—American Standard Code for Information Interchange. A code used for representing English characters, including punctuation symbols, as numbers. It is the most common format for text files in computers and on the Internet.

ASP—An acronym that has two references: Application Service Provider and Active Server Pages. An *Application Service Provider* is a company that rents software solutions over the Internet or a private network. *Active Server Pages,* a combination of code, *HTML,* and scripting, allow dynamically generated Web pages (pages with tailored information based on user interaction).

Authentication—The process of identifying an individual, usually based on a user's name and password. In security systems, authentication is distinct from authorization, which is the process of giving individuals access to system objects, based on their identity. Authentication merely ensures that the individual is who he or she claims to be. It says nothing about the access rights of the individual.

Auto-responder—An *e-mail* message that is automatically distributed to senders of incoming messages. Auto-responders can be customized to send a specific message "on demand," depending on the sender's address, a specified recipient address, or the message subject header. Auto-responders are used to enhance customer service, save time, or to drive *Web* site traffic. *Internet* users can create their own auto-responders in their *e-mail client* (e.g., Microsoft Outlook, Eudora, Netscape Communicator) or their ISP may offer this service.

B2B—Business-to-Business; refers to the exchange of products, services, and information between businesses.

B2C—Business-to-Consumer; refers to the exchange of products, services, and information between businesses and consumers.

Backbone—The physical connection that transmits data between two or more networks. A backbone is often composed of fiber-optic cables or other transport media that support high speeds.

Bandwidth—The amount of data—text, images, audio, or video—that can be transmitted via a communications path in a fixed amount of time.

Banner—An interactive advertisement, typically rectangular in shape and placed across the top, side, or bottom of a Web page. A banner is linked to an external advertiser's Web site or another internal page within the same Web site. Banners often include animation and graphics to entice site visitors to *"click through."*

Banner exchange—An advertising network where participating Web sites display and rotate the banner ads of other participants in the network. Examples of banner exchange networks are:

The Banner Trader	www.thebannertrader.com
Banner Women	www.bannerwomen.com
BannerSwap	www.bannerswap.com

IT Banner Exchange	www.itbannerexchange.com
LinkBuddies	www.linkbuddies.com
VirtuAds	www.virtuads.com

Bitmap—Image format; a collection of pixels that forms an image.

Bluetooth™—Wireless technology, developed by a consortium of companies (3Com, Intel, Toshiba, Ericsson, IBM, Lucent, Microsoft, and Nokia), that links Bluetooth™-enabled portable PCs, wireless phones, *PDAs*, *MP3* players, and digital cameras.

Bookmark—A Web page "flag" or marker, usually stored in a "folder," that allows you to return to the Web page without having to memorize the domain name.

Brand—Refers to an assurance of value from a company; it is the way that a company is depicted by its target audience and/or the general public. The act of branding involves creating an association between a company's name, colors, logo, and overall image with a promise of value, or the solution to a challenge facing the company's target audience.

Brick-and-mortar—Storefront, office-based, or home-based business that sells its product or service strictly via traditional methods.

Broadband—Broadband services include cable, satellite, *DSL,* and *wireless*. Broadband technology, which is powered by digital wiring or fiber-optic cabling, provides data transmission at ten times the speed of dial-up connections, provides an "always on" connection to the Internet, and doesn't tie up subscribers' phone lines (so there are no missed calls while you're connected).

Browser—A software application that allows you to view Web sites. The most popular browsers are Microsoft's Internet Explorer and Netscape's Navigator. A browser locates a Web site's files on a server (based on the Web site address that you type in), arranges the content according to the coded instructions, and projects the requested page on your screen.

Business model—A business's means of generating revenue and providing value to its customer base.

Button ad—An interactive advertisement—typically, square in shape and placed in the left or right margin of a Web page—that is linked to an external advertiser's Web site or an internal page within the same Web site. Buttons, like *banner* ads, often include animation and graphics to entice site visitors to "*click through.*"

Cache—The act of saving a Web page in a temporary file so that your computer can quickly reload it without actually downloading the Web page files from the server again. Recently visited Web pages are "cached" (or stored temporarily) on a user's hard disk to speed up Web surfing. Web page files are cached for a specified amount of time or until the cache directory reaches its specified file size limit, at which time the directory is emptied.

CD-ROM—Compact Disc-Read-Only Memory, a type of optical disk that can store the same amount of information as 700 floppy disks. CD technology also includes CD-R (CD-Recordable) disks, which enable you to record information on them once, and CD-RW (CD-Rewritable) disks, which enable you to record information on them several times.

CGI—Common Gateway Interface; a program that allows dynamically generated content on Web sites, based on a user's input (often via forms).

Chat room—A virtual room where visitors can communicate in *real-time,* using text and symbols.

Click-and-mortar—A traditional *brick-and-mortar* business that establishes an *Internet* presence. Also refers to the results of transforming an established or *brick-and-mortar* operation, business process, or business model into a technology-enhanced concept, powered by the Internet.

Click-through—Used to describe when a site visitor clicks on an ad *banner* to view the advertiser's Web site.

Co-location—Refers to a hosting situation in which a company purchases its own servers and places them at an ISP's site to obtain high-speed, dedicated Internet access.

Community technology center—Locally based, often grassroots organizations that provide free or low-cost access to computers, computer-related technology, and training.

Configure—To set up a computer system to work properly with a particular software application.

Convergence—Refers to the efforts underway to combine personal computers, telecommunication, and television into a user experience that is accessible to everyone. WebTV is an example of convergence.

Cookie—A text file placed on your computer by some Web sites that you visit. Because cookies only contain text, they cannot transmit a virus or do damage to your computer system. Internet cookies can be used:

> As an anonymous code so that *Webmasters* or Web site owners can see how many users return at a later time. (These "persistent" cookies are configured to stay on your system for months or years.)

> To identify you after you register on a Web site. The site could keep a detailed account of pages visited, items purchased, and so on, and could combine this with information from other sources once your identity is known.

To maintain a list (or "shopping cart") of items you purchased on a Web site. (These "session" cookies typically expire when you log out.)

To maintain your personal preferences after you register on a Web site. (This can be anonymous or linked to personal information obtained during the registration process.)

For more information about cookies, go to www.cookiecentral.com.

Cost per click—An online advertising term used to describe the cost per *click-through* of an ad to an advertiser's Web site.

CPM—Cost Per Thousand; an online advertising term used to describe the cost per 1,000 ad impressions.

CPU—Central Processing Unit, aka *microprocessor,* refers to the central unit of a computer, where most of the calculations and instructions take place.

Cramming—A type of scam that involves billing unexplained charges on a person or company's phone bill for services never ordered, authorized, received, or used. Charges may range from $4.95 to $30 per month. Examples of crammed charges include travel club memberships, *Internet* access, calling cards and voice mail service.

For more information on cramming and how to safeguard your business, contact:

Federal Trade Commission (FTC)
Phone: (202) 326-3134
www.ftc.gov

National Consumers League (NCL)
Phone: (202) 835-3323
www.nclnet.org

National Fraud Information Center (NFIC)
Phone: (800) 876-7060
www.fraud.org

CRM—Customer Relationship Management; refers to software and methodologies used to streamline sales and marketing processes, allowing a company to better manage its customer relationships.

CTR—Click-Through Rate; measurement used to describe the effectiveness of a banner ad campaign. The rate is determined by dividing the number of times that site visitors clicked through to the advertiser's Web site by the total number of times the banner is viewed. For example, a 1 percent CTR means that 1 percent of each 1,000 banner views (or 10 visitors) have clicked through.

Cyber café—A coffee house or café that provides free or low-cost access to personal computers and the Internet.

Cyberpiracy—See *Cybersquatting*.

Cybersquatting—A practice where an individual registers a Web site address that is identical or similar to celebrity, corporate, or trademarked names, for the sole purpose of extorting profits.

DDoS attack—Dedicated Denial of Service attack; refers to a *hack* attack on a network that floods the system with messages, causing it to shut down and deny access to authorized and legitimate users.

Dedicated hosting—Web *hosting* that provides the rental and exclusive use of a server to one client (versus *virtual hosting* or *shared hosting*). Dedicated hosting is typically reserved for highly trafficked Web sites.

Desk rage—Expressing anger at work, often associated with stress-filled environments, coworker disputes, or frustration with equipment. This rage takes the form of yelling, verbal abuse, attacks on office equipment (usually computers), and fights with coworkers.

Dial-up networking—Method of connecting your personal computer to a *network* (like the *Internet*) using a *modem*.

Digital Divide—Refers to the disparity between those persons and/or communities who have access to telephones, computers (hardware, software, peripherals), and *Internet* technology, and those who do not.

DNS—Domain Name System; used to locate and identify computers connected to the *Internet*. It is essentially a naming convention that converts numeric *IP addresses* into Web site addresses that are easy for people to remember.

Docking station—Hardware and electrical interfaces that enable a laptop to serve as a desktop computer, allowing it to attach to a *LAN* or to use *peripheral* devices.

Domain name—The unique name of a Web site, like att.com or microsoft.com.

dot-com—Refers to a business that is named after its chosen ".com" *Internet* domain (e.g., amazon.com, pets.com). The term is also often used to describe venture capital-funded, new media businesses.

Download—The transfer of information from the Internet to the browsing computer.

DSL—Digital Subscriber Line; a broadband technology that allows high-speed *Internet* access over regular copper telephone lines.

DVD—Digital Video Disc; type of optical disk that holds 28 times as much information as a *CD-ROM* (up to 4.7 *gigabyte*s), or enough video, audio, and other information to store a full-length movie.

e-Commerce—The buying and selling of goods and services across the *Internet*.

e-CRM—Electronic Customer Relationship Management; eCRM involves the integration of Web-based functions that allow interaction directly with clients, prospects, and business partners.

EFT—Electronic Funds Transfer.

e-learning—Refers to online training or distance learning that requires the use of *network* technology for content delivery in static form or *real-time*.

Electronic Frontier Foundation—A nonprofit, nonpartisan organization founded in 1990 to work in the public interest to protect fundamental civil liberties, including privacy and freedom of expression in the arena of computers and the *Internet* (www.eff.org).

Electronic mailing list—An e-mail distribution list, often based on a specific subject or industry. When an e-mail message is sent to the list's primary address, it is automatically forwarded to the e-mail addresses of all list "subscribers." Yahoo! Groups, ListBot, and Topica are examples of electronic mailing list services. Also see *"listserv."*

E-mail alias—A forwarding e-mail address that allows you to use a preferred or branded e-mail address (name@yourcompany.com) to receive e-mail. An e-mail alias does not provide a second e-mail account; incoming messages are forwarded to your actual e-mail address (screenname@anyisp.com).

E-mail forwarding—The process of redirecting e-mail messages to one or more different e-mail addresses.

E-mail reader—Software program that allows the user to access, read, distribute, and filter electronic mail (e.g., Eudora, Microsoft Outlook, Netscape Messenger). Also called an "e-mail client."

E-mail spoofing—The practice of changing your identity in e-mail so that it looks like the e-mail came from somewhere (or someone) else. *Spammers* often use e-mail spoofing to mask their real identities, which is illegal. E-mail spoofing is also done legitimately for users with more than one e-mail account. Basically, you change the "Identity" information (under Mail Preferences) in your *e-mail reader* so that all e-mail responses go to a specific e-mail address. (For example, if you want your e-mail responses directed to you@yourcompany.com and you want outgoing messages to look like they came from you@yourcompany.com but you send and receive e-mail as you@anyISP.com, you can spoof yourself.) NOTE: It is illegal to spoof anyone but yourself.

Encryption—The process of converting data into an unreadable form so that it cannot be interpreted by unauthorized persons. Decryption, the process of converting encrypted data into plain text, often requires the use of a password.

Ergonomics—The science of optimizing work environments for the purposes of minimizing injury and increasing comfort and productivity. For more info, go to Healthy Computing (www.healthycomputing.com) or ErgoWeb (www.ergoweb.com).

ERP—Enterprise Resource Planning; refers to software packages and consulting services that integrate a wide range of business activities, including inventory management, employee training, customer service, order tracking, purchasing, human resources management, and financial management. ERP systems are typically supported by a multimodule application software that centralizes all company departments and functions.

e-tailer—Online or electronic retailer.

Ethernet—The most widely used local area network (*LAN*) technology; originally developed by Xerox and enhanced by Xerox, DEC, and Intel. Ethernet typically uses coaxial cable or special grades of twisted pair wires, and supports data transfer rates of 1 gigabit per second.

Extranet—A private *network* used to share information with authorized business partners, customers, vendors, and suppliers.

E-zine—Electronic magazine. Often subject-specific. Also refers to major content *portals* and Web sites for print magazines.

FAQ—Frequently Asked Questions; a subject- or site-specific list of questions and answers found on Web sites, in *newsgroups* and *electronic mailing lists*. FAQs are used to acquaint *Internet* users with the respective site's/newsgroup's/e-mail list's rules of interaction.

Firewall—A system designed to protect a private *network* from unauthorized access.

Flame—To send a verbal attack via e-mail.

Flash—Software developed by Macromedia (www.macromedia.com) and used to create animation. To view animation created with Flash, *browsers* must be equipped with the Macromedia Flash *plug-in*.

Freeware—Software that is copyrighted and given away free of charge. Freeware can be found on a variety of Web sites, like www.jumbo.com.

FTP—File Transfer Protocol; used to send and download files—text, images, Web pages—over the *Internet*.

GIF—Graphics Information File; a popular image format that supports a 256-color palette, simple cell animation, and a transparent background color. Often used for icons, logos, banners, and button ads.

Gigabyte—1 billion bytes (or 1,000 *megabytes*); abbreviated as "GB."

GUI—Graphical User Interface; a graphics-based, rather than text-based, computer interface. A Web *browser* is an example of a graphical user interface, as are Windows and Mac desktops.

H1-B Visa—Commonly referred to as a "work visa" or "work permit"; enables a foreign worker to enter the United States to work temporarily in a professional capacity.

Hacking—The act of illegally accessing a private *network* and modifying programs and files. (Hackers have been known to work with the government, software manufacturers, and security companies for the purposes of finding holes in *firewall*s and network security systems.)

Hit—A measurement used to record all files on a Web page (including image files) that are accessed by a site visitor.

Home page—The main page of a Web site; typically, the first that a site visitor views. Usually located at the *site's top level domain*—www.yourcompany.com or www.yourcompany.com/index.html.

Hosting—Aka "Web hosting"; refers to the business of storing, serving, and maintaining files for one or more Web sites.

HTML—Hypertext Markup Language; the standardized language that allows Web *browser*s to interpret and display Web pages.

HTTP—Hypertext Transfer Protocol; used for exchanging files on the *World Wide Web.*

Hub—Central communication point in a network, where data arrive from one or more locations and are distributed to one or more other locations.

ICANN—Internet Corporation for Assigned Names and Numbers (www.ICANN.org); an international nonprofit, private-sector organization created to coordinate four key functions for the *Internet:* (a) the management of the domain name system, (b) the allocation of *IP address* space, (c) the assignment of protocol parameters, and (d) the management of the root server system.

ICQ—An instant messaging program, developed by Mirabilis (www.mirabilis.com), that is often used as a conferencing system. An ICQ user can add other users' ICQ identification numbers to his or her address book so that when these users access the Internet, he or she is notified and may contact them via ICQ for live communication.

Image map—An image on a Web page that has certain regions mapped out as links to other Web pages.

Impression—A measurement used to record the number of times a *banner* advertisement is viewed by Web site visitors; aka "ad views."

Instant messaging—A communication system that allows users to exchange immediate messages with other users on the same instant messaging system. America Online's Instant Messenger (AIM), Microsoft's MSN Messenger, and *ICQ* are all instant messaging systems.

Internet—A worldwide system of computer networks; a global network of millions of computers that allows users to exchange information. Originally conceived by the United States Government in 1969 (and called "ARPANet" at that time), for the purposes of research communication. The most widely used parts of the Internet are electronic mail (e-mail), the *World Wide Web,* and Internet Relay Chat (*IRC*).

Interstitial—An interactive advertisement that appears in a separate *browser* window while you wait for a Web page to load.

Intranet—A private *network* used to share information within a company. Information is typically shared via Web pages uploaded to the private network. Access is generally given only to employees, and a *firewall* is used to prevent unauthorized access to outsiders.

IP address—Internet Protocol address; a global, standardized scheme for identifying machines that are connected to the *Internet.*

IPO—Initial Public Offering; also referred to as "going public." An IPO is a first and one-time fundraising opportunity for a privately owned company to sell shares of its stock to public investors.

IRC—Internet Relay Chat; the most widely used protocol allowing people to "chat."

IS—Information Systems; typically refers to the internal department that is responsible for a company's computers, network, and information management. Also referred to as *IT* or *MIS.*

ISDN—Integrated Services Digital Network; a digital transmission standard allowing high-speed *Internet* access (up to 128,000 bits per second) over regular telephone lines.

ISP—Internet Service Provider; a company that provides access to the *Internet* through telephone lines and other equipment. Some ISPs provide server space for Web site hosting. Aka "Internet access provider."

IT—Information Technology; refers to all systems and applications used to process (create, modify, store, transfer) and manage information. IT includes telephony, computers, and peripherals.

Java—A high-level, object-oriented programming language developed by Sun Microsystems in 1995. Java is used to create *applet*s or complete applications that run on a single computer or across *network*s.

Javascript—A programming language developed by Netscape; used in Web development, and shares many features of the *Java* programming language.

JPEG—An image format that supports a palette of more than 1.6 million colors. On the Web, it's the most popular format, next to *GIF,* for photographs and illustrations requiring a broad palette. Unlike *GIF* files, JPEGs do not support animation or transparency. The JPEG acronym stands for Joint Photographic Experts Group, the committee that developed it.

Keyword—A word used to search for information.

Kiosk—A booth with a display screen; often found in malls, airports, and trade shows. Kiosks provide local information or directions, and sometimes offer computer and Internet access.

LAN—Local Area Network; a *network* of computers and shared devices usually found in the same building or geographic area.

Leased line—A special-purpose telephone line, composed of copper wire or fiber-optic cable, that's used exclusively for high-speed digital transmission and linking large networks to the Internet. T-1 and T-3 are run on leased lines. Because leased lines are maintained at a much higher service level than are regular voice lines, they are very expensive to rent.

Link—An electronic connection between two documents; typically refers to a connection, between Web pages, that allows you to click on content or an image to access another Web page. Also called a "hot link" or "hyperlink."

Linux—A popular, freeware version of the Unix operating system.

Listserv—A popular *electronic mailing list* program, founded in 1986. The term "listserv" refers to a specific mailing list server but is often mistakenly used to refer to any electronic mailing list.

m-Commerce—Mobile Commerce; the buying and selling of goods and services, using wireless devices such as cellular phones and *PDAs.*

MAP—Merchant Account Provider.

Media player—Device used to run audio and video files on a computer (e.g., Apple's Quicktime, Real Player, Windows Media Player).

Megabyte—One million bytes; abbreviated as "MB."

Merchant account—An account established with a bank, or other payment processor, to settle credit card transactions. Approved businesses receive a Merchant ID and Terminal ID.

META tag—A type of code used in *HTML* to provide information about a Web page; often used specifically for search engine and directory listings.

Microprocessor—A computer processor that performs all of the logical instructions (e.g., calculations) received from the *operating system;* often, used interchangeably with *CPU.*

MIS—Management Information Systems or Management Information Services; refers to the central computer system and applications that manage a company's operations.

MP3—Audio compression format for *MPEG*, layer 3; audio files with the ".MP3" extension can be downloaded from the Web and played on your computer.

MPEG—Moving Picture Experts Group; a standard for digital video and audio compression.

Modem—A device that enables a computer to transmit data over telephone lines. Modems can be internal or external, and they can provide regular dial-up, ISDN, DSL, or cable access to the Internet. Modem speeds are measured in bits per second (bps). The fastest dial-up modems run at 57,600 bps. (Older models ran at speeds of 2,400; 4,800; 9,600; 14,400; 28,800; or 33,600 bps.)

MSP—Management Service Provider or Managed Service Provider; a company that manages *IT* functions for other companies, either internally or via an *ASP*.

Netiquette—Internet etiquette; guidelines for online interaction.

Netizen—An Internet veteran; an experienced Internet user.

Network—Two or more linked computer systems; types include *LAN* and *WAN*. Computers and other devices connected via a network are called nodes. The computers and devices that allocate resources for a network are called *servers*.

New media—All forms of electronic communication.

Newbie—Someone new to the Internet.

Newsgroup—An online discussion group devoted to talking about a specific topic. Also referred to as "Usenet newsgroups." Currently, there are over 15,000 newsgroups. To participate in a newsgroup, a user must have a news reader program, usually provided with a *browser* and *e-mail reader*.

Node—A single computer or other device connected to a network.

Non-virtual hosting—Web hosting provided by an *ISP* that stores each customer's Web files as a subdirectory of the ISP's domain (versus allowing the customer to use his or her own registered *domain name*). In other words, a customer's domain might look like www.ispdomain .com/yourcompany. Yahoo! Geocities, Lycos Angelfire, and Tripod are three of the largest and most popular companies that provide non-virtual hosting.

Opt-in—Refers to the act of authorizing the receipt of promotional e-mail. Direct e-mail distributors are encouraged to purchase lists of e-mail addresses for Internet users who have "opted" to receive promotional information, rather than sending unsolicited direct e-mail.

Optical disk—A high-capacity storage medium; like *CD-ROMs*, laser-written.

OS—Operating System; computer program that manages and runs all other programs. Examples of operating systems: DOS, Windows, Apple Macintosh OS, Unix, and Linux.

P2P—Peer-to-Peer; a *network* communications model that allows each node of the network to have equivalent responsibility. In other words, each node can directly exchange files with other nodes, without the need for a dedicated *server.*

Page view—A measurement used to record the number of times a Web page is viewed by site visitors.

Partition—Division of memory or storage. Sometimes, users partition hard drives to improve disk efficiency, run different *operating systems*, or manage multiple user files.

PC Card—Personal Computer Card, aka *PCMCIA* Card; a credit-card-size device used typically for laptop or notebook computers; provides memory or data transfer capabilities.

PCMCIA—Personal Computer Memory Card International Association; an industry group organized to create a standard for PC Cards.

PDA—Personal Digital Assistant; a small handheld device used for computing, scheduling, contact management, and data transfer. The most popular PDAs are 3Com's PalmPilot models.

PDF—Portable Document Format; a file format created with Adobe Acrobat software. Captures and saves as a single document formatting information from a variety of desktop publishing applications. The document is then easily transferable over the Internet and appears on the recipient's screen or printer as it was intended. PDF documents are viewed with Adobe Acrobat Reader, a freely available software application (www.adobe.com).

Peripheral—An external device attached to a computer; a mouse, scanner, printer, *modem,* keyboard, monitor, or disk drive.

PGP—Pretty Good Privacy. A public domain *encryption* technique, commonly used to protect messages sent via the *Internet.*

Pixel—A pixel is the most basic component of any computer graphic. It corresponds to the smallest thing that can be drawn on a computer screen. Every computer graphic is made up of a grid of pixels. When these pixels are painted onto the screen, they form an image. This grid of pixels is called a *bitmap.*

Plug-in—Applications (or hardware) that are easily installed into a computer and add extra features. Some of the most popular plug-ins are loaded from Web *browsers* like Adobe Acrobat.

POP—Post Office Protocol; a format for retrieving e-mail messages. Also refers to "Point of Presence": a telephone number that gives a user *dial-up* access to the *Internet*.

Portal—A Web site that serves as a gateway to the Web and to a variety of *Internet* services, including e-mail, news, entertainment, and shopping. Typically, portal sites are "starting points" for Web surfers; they serve as the default home page when the user's *browser* is opened. Examples of portals include NetNoir, AOL, BlackPlanet.com, and Yahoo!. Portals may offer general information, but some (referred to as "*vortals*") are subject- or industry-specific. Nowadays, most search engines, directories, magazines, and sites targeting women or people of color have been transformed into portal sites.

Privacy policy—A policy for protecting the privacy of individually identifiable Web site visitors' and customers' information, including e-mail address, contact information, and financial information.

RAM—Random Access Memory; any currently used programs and data are stored in a computer's RAM for easy accessibility. Like a human being's short-term memory, all programs and data are retained only while in use.

Real-time—Refers to a computer process that responds or occurs immediately.

Registrar—A company or organization that processes Internet *domain name* registrations (e.g., Network Solutions—www.networksolutions.com).

Rich media—An Internet advertising term; describes online ads that use advanced technology, such as streaming video and applets, to interact with site visitors.

RingMaster—A person who owns or manages a *Webring*.

ROI—Return on Investment.

ROM—Read Only Memory; the part of a computer that stores the operating system and the files needed to boot up the computer. Unlike *RAM*, ROM retains its contents, even when a computer is turned off.

ROS—Run of Site; an ad-buying option in which ad placements may appear on any page of the target site.

Router—Software, or a device, that connects *network* systems and determines the path of data that are transferred between the connected networks and nodes.

SAP—Systems, Application and Products in Data Processing; the world's largest inter-enterprise software company and the world's third largest independent software supplier (www.sap-ag.de). SAP employs over 23,000 people in more than 50 countries. The company was started in 1972 by five former IBM employees in Germany. SAP launched mySAP.com to target new-economy businesses with its e-business applications.

SCSI—Small Computer System Interface; pronounced "scuzzy." Refers to a set of standard electronic interfaces that allow personal computers to connect to and communicate with *peripheral* devices such as disk, tape and *CD-ROM* drives, printers, and scanners faster than parallel or serial ports. Originally developed by Apple Computer, most PCs have SCSI ports and they're supported by all major operating systems.

SDRAM—Synchronous Dynamic Random Access Memory. A type of *RAM* that is synchronized with the *microprocessor*'s clock speed, which increases the number of software instructions that the processor can perform in a given period of time.

Search engine—A program that maintains a massive index of Web site addresses, allows a user to search its index with *keyword*s, and returns results upon request. Search engines use *spider*s to crawl through the Web in search of new sites to be added to its index. Examples of popular Web search engines are Lycos (www.lycos.com) and Alta Vista (www.altavista.com). Search engines are commonly confused with Web directories, which maintain categorized indexes of Web site addresses. The most popular directory is Yahoo! (www.yahoo.com).

Server—A computer that holds data, files, or programs so that multiple users can have access to them. A server can also provide a *link* to a shared resource such as a printer.

SET—Secure Electronic Transaction.

Shared hosting—*Virtual* or *non-virtual Web hosting* provided by an *ISP* that stores a number of different Web sites on a single *server.* This type of Web hosting is very inexpensive. It is reserved for personal or smaller business sites with low traffic.

Shareware—Software that is distributed free of charge, on a trial basis. If users decide to continue usage beyond the trial period, or if they prefer the enhanced version of the software application, they pay a small fee. One source for finding shareware programs is www.shareware.com.

Signature file—Aka "tag line." A text file appended to the end of e-mail messages; it often includes contact info for the sender. An example of a signature file:

++

Black Data Processing Associates

Information Technology Thought Leaders

9315 Largo Drive West, Suite 260, Largo, MD 20774

(800) 727-BDPA   (301) 350-0052 fax

www.bdpa.org

++

Slamming—The illegal practice of changing a telephone subscriber's pre-ferred telephone company without the subscriber's knowledge or ex-plicit consent. In 2000, the Federal Communications Commission implemented several regulations against slamming. To read more or to file a complaint, go to www.ftc.gov/slamming, or call 1 (888) CALLFCC.

SMTP—Simple Mail Transfer Protocol; a format for sending e-mail messages. E-mail readers receive messages using the *POP* format.

Software piracy—Unauthorized and illegal duplication, use, or distribu-tion of software.

Spam—Unsolicited commercial e-mail, usually sent to a large group of e-mail addresses.

Splash page—An introductory Web page, often including music and/or animation, that leads into the Web site's main (home) page. Splash pages are often used on entertainment and gaming sites, and they may include promotional content.

Spider—A program that searches the Web to capture Web site ad-dresses for search engine and directory sorting. Aka "Web crawler."

SSL—Secure Socket Layer; an *encryption* technology on the server that scrambles important data such as credit card numbers and order infor-mation when they are being stored or passed from one computer to an-other.

Sticky—"Sticky" sites are those where the visitors stay for an extended period of time.

Streaming media—Technology that allows the "on demand" distribution of audio, video, and multimedia over the *Internet*. Streaming technology allows for *real-time* transfer of multimedia files to users with low- or high-speed access. Although multimedia files tend to be rather large, streaming allows a user to view such files as they are being downloaded (as opposed to waiting for a complete download for viewing). A *plug-in* is required to view streamed files. It's also important to note that because streamed files are viewed in real-time, no content is stored on the user's hard drive. For more info, go to www.streamingmedia.com.

Surge protector—Aka "surge suppressor"; a device that protects a computer's power supply from electrical surges.

T-1—A digital line that uses copper wire and supports data transfer rates of 1.54 megabits per second. T-1s are often leased by businesses and *ISPs* to connect to the *Internet*.

T-3—A digital line that uses copper wire and supports data transfer rates of 44.73 megabits per second. T-3s are mainly used by *ISPs*.

Tag line—See *Signature file*.

Terabyte—One thousand *gigabytes*.

Thread—An ongoing conversation in an electronic mailing list or Usenet newsgroup.

TLD—Top Level Domain; refers to ".com," ".net," ".org," and other newly approved *domain name* extensions. It is usually the portion of the domain name that appears farthest to the right. Country-code top level domains are two-character abbreviations that are associated with a specific country or region of the world (e.g., ".us" for United States; ".za" for South Africa; ".jp" for Japan; ".ca" for Canada, ".uk" for United Kingdom).

Trojan—A program that pretends to be something else and causes damage when the infected file is executed. Trojans are commonly confused with *viruses*, but they are not the same.

TRUSTe—An independent, nonprofit privacy initiative dedicated to building users' trust and confidence in the Internet and the accelerating growth of the Internet industry (www.truste.com).

Unified messaging—The consolidation of voice, fax, and e-mail messaging into one mailbox, allowing a user to access information via telephone or the Web.

UPS—Uninterruptible Power Supply; a device that contains a *surge protector* and a battery that maintains power for several minutes after a power outage, allowing users to save any data and log off without losing any information.

Urban legend—A type of folklore; a popular story, alleged to be true, that is sometimes sad, humorous, or gory, and is passed along orally or via fax, mail, or e-mail. To add credibility, urban legends often cite "A Friend" as the source of the information.

URL—Uniform Resource Locator; aka "Web site address."

User session—A measurement for recording the time spent and the pages viewed by site visitors on a single Web site. The session begins when the visitor, logs on and ends when he or she leaves the site or logs off.

vCard—Virtual business card. See *Signature file.*

Venture capital—A common form of high-risk financing for fast-growing businesses; used for start-up, development, or expansion. In exchange for their cash investment in a private company, venture capitalists (VCs) typically acquire shares of stock and management positions (to offer assistance and to monitor their investment). VCs expect a high rate of return; typically, they depend on the company's sale or an *IPO* to fulfill their expectation.

Viral marketing—Refers to e-mail campaigns in which recipients are encouraged to forward the message to others, in order to increase the reach of the marketing message.

Virtual—Refers to something that exists but not in physical form; a concept.

Virtual hosting—Often synonymous with "Web hosting"; refers to hosting services, provided by an *ISP* that allow a company to use its own domain (www.yourcompany.com). With virtual, *non-virtual* and *dedicated hosting,* a company does not have to purchase and maintain its own Web server and connections to the Internet.

Virus—A program designed to spread itself by first infecting executable files or the system areas of hard and floppy disks, and then making copies of itself. Viruses spread when files are shared via floppy disks, *CD-ROMs*, e-mail, or computer *networks*.

Vortal—A specialized portal, often focusing on a specific topic or industry.

VPN—Virtual Private Network. A *network* of computers that uses public telecommunication wiring to connect the network *nodes*. Data sent through VPNs is encrypted to safeguard the sender, recipient, and message content.

WAN—Wide Area *Network;* a group of *LANs* connected via telephone lines and radio waves.

WAP—Wireless Application Protocol; an informal industry standard that allows users to access the *Internet* using wireless devices, such as cell phones and *PDAs*.

Webcast—A live information broadcast over the *World Wide Web.*

Webmaster—A person who designs and manages a Web site and its content. Aka "Web designer."

Webring—A group of subject-specific Web sites linked together.

Wireless—A technology that uses electromagnetic waves (versus wires or cables) to carry signals and transfer data. Examples of wireless devices include cordless telephones, garage door openers, cell phones, and pagers. Wireless devices can be fixed (e.g., wireless keyboard) or mobile (e.g., cell phone).

World Wide Web—Aka "Web." A networked system of Internet *servers* that supports the Hypertext Transfer Protocol (*HTTP*). (Not all Internet servers are part of the World Wide Web.) Web pages are formatted in Hypertext Markup Language (*HTML*) and are viewed with Web *browser* applications like Microsoft's Internet Explorer and Netscape Navigator.

Worm—A self-replicating program, like a virus, that does not alter files but resides in active memory and duplicates itself.

NOTES

Introduction:

1. More specifically, the Digital Divide refers to the disparity between those persons and/or communities who have access to telephones, computers (hardware, software, peripherals), and Internet technology, and those who do not.
2. "Falling Through the Net: A Survey of 'Have Nots' in Rural and Urban America" (July 1995).
   "Falling Through the Net II: New Data on the Digital Divide" (July 1998).
   "Falling Through the Net: Defining the Digital Divide" (July 1999).
   "Falling Through the Net: Toward Digital Inclusion" (October 2000).
3. The NTIA's efforts were spearheaded by Larry Irving, former NTIA Administrator and Assistant Secretary of Commerce for Communications and Information. After leaving his position at NTIA, Larry Irving accepted the CEO position at UrbanMagic.com.
4. Vanderbilt University, 2000.
5. NUA Internet Surveys (www.nua.ie).
6. NTIA, "Falling Through the Net II: New Data on the Digital Divide" (July 1998).
7. In the United States, gender is no longer a major issue. Women have surged forth to surpass their male counterparts in acquiring and utilizing Internet access.

Chapter 1

1. Personal Digital Assistant, aka handheld PC.
2. Condensed (or "compressed") files have been reduced in size for easier storage or transfer. Files are often compressed using PKWARE's PKZip (www.pkware.com), WinZip Computing's WinZip (www.winzip.com), or Aladdin System's StuffIt (www.aladdinsys.com) software.
3. *Minority Businesses' Use of Internet Technology.* Sponsored by the U.S. Department of Commerce's Minority Business Development Agency (MBDA), Wells Fargo Bank, and the QWEST foundation. The study used interviews with 1,673 business executives from Latino, African American, Asian American, and Native American-owned firms. These companies had annual sales between $3.3 million and $4.9 million and employed between 22 and 34 persons full time.

Chapter 2

1. PowerPC is a joint effort among IBM, Apple Macintosh, and Motorola.
2. Configuring an application so that it runs more quickly or takes up less space on the hard drive.
3. Please note that software piracy is against the law. Software piracy refers to the unauthorized duplication, distribution, or use of computer software. This includes making more copies of software than the license allows, or installing software licensed for one computer onto multiple computers or a server. Copying software is an act of copyright infringement and is subject to civil and criminal penalties. It's illegal whether you use pirated software yourself, give it away, or sell it. And aiding piracy by providing unauthorized access to software or to serial numbers used to register software can also be illegal. For more information, contact the Business Software Alliance (1.888.NO.PIRACY or www.bsa.org).
4. Zip and Jaz are registered trademarks of Iomega Corporation (www.iomega.com).

Chapter 4

1. According to the American Electronics Association's *CyberStates 2001* report, high tech employment in the United States totals 5.3 million.
2. As of June 2001.
3. The H1-B visa, commonly referred to as a "work visa" or "work permit," enables a foreign worker to enter the United States to work temporarily in a professional capacity.
4. Data are from Bureau of Labor Statistics.
5. As of May 2000.
6. Federal law prohibits employment discrimination based on race, color, religion, sex, or national origin.
7. Salaries listed in most reports do not reflect bonuses, stock options, or benefits.

Chapter 5

1. Top-level domains are approved by The Internet Corporation for Assigned Names and Numbers (ICANN)—www.icann.net.
2. Network Solutions (www.networksolutions.com) is the premier domain registrar ($35/yr), but several companies now offer domain name registration (at much cheaper prices—$10–$20).
3. A broken link is a hypertext link that doesn't work; it leads to an error message or to the wrong page.

Chapter 6

1. Modern-day slang meaning "great," "wonderful," or "the best." A variety of tech and mainstream publications utilize the phrase "killer app" to refer to any widely used and beneficial software application.
2. Unsolicited commercial e-mail, often distributed to thousands of e-mail addresses at once.

3. The ListBot free electronic mailing list service (www.listbot.com) was discontinued as of August 6, 2001.
4. See Lena West's article, "Tech Support Insanity: How to Turn Nightmares into Sweet Dreams" @ www.smallbiztechnology.com/techsupportinsanity .htm.
5. The Internet Advertising Bureau, originally called IAB was founded in 1996. IAB has created a set of voluntary guidelines to simplify ad rate development for Web publishers and to provide marketers with a number of options for displaying their online messages.

Chapter 7

1. A "cookie" is a small computer file placed on your hard drive by some Web site servers to track your Web surfing patterns. Cookies are also used for security, online ordering systems, Web site personalization, and targeted marketing.

INDEX

TAKE ONE STEP CLOSER TO FINANCIAL EMPOWERMENT

Introducing the BLACK ENTERPRISE **Wealth Building Kit**, a step-by-step guide to financial empowerment from the nation's No. 1 authority on black business. To get your free kit, log on to blackenterprise.com and visit our personal finance section or call toll free **1-877-WEALTHY**

BLACK ENTERPRISE
YOUR ULTIMATE GUIDE TO FINANCIAL EMPOWERMENT